In Search of Living Knowledge

Marja-Liisa Swantz

MKUKI NA NYOTA
DAR – ES – SALAAM

PUBLISHED BY
Mkuki na Nyota Publishers Ltd
P. O. Box 4246
Dar es Salaam, Tanzania
www.mkukinanyota.com

© Marja-Liisa Swantz, 2016

ISBN 9789-9877-53-40-6

Visit www.mkukinanyota.com to read more about and to purchase any of Mkuki na Nyota books. You will also find featured authors, interviews and news about other publisher/author events. Sign up for our e-newsletters for updates on new releases and other announcements.

Distributed world wide outside Africa by African Books Collective.
www.africanbookscollective.com

Contents

Foreword

I am pleased to see the ideas and thoughts of Marja-Liisa Swantz published in a single volume that does justice to the breadth and depth with which she throughout her life has approached the challenges of knowledge formation in and about Africa. She is truly a portal figure in the study of development whose insights have yet to be fully acknowledged and appreciated because as a person and professional she has always adopted a low-profile position. Yet, as this book clearly shows, she has been a pioneer in promoting what she refers to as "cognitive justice", i.e. an approach that recognizes the contribution to knowledge that those who we typically label" research objects" make. Theoretical knowledge is important but theory is and should not always be King. Such a situation creates an unequal relation between the researcher and those who are studied. It also limits the extent to which the voice is heard of those for whom the research often matters most.

Living knowledge, according to Swantz, is one that always evolves in relations between people. Citing the work of Steve Feierman in the Usambara Mountains, northeast Tanzania, she argues that there is a process of knowledge formation even in contexts where mainstream social science is least likely to look for it. The peasantry has its own intellectuals and rationality is not confined to modernity only. It exists in its own way also in societies where symbols rule the minds and understanding them is crucial for how these entities are governed. There are at least three good reasons why the ideas presented in this volume are important.

The first is how these ideas reveal the limits associated with the type of knowledge formation that is useful for governments and donors. It prioritizes systematization of knowledge in relation to specific goals or objectives, be they formulated at project, program, government or international level. It is formulated in ends-means relations and little else is of interest outside the specific parameters of these activities. Development is a captive of the global policy community and as such treated in a way that limits the opportunity for others to engage in creative thinking, which may result in progressive outcomes. Even international NGOs that typically have a close relation with local populations operate on the assumption that their mission is to make these people embrace a Western outlook and epistemology. They cannot fathom development without rationality and reflexivity as conceived in a Western enlightenment episteme and therefore easily turn into secular missionaries of a creed that with the exception of a small minority of educated people is alien in the African context.

Development in this way of thinking is meant to be both beneficial and benevolent. Those who already know, lead the way. Their ideas are the blessing of all. Universalism is sacred. There is no need to incorporate insights from other sources. With the world getting smaller through globalization and issues critical to the future of mankind are embraced with increasing urgency, the monopoly of knowledge formed in formal scientific and policy processes tend to prevail with even greater strength. The Millennium Development Goals is a case in point. Although the newly adopted Sustainable Development Goals (SDGs) were preceded by an extensive process of consultation around the world, the framework for what should be included in the final statement clearly determined what kind of inputs that were eventually adopted.

The problem with both the MDGs and the SDGs is that they do not go halfway to meet the actors for whom development is most valuable. There is no readiness to look at the world from their perspective; no interest to take the time to learn from them. This artificial rush to progress leaves the population in Africa without a chance to learn on terms that are congenial to their own circumstances. Not only is their own knowledge brushed aside but so is their integration into a knowledge system in which they are doomed to remain at its lowest ramp. Especially harmful to the ability of local people in Africa learning about development on their own terms is the pressure to monitor progress through a set of indicators within a narrow timeline. If the international community is serious about its talk of local ownership and "going with the local grain", i.e. allow a process of development that begins with already existing institutions, it should allow member countries, like those in Africa, to advance on their own terms from their own particular circumstances. The objective should not be meeting global targets as if they are sacred but instead measure progress in terms of how far a particular country has been able to move from a specific baseline. The approach should not be to fall back on standard global indices but instead encourage monitoring and evaluation based on a trajectory approach. Doing it that way would give room for ownership and promote a process of learning that incorporates local insights and thoughts. It would help to put African agency at the front. It would promote the kind of cognitive justice that Swantz is pleading for.

The second reason is to emphasize that the type of participatory research which she pioneered in her research in Tanzania in the 1960s and 1970s and has continued to advocate over the years is quite different from the quasi-participatory approaches that have mushroomed as part of efforts to bring people into forms of conventional development design and evaluation. With due respect for the important contributions that Robert Chambers and others have made to making the voice of the people part of formulating development policy, programs and projects, these approaches are first and foremost aimed at incorporating local knowledge on the terms of the policy analyst. They do not promote understanding of local people and their knowledge systems but integrate such ideas and insights into models or theories of change that are driven from the outside. Participatory analysis, whether in the form of Rapid

Rural Appraisal or any other version, is essentially a form of hijacking of Swantz's approach to participatory research as developed in her work in various regions in Tanzania, perhaps notably in Bagamoyo District, Coast Region.

The third reason is that the participatory research that she developed alone as well as in collaboration with others like Bud Hall, a Canadian of the same persuasion, evolved in the shadow of the neo-Marxist wave that struck the academic scene in Tanzania in the 1970s. As a result, it never received its immediate recognition as a true intellectual revolution. Unlike the progressive ideas of Marx and other Gods in the Marxist Pantheon, those that were born and nurtured by Swantz in the soils of Bagamoyo, Mtwara and other locations in Tanzania developed into a movement with a range of manifestations, all of which had a resemblance with its original creation. She is the pioneer that placed Tanzania on the map of development research by highlighting the important role that indigenous ideas and insights play in knowledge formation. She shares a rightful place on the prestigious podium of "alternative development thinkers" with better-known figures like Eric Schumacher ("Small is Beautiful") and Gustavo Gutierrez (Liberation Theology). It is appropriate, therefore, that this book is first published in Tanzania, the birthplace of the participatory research revolution.

Let me finally add that although the book is written as an intellectual life story, it contains more insights than one can usually gather in a regular textbook. Any one with interest in how greater justice and equality can be achieved in development should read this book and it is my hope, therefore, that it gets to be read widely by students and practitioners of development, be they Tanzanians or from other countries around the world.

Goran Hyden

Preface

This book is an account of some of my personal research history. My scientific search has followed a long road with converging paths, initially deriving its scientific base from the study of ritual symbols in participatory research. It led me to a search for meaning according to the hermeneutical approach and to the paths of development.

My work was part of a phase in anthropology when many social scientists were dealing with the concept of symbols, and Victor Turner, who worked within the social-functional school, influenced me. According to Edith Turner, Victor Turner's doctoral work was still under the influence of Max Gluckman's Manchester School of Anthropology, interpreting rituals to reflect social structures. She suggested that he was moving towards a wider interpretation of symbols and their meanings (E. Turner 2008).

I framed my doctoral work in the 1960s in terms of the social change that was taking place among the coastal Zaramo in Tanzania and the ritual symbolism reflecting it, and I saw the dominance of death symbolism as a reflection of the transition that the society was going through. The basic symbols that people interpreted and acted out as part of their life made the social processes a cultural process as the symbolic interpretation was well understood by the people.

My initial understanding of the symbolic formulation of thought originated with Susan Langer's *Philosophy in A New Key, A Study in the Symbolism of Reason, Rite, and Art* (1957). It was through Langer's work that I came to believe that symbols preceded rational thought. Susanne Langer pointed out that there were two categories of symbols. The study of symbols had been of interest to linguists, psychiatrists, social and cultural anthropologists, philosophers, mathematicians and students of religion; the meaning given to the symbol as a concept differed depending on the significance of the concept in each field of science. The symbolism of sciences such as mathematics, even linguistics, says nothing about the content of the symbols, and what it is they represent. Language, with its grammatical scheme of expression, requires intellectual activity setting word symbols in a logical order. This kind of use of symbols was *discursive symbolism*. On the other hand Langer, as an anthropologist, would analyse what she called *presentational symbols*. They could contain aspects that many other sciences would regard as subjective experience and feeling. These thoughts continued to underpin my efforts to search out the meanings. In my interpretation, the preeminent social element reflected in Zaramo symbolism was experiencing death in one way or another.

The research path I have followed has been a personal journey: a meaningful "lived experience," drawing on some scholars of philosophy such as Martin Heidegger and his "ontology of understanding." I learned that even if Edmund Husserl could not be hermeneutic with his *Phenomenology of Logical*

Investigations, he understood the significance of the concept "to live it out in practice." I build on Wilhelm Dilthey's intent to unite theory and praxis and his structural analysis of the basic category of meaning together with the other categories of "sense, value and purpose." The meaning of ritual symbol in the hermeneutic field, "deciphering the hidden meaning in the apparent meaning" (Bleicher 1980), was the central focus in my *Ritual and Symbol* (1970). I still consider the specific cultural understanding of the meanings to be the key in appreciating the cultural base of a community and its social development.

In the words of Susan Langer, "The importance of symbol-using, once admitted, soon becomes paramount in the study of intelligence" (1957, 33). That has led me to believe in the need to move forward with this thinking, to move beyond, as Bernard McGrane states it in the name of his book *Beyond Anthropology,* with the subtitle *Society and The Other.* Anthropology had become the "way of seeing The Other, as both fundamentally and merely, culturally different" yet "disintegrating before our eyes." The questioning of Foucault's *The Order of Things* (1970, 78) could relate to the theories of kinship, when the Western scholar tried to find the "Other," reflecting the "order of things," which differed from his own. In this book, I return to some of the old constructions of The Other, but I also strive to increase the understanding of the "modern" when it appears with the new Other whilst the "ancient" is stuck in its passing modernity.

With scarce literary resources on contemporary anthropology available to me whilst carrying out my first research in Dar es Salaam, I was unaware that I was one of the many at the time trying to decipher the meanings of symbols. Philosophers and anthropologists were interpreting "meaning" as the concept in the wider sense when it was discussed in a seminar from which Keith Basso and Henry Selby published ten presentations under the main theme *Meaning in Anthropology* in 1976. According to the introductory statement by Douglas Schwartz, the symbolic character of cultural phenomena was at the time, "of greater interest than at any other time in the history of anthropology." My exploration of meaning in its relationship to symbols started in 1965. In writing this, I return to them in an historical perspective searching for new meanings for them in the modernizing Tanzanian society. The answer to the question of meaning was a set of assumptions about the nature of culture and the aim of ethnography. Among the participants in the seminar on the concept of meaning were the well-known anthropologists David Schneider and Clifford Geertz, who I have referred to in this book in relation to the acceptance of the concept of culture in anthropology.

The chapters of this book return to the studies made in the course of my career as a researcher whose focus on anthropology was side lined by the necessity of addressing questions of development because of the central role it played in a newly emerging nation like Tanzania. The Ministry of National Culture in Tanzania, with which my research was carried out, after I completed my first study of symbolic meanings, could not take on the study of culture without relating it to the central aim of the nation regarding development. In this book, I return to the anthropological context of the past studies and relate them to the developments that have taken place within them.

Experience has taught me, with first-hand participation in developing situations, that scientific work relating to people cannot be separated from their practical life. The political and social situation of a newly independent country aspiring to achieve national unity was bound to have an influence on the way the research was carried out. This meant that anthropological research which had from its beginning as a science been close to people, could relate to the aspirations of the society, thus moving from the objectifying concept of science to interpretative, phenomenological and hermeneutic search for meanings in the new and changing situation. Research had to take on the task, which the decision makers missed. I understood that the participatory research was necessary to gain a *deepened understanding* of the society and the social processes in action. Theory should emerge from society, yet I realized that by taking such a position it also presupposed theoretical positioning, even if this was not yet worked out.

Participatory Research (PR), which later came to be known as Participatory Action Research (PAR), became for me a personal response to the political direction that Tanzania had taken but was not implementing in practice. It led me out of the concentration on the symbolic understanding of phenomena, which the people I worked with had less interest in. People would need to understand the changing situation they were in and learn to join with conscious participation in decision-making. If they learned to participate by formulating their thoughts in cooperation with a researcher this would develop into questions for further research. This involved expressing thoughts and problems that related to their lives and a realization that such research was significant. Participatory research, in which the different categories of people share their knowledge in the research process, is a research tool for thinking and for deepening the understanding of the situation, both for the scholar with her tools of thought and action and for the people who shared the situation. This affects the problem of power and the issue of steering people towards the researcher-led direction, developing debates and analysis, as well as analysis in cooperation with people. As an anthropologist, the researcher understands that she is, as such, a student and needs to learn, because she cannot direct the discussion with questions that are formulated from her thought structure and context, as is commonly the case in the methodology of other social and political studies, aside from economics.

Participatory Research can become Participatory Action Research and equip some people to participatory planning, which potentially becomes part of the political process. Since 1998, more people than before could become involved in the process with the decentralization of the Government in Tanzania.

Participatory planning, made part of local politics, was another shared search at the primary level for understanding the new communal life situations. It was given little attention but relating closely to people's cultural expressions when they recognize their significance. Participatory research meant also giving expression to the hidden *less rational cultural meanings* which the external researcher too readily misses and fails to make space for.

Participatory research has theoretical consequences. The line of thinking *brings differing forms of knowing into contact with each other*. There does not need to be clear lines of difference between scientific and everyday knowledge in the pursuit of commonly shared knowledge. A significant point is that *knowledge is a continuum*. PAR is not a utilitarian method. Its primary purpose is not to apply scientific knowledge into practice by using applied science. Its purpose is to deepen the participants' understanding of her or his life situation in relation to development efforts going on, as part of the overall changes taking place.

The problems that arise in people's lives are not there for the researchers to solve. Participation means a common search for common understanding and knowledge creation in which different participants from different levels share. The support, which I have received from former colleagues has been invaluable, some have been mentioned in the course of the writing. They deserve much more recognition than what I offer in the book.

Brief introduction to the contents of the book

Participatory Research Approach and later Participatory Action Research form the core of the analyses and reports in this book. I have divided the book into three parts, leaving the earlier experiments in the use of participatory research to the second part of the book. The chapters describe and analyse the use of participatory research from different perspectives. The main theme in the book is the necessity in the development context to involve the researched community in the research as participants, whose problems and line of thought are consciously woven into the research problematic and into the ways of studying them. The anthropological emphasis plays a role in the need to deal with the social and cultural often neglected contribution in the development context.

The first chapter introduces what I long called "living knowledge." I hope that by documenting something which has been a lived experience, it would not take on a rigid scientific form. The book tells the personal story of research with its shortcomings and rich experiences. It introduces the scholars who have influenced my research and how I came to apply different shades of participatory research and initiate it at the time when there were no models yet. The whole book is a story of developing it and its significance as the mediator between the science and practice yet not being applied science.

The second chapter discusses the reasons why anthropologists have shied away from actual participation even when their method has been participation in people's lives.

The third chapter is entitled "Paths to Participation in Development Research." This chapter focuses on the use of participatory research in development studies. Anthropologists have a reputation of being conservative and their analysis of the developing cultures have come too close to the reality of people who want to look at their societies from the perspective of development.

In contrast to the descriptive parts of the project work, the fourth chapter, "On Whose Culture Is Development Built," summarizes some theoretical and historical phases in the development of the Participatory Action Research and its relation to development studies. The research context in the book is development, which only seldom highlights the cultural and social aspects of shared life. The old issues in the background reflect the former colonial rule, globally set development policies and the role anthropology has played even if they are not brought out in daily political discussion. The Western way of setting the problems dominate. The chapter brings to the fore the role of development anthropology in Participatory Action Research, leaving room for the discussion on the role of anthropology in development more broadly in the following chapters. The chapter takes up historical glimpses of how anthropology has looked at the other cultures and cites anthropologists who have taken a critical look at the missionaries influence on cultures they have also studied.

In chapter five, "Women's ways of sustaining life," the extensive role of women in development is described and analysed. It relates to experiences in the 1990s and in the new millennium in Mtwara and Lindi regions and in Singida Region in Iramba District with comparative material from Northern Kilimanjaro and Pare mountain areas. The utilization of PRA in women's projects shows the differences in development tasks by men and women. The near-total neglect of women in the Government agricultural program is contrasted sharply to the central role women play in cultivating their families' subsistence. A particular strength of the women is their sharing of work and earnings within a variety of savings groups. Community-Based Research, also recently introduced to East Africa, gives hope of a new beginning with a role for participation in research of societies and their cultural inheritance.

The sixth chapter "Between the 'Traditional' and the 'Modern'" deals with the changing world, which affects the different sectors of the society in a variety of ways. Loosing traditional values means also change in the cultural background of society, yet the old customs affect people's living. It brings up the values, which traditions hold up in different sectors of society and their significant role in building social and cultural continuity.

The second part of the book includes the first case studies in which I initially started experimenting with PR in different fields of development. The first project in which I applied a participatory approach is recorded in the chapter, "First Steps in Participatory Research," which returns to the years 1972-75 when I was employed as a Senior Research Fellow in the Bureau of Resource Assessment and Development Planning (BRALUP) (later IRA, Institute of Research Assessment) at the University of Dar es Salaam, which was then starting the second decade of its existence. It provided the opportunity to experiment with what I then called Participative Research Approach in projects, which combined training of thirteen student assistants in the use of the new way of doing research. It involved participation of school leavers with whom the students worked initiating potential income earning projects. "Putting Participation into Practice" includes brief accounts of these experimental projects, which caused some stir among other foreign research staff.

The eighth chapter describes the first extensive research project, Jipemoyo, that has had international attention more than any of the earlier or later projects. It was an interdisciplinary research for four years using Participatory Action Research, carried out in the Western Bagamoyo district in 1975-79. After the four first years as a family in Dar es Salaam we returned to Finland in the autumn 1975 as I got the post as a lecturer in the Science of Religion faculty in the University of Helsinki, a position related to the humanities and theology faculties. However, before leaving Tanzania, the Director of the Ministry of National Culture and Youth had invited me to join and plan research cooperation. This gave me the opportunity to initiate a research project on the theme "The Role of Culture in the Restructuring Process of Rural Tanzania," for which the Academy of Finland's Department of Humanities was ready to provide its share of funding as its first extensive development research project. It included the cooperation with the pastoralist Parakuyo Maasai and with farming villagers, paying attention to the role of women in the development process. A team of Tanzanian and Finnish researchers carried out the extensive project in Western Bagamoyo District applying Participatory Research Approach consisting of different ways of applying participation.

Another participatory research, which I conducted in cooperation with staff and female students in their home district in Central Kilimanjaro, was on the potential causes of spreading malnutrition of children. This is described in Chapter 9, "Participatory Research in Support of Public Health Training." The concept of malnutrition was broadened when the social problems involved in feeding were shown to be crucial (M-L. Swantz 1975; 1985). The research mode was new, as the traditional research had concentrated on the nutritional feeding methods as such rather than considering also the role of the home conditions of the children and their neighbourhood. A further experimental project, with the extensive use of participation by villagers, was focused on the education and skills of the villagers in three divisions, Western Bagamoyo, Usangi in the Pare-mountains, and Kyela in the Southern Highlands. The project was funded by ILO and initiated by the Development office of the Government, but the research approach was totally new. The follow-up in Usangi reflects the critique of development included in this book. The concluding Chapter 10 in Part III revisits key themes explored in the book.

I have made use of some data that became available while I participated in an extensive RIPS project in the southern regions over a six-year period in the 1990s, but I have differentiated between the use of Participatory Action Research (PAR) as an approach to research and Participatory Rural Appraisal (PRA) as a tool in development planning. I briefly respond to the critique of participation when directed to the use of PRA as a research method. I have been involved in the use of both and am aware that the main proponent of PRA, Robert Chambers, has promoted the approach also as a research method (Chambers 2008).

I end this Preface with the question of what I mean by suggesting that there is a way for creating living knowledge. The question brings us to the theme of this book. Can participatory research be worked out, in which the problems of research are commonly laid out and discovered, while knowledge is consciously mutually shared and created together with those who earlier have been the subject of research or informants? Could answers be more consciously sought in a mutual researching relationship in a commonly recognized way of doing research? The book seeks to answer this question.

PART

I

CHAPTER 1

Introduction

Preliminary reflections

This book tells my personal research history spanning fifty years. Other scientists, having reviewed their life's work, encouraged me to review mine and recount my story, to recall the paths I have travelled while developing the approach to research in which knowledge is produced together with the studied people as co-researchers and research partners. In this book, I make my contribution to the library of work written by those who have crossed disciplines and looked for ways of interpreting the "lived world."

I reflect upon my experiences following my initial studies in the Finnish language, literature and folklore, including the science of religion. My early Master's thesis focused on the work of the Finnish language by Professor August Ahlqvist, who criticized the language of Aleksis Kivi, the early master of Finnish literature. I travelled far from the beginnings of my scholarship, but over the course of time I found that the acquaintance with my own background – that of a small country struggling to have its cultural contribution recognized in the global context – has been most helpful when learning to understand the life in emerging independent countries in Africa. Interestingly, the history of anthropology suggests that many leading scholars come upon anthropology after carrying out scholarship in other fields, which may benefit them.

The name of the book, *In Search of Living Knowledge*, refers to both the author's fifty-years long research journey, as well as the people I lived among and became acquainted with over that time. These people have had a recognized role in the process of knowledge creation, while I have articulated my thoughts into the language of human and social science.

I set out on my research path while my family and I were living in Dar es Salaam in the 1960s. In a country about to reach independence, in the service of the local Lutheran Church, we were facing the growing challenges of fast urbanization whilst meeting people migrating from rural settings and from different levels of society. The coastal Islamic groups, who belonged to diverse ethnic backgrounds, felt at home in Dar es Salaam, but were at the time facing an invasion of upcountry people with different ethnic and cultural backgrounds. The pioneering ministry in the urbanizing society became the job of my American husband, but as the wife and mother of three small children, the last one born in Dar es Salaam, I had the freedom to find my own way. My 1961 notebooks were filled with questions and reflect the same awareness of the unequal social situation in Dar es Salaam, raising similar questions which development workers ask today.

In the fall of 1965, after returning from home leave after the first four years of service, I had an entirely new experience as I became acquainted with a group of coastal people in the area around Bunju village north of Dar es Salaam. I shared life with these village people for five years, resulting in my doctoral dissertation entitled, *Ritual and Symbol in Transitional Zaramo Society with special reference to women* (1970, reprinted in 1986).

Soon after I had become acquainted with the people in Bunju, it became obvious that I was not only there to observe their lives as the traditional anthropological term "participant observation" indicated. Instead, I participated in their lives and became adopted into their community. The search for understanding their different ways of life became an integral part of our communication. This experience not only changed my relationship with people, it changed my thinking as to what the research was about and, ultimately, it changed the course of my life.

Gaining its independence from Great Britain in 1961, Tanzania initially built its politics on a non-Marxist socialist orientation, as outlined by the country's first president, Julius Nyerere. The national politics emphasized the concept of self-help, based on *ujamaa*, familyhood. It drew its philosophy from the people's traditional communal social cohesion based initially on kinship, and with a vision that it could be extended to other social relations. This placed new demands on research. The anthropological research approach as an inquiry involving participation facilitated a common search for understanding between researchers and people of their changing situation.

The experience of participatory research in Bunju formed the foundation for the many encounters that followed in my life. Contact with people during later encounters was no longer as enduring, nor as personal, as before, but there was an awareness of the significance of the human contacts in the ongoing communication between people initially alien to one another, and above all the significance of close human contacts in the research process. The primary concern was not how "value free," "objective," or "scientific" the research was, or whether the needed distance was retained in the relations between myself, as the researcher, and the people with whom I communicated.

On my return to Tanzania after a break of two years, I was employed as a Senior Research Fellow at the University of Dar es Salaam for three years (1972-75). I recognized that I was in search of deeper concerns, of knowledge and meaning, not only for myself, being charged with knowledge production, but above all for the people with whom we cooperated as a research community. A new path had started in my life.

On the path to participatory research

While reflecting on our past, we do not remember events in minute detail. We relate later experiences to earlier ones, associating the subsequent events with the earlier ones, thus allowing the latter to influence their interpretation. When I was reminiscing about my career and the meaning of the different research paths I had taken, the book *Minnena ljuger* (Memories Lie) by the Swedish author Kjell Espmark caught my attention because of its enticing name. They gave fresh impetus to my thoughts (Espmark 2010). In his words, "What I really have wanted to arrive at is something that goes beyond the individual fate – how we reformulate our memories into myths which *give structure and meaning to our existence*" (my italics and translation from Swedish). The author reformulates events of his own life in a way that gives structure and meaning to his existence, allowing the later experiences to deepen the meaning of the earlier ones. He recognizes that in the reinterpretation of the old there is an element of "deceit," but in light of later experiences it deepens the meaning. The same is the case when interpreting the research as one's life's work.

In writing my research history I am bound to give new meanings to what was done over the course of a half a century. I seek to deepen the meaning of common existence without distorting the facts. Reading gave me a new intent for reflecting on my research experiences, instigated in 1964 and continued in one way or another until now. These experiences have covered different research situations while seeking to deepen contacts with people. I look for the common inner intent in the ways in which I have implemented the research, the ideal I set before myself, the factors that have influenced my wanderings, and what have been the lessons learned when winding up my life's work.

The intent and the time span in carrying out the different research efforts have varied, but this perspective helps to give the writing *structure* and *meaning*. History plays out meanings to past experiences, and when they are relived they gain new meanings. I am reminded of Marshall Sahlins's *Historical Metaphors and Mythical Realities* (1985) from the Early History of the Sandwich Islands, in which the history repeats itself in terms of the myths, which carry the history forward (1985). The structure is one of repetition, similar experiences and lines of thought repeat themselves and I question whether the meaning deepens and broadens with new layers or whether it ends in repetition. I spell out some leading visions that have guided the way, how I have experienced and comprehended the context of the research I have been involved in, the theoretical points which the different phases of research have brought up, and how it has broadened and deepened my view of life in Africa, still leaving me as an inquirer.

I had been in the coastal area and communicated with people for four years in Dar es Salaam city when evangelist Mwakalasya's wife Emma invited me for a visit to Bunju on the way to Bagamoyo. Bunju with its sub-villages was beyond the commercial fields of Boko, up from the low land, where the evangelist had his church, at that time still far from the city and its suburbs. Bunju was a village of farmers and fishermen, who walked down daily to the shores of Indian Ocean. They identified themselves as Muslims, but lived their lives with traditional rituals and beliefs. Not giving me any warning, Emma had invited a group of women to meet me and inquired from them what they would want me to share with them. Their response was to teach them to read.

I had to agree and made trips from town, meeting with them as well as with Emma. I sat, taught, and talked with the eager women of different ages. Soon they invited me to share in their rituals and they began to reveal their ritual secrets. Eventually we became close friends and I came to know their wise diviner-healer woman (*mpiga ramli*), Mwawila. I became adopted as a daughter of the healer (*mganga*) Salum Mhunzi, and was from thereon identified as *Binti Salum*, the daughter of Salum. I shared life with the people in Bunju off and on for five years. We built a Swahili house there, sharing it with the Zaramo friend Emma's family, and brought my family and even visitors there during weekends and holidays.

At the same time, I sought theoretical grounding from different tutors as a research associate at the University of Dar es Salaam. I was fortunate to be able to sit in the seminars of Professor Terence Ranger, to meet other famous historians, talk to anthropologists during their period of field research, attend East African social science conferences and communicate with visiting professors such as Steven Feierman, Aylward Shorter, Marcia Wright, John Iliffe, Ronald Frankenberg and John Sutton among many others, before Africans took over the positions. In 1970 Ulf Himmelstrand, professor of sociology in the University of Uppsala and visiting Dar es Salaam at the time became interested in my work and offered to be the second opponent. There were no African studies in Finland and anthropology was taught as one course in sociology. I found the best specialist on Africa and Tanzania in Sweden, Professor Bengt Sundkler, who directed my dissertation and who made it possible for me to write my dissertation at the University of Uppsala. He had acquainted himself with anthropology in Africa but he was from the Theological Faculty, so to qualify I presented a licentiate thesis in Science of Religion and took another examination on African religions. On my visit to Uppsala in 1968, Professor of Ethnology Stig Lagercrantz from Uppsala University gave me advice on relevant literature.

Professor Kjell Espmark, the chairman of the literature committee for Nobel laureates, claimed to be of the first generation of tutors who gave regular guidance to his doctoral students. His teachers had been learned men, but they did not influence the way their doctoral students progressed in their research. Bengt Sundkler belonged to the same generation but he was keenly interested in my research and he enthusiastically accepted my approach. I learned that the first step in research was for a researcher to know the studied people as interesting individuals. As the researcher I did not only have a role in the community I was studying but there was a further cognitive point whereby "human essence could be understood only by human essence" (M-L. Swantz 2002, 2009).

The significance of the contacts with people offered the basic inspiration in research. Knowledge is not created only through components in a rational language or a systematic thought structure, knowledge can be created through communication between people who are alive in their minds and thoughts. In preparing a lecture for the 100-year birthday celebration of Professor Bengt Sundkler, I was aware that my work bore similarities with his scholarship in this regard. The personalized approach to research develops when the scientist distances him or herself from the role as a scientist and takes the studied people as humans, as neighbours, not as informants and objects of research, yet s/he converts the knowledge so gained into a degree of scholarly analysis. Unexpected events in life turn to occasions of new learning and become overtures to new scientific vistas but such occasions must not turn to hidden exploitation of the counterparts' knowledge.

Contacts between people form a key to participatory, engaged research. The contacts and communication come first and are crucial before they turn to research on specific issues. Peter Rigby, a research partner referred to in Chapter 8 on Jipemoyo, expressed this point succinctly, when he described communication in every day life as his research approach (Rigby 1977, 24-79; 1985, 25-47). Stephen Diamond and Johannes Fabian have expressed similar views. The contacts led to the significance of engagement and shared participation in knowledge production, in which the human contacts turn to mutual learning and lead to analysing thought structures and meanings with common understanding. This cannot be the experience in all the contacts but it sets the basic tone in cooperation.

In this book and during my scholarly career, I have struggled to find what support I get as an anthropologist as well as a student of religion and development studies from these disciplines for a better understanding of the lives of the rural people in Tanzania, so that the research contacts could sustain and enrich their lives as they do mine. In these research efforts the foremost goal has been to understand people, women and men, young and old, their life situations, their joys, sorrows, and beliefs, their social relations and contacts, where and how they find their subsistence, what sustainable livelihood means to them and together with them gain fruitful ideas as to how they could improve their living. The question here is how the knowledge system we use serves the people cooperating with us, and us as researchers, in increasing our understanding and knowledge and how the people we relate to could recognize their role in the process and find ways of improving their lives. I am aware of the gap between the ideal and the practice, at times caused by the external or even disciplinary premises for research, or the limited time preventing deeper penetration into the topics raised and the problems met. The basic tone plays a part even in shorter encounters.

The time and the context in which the research is done are significant. Today the abundance of global scientific and literary writings overwhelms any reader and student of human and social life. Yet everyone has his or her own angle from which to look at the world and its development. My former experiences covered the colonial period. I taught female students about the colonial government's plans and the failed implementation of development projects in 1952-1956. I followed the country's steps towards independence with the people's hopes and dreams of a better life, their struggle toward self-reliance. I was at the national stadium in 1961 and saw the flag of independent Tanganyika open, the British flag lowered and colonial power brought to an end. The desire of people to live a better life was palpable, but in time it brought disappointment, which became evident in the research I shared with villagers.

Participation with whom and how to keep the balance are questions with which I was concerned. It brings up the issue of normativity the researcher faces. With whom does the researcher identify? In whose lives does she participate and how? Development as such is a normative concept as it assumes that the existing state needs to change for better, but when and how, in which aspects of economy, social life and people's culture.

How did I increase my understanding and knowledge of these and other related questions? In many of the projects the training aspect has been an integral part of the research process, considered to be important with regards to the developing situation of the country, and also for the researcher. But the time and resources needed for the scientific analysis of the political, economic and human relations and different lines of thought have remained a lifetime process. The participatory approach has enriched the research contacts, yet every time when tackling a task there was more to know and much deeper to probe. As I write these reflections at the end of five decades of academic pursuit closely relating to Africa there is a sense of accomplishment, yet I also feel that I am still at the threshold of deeper understanding while sharing people's lives. I am overwhelmed by the large amount of detailed handwritten research notes I made over my career and the wealth of unused knowledge and hidden wisdom.

This book is an effort to untangle the lessons learned during these long years, to delve into the treasure house of experience and to sort out the factors which have influenced my scholarly work in moving between different forms of knowledge: the practical everyday experiential knowledge of ordinary people and the theoretical knowledge, which has accumulated on my library shelves. There is no need to privilege one form of knowledge over the other, but there is a need to clarify the requirements for their interaction in search of what the author has called "living knowledge." Concentration on learning and training whilst doing research has weakened the theoretical analysis, but the personal understanding has deepened with the continued reading of related philosophical reflections.

When leafing through the books and numerous articles, lectures and speeches written and delivered, the question arises as to what significance my work has been in the field of science and development. What has been the meaning of my work to the people I have been engaged with and to the communities which have striven for the goals they set for themselves when becoming aware of their possibilities? Or has this work remained an effort to fulfil my own inner need to understand and analyse life? I am astounded by the similarity between the questions I asked when my research career commenced and those that still puzzle me as existential problems. Although the nature of the problems changes, they re-emerge because the solutions do not last. The role played by those as the actors in the research is repeatedly the aspect most neglected.

On initiating my research, I focused on the active role played by women in rituals and, time and again, I returned to the situation of women within different contexts. It is evident that there has been visible upgrading of women's legal rights in Tanzania and their role has increased in public life, but it has not played out in the same way in the domestic sphere or even, despite the rhetoric, in the policies of the state. This is visible especially in the agricultural program of the state. Agriculture is still the core engagement for the majority of women, but this fact is almost totally ignored in agricultural planning.

While writing these reflections, I have come to realize the influence that early wartime history and basic academic training have had on my thinking. Lately, my thoughts have turned to the term folklore, and what it has consisted of as "people's knowledge." In Finland *rahvas,* corresponding with "peasants" in today's Africa, became *kansa* (folk, nation), when people's cultural inheritance was discovered in hundreds of thousands of conserved verses of poetry, epics, songs, proverbs and phrases, which inspired national artists and musicians.

In Africa, the country folk have been politically referred to as *peasants*, and their *poverty* is still in the centre in all development discourse, especially so after the universally agreed Millennium Development Goals (MDGs) and the Paris Declaration. Neither of these terms applies to people in these writings. Instead of "peasants," people are called villagers, farmers, and pastoralists. In Chapter 4 which questions on whose culture is development is built, the dominant concept "poverty" in "aid" discussions is called into question.

The intention is to bring out the wealth of people's common knowledge, the astonishing richness of ritual and symbolic understanding of life and the women's role in them, so frequently ignored in studies. Women are remembered when poverty is discussed, yet women have been the carriers of tradition and they not only maintain life, but the domestic and social continuity in villages. The Zaramo myth tells us that it was the *progenitris* who discovered all the plants they customarily eat, cooked them and as a wife gave to the husband to taste (M-L. Swantz 1986, 260).

The significance still found in the traditions becomes evident in several chapters.

A reminder of how contacts become alive touched me when arriving in Dar es Salaam in 2010. A student came to meet me at the airport in the car he had bought on a loan allotted to doctoral students in the University of Dar es Salaam. On the way to the city he decided to drive via the area earlier called Buguruni, traditional living quarters for the Zaramo, with whom I had closely shared life. To my great surprise the entire area, including the modern buildings and institutions on the other side of the main street, had been renamed and were now called *Kwa Malapa.* We turned right into the narrow streets and crooked corners - which the city planners had mercifully saved from being standardised, thus still allowing the accommodation of the traditional Zaramo dwellings. An old man did not hesitate to step into the car and sit next to the *Mzungu* (European) woman to guide us to the original *Kwa Malapa*. Everyone familiar with Buguruni knew Malapa's house and bar. Now there are only faint lines left of Malapa's name on the bar walls, remnants of the large painting of Malapa himself sitting before the elephants and hippopotamus, and new people were renting the rooms on both sides of the corridor of a typical Swahili house. But Malapa, the barkeeper, had left his name as a lasting memory for the extensive ward.

Before Malapa arrived here and before Dar es Salaam existed, in fact before the Germans chose Dar es Salaam as the capital, the place was called Kwa Binti Madenge; the woman innkeeper Madenge being well known to the Zaramo. They came to the settlement near the harbour to sell their produce using the road built by a British constructor MacKinnon with the help of Indian elephants. The seventy kilometres of finished road through the Zaramo lands were enough to facilitate their trade in gum copal before the elephants, and gradually the trade, died. Better ingredients replaced the gum, but a Zaramo elder, Abdurahamani in Bunju originating in Msanga on the way to Maneromango, claimed that people began to mix sand in the copal and the poor quality lessened the interest of the Indian traders.

What else do we know about Malapa? He was a man of South African descent who had married my classificatory sister Binti Salum, a daughter of a famous *mganga*, medicine man Salum Mhunzi in Bunju, who adopted me as his daughter as a way of integrating me into the village society. Upon my visit, his grandson happened to be there with his motorcycle. He was now the Vice President's assistant for setting up his communication media. He was building a house in Bunju and invited us to come and see it. The history of *Kwa Malapa* might not be written in tourist guides of the city but it lives in the minds of the people. The elder who took us through the winding narrow lanes would tell a different story from that of the historians as the city planners look toward the high-rises and the white maritime architecture.

Early guides on the way

Before starting the process of participatory research, I experienced some helpful visions, which coincided with my study process. The book *Patterns in Comparative Religion* (1958) by Mircea Eliade had made an impact on me. It drew my attention to the basic universal themes repeated in most cultures and religions. The symbolic patterns in reference to the sun and moon, water and earth told me something about human beings in general. Their significance was to gain depth when I became acquainted with the wise men and women in Bunju where the water and earth were a central part of the symbolic theme of the Zaramo. It was possible to relate Carl Jung's interpretation of water as symbolizing the unconscious to the experience of the *mganga* Ndamba, whose descent into the depths of water gave him the basic experience leading to his life's task as a wise-man and spirit healer (Jung 1964; Swantz 1986). It led to the key realization that symbolism was at the heart of knowledge creation and central to different knowledge systems. It formed the key to understanding the culture in the participatory research process.

The readings of Carl Jung, Sigmund Freud (1961) had potential applications to psycho-analytic concepts in the analysis of the actions of the wise woman Mwawila and men, *waganga,* I communicated with in Bunju, not least to Salum Mhunzi, which also led me into the interpretations of psychiatrist Martti Siirala, the initiator of the Terapeia Foundation in Finland, and his theologian brother Arne Siirala, who both took an interest in my study (A. Siirala 1964; M. Siirala 1964, 1965, 1986). The readings led me further to the realization that research requires imagination. C. Wright Mills's *The Sociological Imagination* (1959) released me from my inner dread of high theory, in his case of the theory of Talcott Parsons. Another initial vision came from Lévi-Strauss's (1963) synchronic knowledge illuminated in two comparisons: the way of comprehending the structure of an orchestra with one glance by following the notations for all the instruments of a symphony orchestra on one sheet; and even more familiar to me, the Olduvai Gorge, where when standing at the bottom of the valley one can see at a glance the structure of the precipice through millions of years. The structure was not an edifice built by minute structural elements, but rather could be comprehended with one's imagination, bringing into the picture the whole geological history. It makes it possible to encompass the existentially unique in the conceptually familiar and to embed the present in the past as Marshall Sahlins has done with the history of the Cook Islands (Sahlins 1985). Such flights of thought made it possible to envision the symbolic communication of the befriended villagers. This vision did not prevent me from going into historical details and exploring in more detail the structural elements guided by Lévi-Strauss's effective symbols, Mary Douglas's *Purity and Danger, Natural Symbols,* and *Implicit Meanings* (1966) and Victor Turner's imaginative interpretations of symbols in *The Forest of Symbols* (1967).

I came to understand the significance of Susanne Langer's *Philosophy in a New Key* (1957). The book became a key influence in my interpretation of the symbolism of the Zaramo, which opened up during my research. I was introduced to Langer's thought of symbol preceding the rational thought by University of Helsinki Professor of Theology, Aarne Siirala. The illness of an individual suffering on behalf of their nearest in a social context can be interpreted as an experience requiring social cure and care of the wider social group. This both influenced my thinking and deepened my understanding of traditional healing. It also opened up the possibility of relying on sensory data. There were vast areas of experience which did not yield either to quantitative measurement or even to expressions in discursive language. Human beings' needs and their capacity for symbolism became central to the interpretation via Zaramo symbolism (M-L. Swantz 1986).

Realizing the significance of symbolism deepened the inner sense of the layers of knowledge, not only based on the rational and systemic thought structures. Knowledge could also consist of a symbolic comprehension of an idea, which becomes alive within a person, even before it has found expression in language. It was my understanding of what Susanne Langer meant when she wrote that symbol precedes rational thought, an idea also found in the writings on Paul Ricouer, in phenomenology and hermeneutics (Ihde 1986, 168).

I came back to these thoughts during my visit to Bunju in 2010 at the meeting with a former *mwali*, a granddaughter of my assigned father Salum Mhunzi and one of the young girls in whose week-long maturity rituals I had taken part in 1967. I pondered how meaningful the symbols could be to her now, if they were recalled amidst her changed life situation. She was now mother of two secondary school boys and a wife of a shopkeeper in Bunju, sitting on a sofa, eyes fixed on TV. I wondered how she would respond now to the meanings that the colours and substances had had when they related to the unified communal experience. Those members of the society, who repeatedly took part in the same inductive rites, learned the symbolic meanings of the colours and shapes of the everyday utensils and containers. This *mwali* had followed other girls' teachings after her own maturity ritual and had remained in the same village, which was now united with the growing city of Dar es Salaam. She did not, however, personally have to face the problem of continuing the ritual as she had no daughters, only two sons. I learned from a neighbour that even in 2010 in the middle of the old Kariakoo housing area in Dar es Salaam, the Zaramo put up a large tent to perform their rituals and the women instructors were in demand even by other ethnic groups for instructing girls who were getting married. It indicates a step from the symbolic interpretation of the ritual to a more practical utilization of the old model of instructing young girls for marriage.

These changes in people's lives lead to the role of culture in development, which forms one of the themes in the book. It leads to the use of culture as a concept, which my early mentor Mary Douglas severely criticized and which I did not have in the glossary or the contents in formulating my ritual analysis in reference to her and to Victor Turner's social anthropological basis. In analysing the role of culture in development I refer to Douglas' criticism of Clifford Geertz's use of the concept. Anthropologists have been divided over the use of the term *culture*. I follow anthropologists who cannot manage without reference to culture, such as Marshall Sahlins, Clifford Geertz and Joel Robbins. Robbins made the point of the centrality of culture in his experience with the Urapmin in New Guinea, having strongly criticized the Comaroffs' conceptualization of religion (Robbins 2004). Even Douglas needed the culture concept in her later writing; it is even in the title of her book *Risk and Culture* (Douglas and Wildavsky 1982) and in *The Risk Acceptability According to the Social Sciences* (1982).

The changes in people's lives lead one to question the extent of their *awareness* of the meanings they act out in human relations or in rituals, which then leads also to the concept of *rationality* in the traditional thought systems. I refer to Terence Ranger and Robin Horton and am aware of the strong criticism the latter has faced on his views of rationality. Both positively commented on my seeing rational thought behind the wisdom of my diviner friend Mwawila, as did my disputant Ulf Himmelstrand at the early phase of my study. I do not find myself among the rationalists, but I come to it in relation to the central concept of *development* and the way I created a framework combining the two concepts in the early phase of my research.

These thoughts take me to the rational component in the process of people's development as an important theme in anticipation of the change from a given state to one in which the members of the society have ability and power to influence intentionally their own state. I use the concept of *space,* translated into Swahili as *nafasi,* with a more specific meaning of *opportunity,* which I later discovered was being argued also by Nobel laureate Amartya Sen. This is a fundamental aspect of social and cultural change giving content to the concept of "development," which was new to the people in Bunju at the time I began my journey with them. I use the concepts *awareness* and *consciousness* of the social and political state and the situation of the people when they discovered themselves to be in the process of unavoidable change with little regard for their capacity to influence it. This state relates to personal and group qualities and conscious choices people make when the situation requires knowledge and rational thought. Also the rationality in the ritual context needs attention, not, however, arguing that the participants in acting out the ritual interpret it rationally. Rituals have many actors in different roles. Consequently, research dealing with such a social process must consider, and not undermine, the conscious element into which the forward-looking members of society are drawn, with the fundamental change in the social policy in the developing situations of any country. I find myself on the border of cognitive anthropology, but feel most comfortable among the hermeneutic scholarship, starting from Edmund Husserl and quoting Alfred Schütz while referring to Habermas' critique of Schütz's demand for connection with practice. It brought me to assessing Peter Rigby and Kemal Mustafa's identification with Merleau-Ponty's existential phenomenology, which claimed not to be transcendental; later readings of his writings provide for different interpretations. I faced strong Marxist methodology during the first substantial research project, which goes by the name Jipemoyo, even when several of us were moving within the phenomenological framework.

Participation, engagement and intention are the key words in this book. Participatory or engaged research can lead to the self-analysis of the community, but it can also become part of the theoretical analysis of the cultural phenomena and contribute to the social goals made common. Participatory community-based research can be part of the process of a conscious change and create a state of people's awareness of the social and political situation and its demands for people from different educational levels of society. It can become a method of critical participation in the society's transformation. To make participatory research an integral part of the social process does not mean forfeiting critical analysis, rather the opposite. The close participation of the researchers in the life of the society, and the incorporation of the people concerned into such research, toward the aim of greater self-realization, give the critical analysis a realistic base.

The story of the involvement in the planning and implementation of different research projects makes this a personal story. The research has been to the author a personal experience throughout her research career, as the involvement of people as active participants in research has also meant personal involvement in people's lives. The intention is to look for the *common intent* of the variety of participants in the implementation of the research; what *the factors have been that have influenced* the selected ways of the practical implementation and formulation of the research; how the implementation of *the participatory research has interacted with practice*; and *what lessons the experience has taught me* when closing my life's work. It means wandering in different directions to review the projects since their intent and the time of carrying them out have differed, but having this perspective will help to *give the writing structure and meaning*, interpreted from the premises set, when drawing the boundaries in the process of creating an understanding of the scientific requirements in an interdisciplinary situation into which participation takes the researcher.

Quest for participatory approach to research

Participatory Research Approach (PRA), which I initiated in 1972 in Tanzania and later changed to Participatory Action Research, grew from the need not to separate the university from the practical reality of the commoners, the actors in development, but rather to facilitate the acquisition and application of knowledge, which pertained to people's actual situations. Participatory Research (PR) and Participatory Approach to Research (PAR), as I initiated in the early 1970s, had no connection with Participatory Rural Appraisal (PRA) or its predecessor, Rapid Rural Appraisal (RRA), which were introduced in Tanzania in the beginning of the 1990s, to which I return.

The danger was evident that the newly established University of Dar es Salaam, literally built on the hills, would, metaphorically speaking, remain there; a separation between the university and people's everyday lives would exist as in colonial times. This would not only create a class base, but also a serious knowledge gap of the real needs of the people. The political situation called for mutual engagement and communication between the researchers and "peasants and workers," as people were called in the political jargon, when workers also included the academicians. The country had set high hopes in establishing the university right after independence. The foreign staff was professionally competent, but foreign, and with some exceptions initially unfamiliar with the needs the developing situation demanded.

With Thomas Kühn, the potential for a new paradigm was breaking into social science, which would make it possible to broaden the knowledge base, in this case with the inclusion of the former objects of research as actors in knowledge creation in some phases of the research process. The new paradigm was a constructive path in the process of nation building, which was the prevailing national motivating theme. President Nyerere demanded that people's voices had to be listened to. He wanted to prevent the formation of an elite class, which would separate itself from the common people. His leading themes were self-help, and building on the national cultural heritage. The problem of being objective in research was obvious in the new research approach, but Gunnar Myrdal's thoughts on objectivity served as an authority in the social sciences. According to him social scientists cannot really claim objectivity, even if they strive to be as objective as possible in the circumstances (Myrdal 1969). However, I also found theoretical defenders of the approach, here I refer to Heinz Moser (1978), whose writings in the German language were not commonly read.

The analysis of the developing situation in the field of knowledge creation was started with the western scientists who held all the senior positions in the University. An initial argument was that the foreign scientists had an advantage in the study of the social situation of the "indigenes," both in technical sciences and in the study of culture. This has continued to be an every day occurrence as one scientist after another is contacted by the media to give answers to problems relating to situations in Africa.

During a session with my close friend, woman diviner Mwawila, another *mganga* Amri Sefu shared the *rungu* exorcism with her. He claimed to have bewitching powers and he even promised to take me to the witches' coven at night. It was too far fetched for me, but I agreed to go with him at midnight to a place where he claimed to get his bewitching medicine. As my husband was doing research at the time on the medicine men in Dar es Salaam, he came along too. The *mganga* ended in a place with a few graves, where he claimed he would get the medicine from a dead man's brains. He did not start digging it from a grave, but rather took a small bottle from his pocket claiming it contained powerful medicine, taken earlier from a grave there. He gave the bottle to me.

The Medical Faculty was using Bagamoyo town hospital for students' practical training while I was doing two Young Child studies for UNICEF in Bagamoyo District in 1974 and 1975. The medical students were taken in a four-wheel drive vehicle to the villages and brought back at night. Their social contact with village people was minimal or non-existent. It happened that a carload of students arrived at a school to give measles vaccinations to the school children to find that only the teachers' children were left at the school while all the others remained at home. They had heard a rumour that the vaccination could kill children. There was no ante- or post-procedural communication, or human contact between the school and the doctoral students. The only information received was that on a certain day the children would be vaccinated.

Visiting the faculty premises in Dar es Salaam, I asked for the reports the students wrote when making visits in Bagamoyo district, based on their practical work in the area. It transpired that the student reports had not been saved. In the teachers' home universities it might not have been necessary, but when information about the local health situation was scarce, the reports would have been valuable. In the field of medicine, the need to relate the academic work to the needs of the country was especially acute. It was a key issue in the maintenance of health, but it also had to do with the growing sense that doctors were a higher category of people. The university students were no longer "peasants," nor would they call themselves "workers." President Nyerere was optimistic in his effort to prevent students being seen as belonging to a different class; this he implemented by sending home the students who demonstrated against the poor quality of food in the university dining hall. It was still a far cry from the present situation when everyone in any position is addressed Honourable (*Mheshimiwa*).

Some influence could be exercised by a parliamentary friend, Barbro Johansson, who left her mission work as the Headmistress in the Girls' School in Kashasha, Bukoba, and twice was elected as a Member of Parliament, MP. She served on the University Council and put forth a request that the policy of applied science be part of the University teaching. After the first participatory research project with the students as research assistants, the Chief Academic Officer, Professor Isaria Kimambo was impressed by their attitudes when reading their research reports from villages. He sent a letter around to the heads of the departments suggesting that the practice oriented approach should be adopted when students were used as research assistants.

The need for a new participatory research approach was evident. Today I could call this approach Community-Based Research (CBR), which actively linked local communities with the research of the scientists for the benefit of the practical needs of the developing community, and involved participation of the members of that community. The same pertained to women's studies. The number of women as students in the university grew gradually and the women's studies required a change of the research and social paradigm, as the prevailing masculine domination in society and in the country's socialist theories needed reworking. Women students became involved in participatory research projects but they were first hesitant to start their own working group for this purpose, as they feared greater isolation and the potential critique of fellow male students. It became the task of Marjorie Mbilinyi to lead the female students within UDSM and to initiate more pointed research on women's rights.

Glimpses of further theoretical inputs

After my experiences while employed at the university of Dar es Salaam, the academic contacts continued through the participatory research programs, first in Jipemoyo research for four years under the Academy of Finland, and then in the programs, projects and evaluations which I led as the Director of the Institute of Development Studies, IDS, at the University of Helsinki once it became officially established. I describe this in further detail in the chapters that follow. The development theories at the University of Dar es Salaam were governed by different interpretations of Marxism, which were fitted into the cultural and social development of the pastoralists and farmers adjusting themselves to the villagization program. The increasing international contacts influenced the applied theories and will be dealt with in the relevant chapters. Anthropologist Peter Rigby, working simultaneously with the Parakuyo Maasai, guided the theoretical formulation for one of the researchers; he was working on the same line of immersion in the community he at the same time studied. The final conference to evaluate Jipemoyo was held in Helsinki and was a significant occasion. It brought together the evaluators of the different subject areas covered in the research, together with the leaders of the European Association of Development Studies Institutes, EADI, for a seminar that was held the day after the evaluation.

Professor Peter Reason from the University of Bath attended a seminar in 1981 organized as a follow-up to Jipemoyo, which led to my close, long-term cooperation with him. Peter Reason, in cooperation with John Heron, had been developing cooperative research in the context of psychological and medical contacts with people. They found similarities in their cooperative approach to my way of working. I was invited, together with them, to contribute to the daylong sessions presenting our related research approach at the annual British Advanced Sciences Conference in Liverpool. From thereon I contributed to the books edited by Peter Reason. I wrote first a chapter in *Human Inquiry in Action, A Sourcebook of New Paradigm Research* (1988) with Arja Vainio-Mattila, a student I had guided and who is now a professor in Canada. Another article in 1996 was a personal position paper in *Qualitative Inquiry;* Peter Reason was an editor together with Y.S. Lincoln (M-L. Swantz 1996). Later I was on the Editorial Committee and contributed to the three volumes *The Sage Handbook of Action Research, Participative Inquiry and Practice,* I, II and III, which Peter Reason and Hilary Bradbury edited. Later attendance at European and Global Action Research world conferences, which included Participatory Action Research, played a crucial role in the promotion of PAR. I attended one in Australia in 1990 and another in Pretoria, South Africa in 1993.

Another highly significant academic cooperation was related to my being a Senior Research Fellow in the UNU-WIDER, United Nations University - World Institute for Development Economics Research, between 1987-1989. It was run under the leadership of Sri Lankan Lal Jayawardena, who invited high academic level scholars to establish and formulate its program. Kumar Jayawardena was also a scholar and she initiated research conferences and research related to women, later with significant addition by the work of Valentine Moghadam, originally from Iran, and Sheila Rowbotham, a notable writer specializing on women in the workplace. They added substantially to research related to women while they were attached to WIDER.

Professor Martha Nussbaum was another well-known scholar who cooperated with Harvard Professor Amartya Sen while in WIDER. Amartya K. Sen later became a Nobel laureate, at the time acted as the Research Advisor and, together with Jean Dreze, produced three volumes on Political Economy of Hunger. Martha Nussbaum and Amartya Sen called together a conference of economists, social scientists and philosophers on the theme of the quality of life, and whether utility was the right unit for measuring the quality of human lives. The international economists, social scientists and philosophers were the speakers and discussants. Among them was the leading Finnish sociologist Eric Allardt whose theory on three concepts of "having, loving and being" was included in the massive volume of the presentations edited by Martha Nussbaum and Amartya Sen as *Quality of Life* (Oxford 1993). It was a great privilege to work in WIDER, and offered the acquaintance of other eminent scholars, such as Eric Hobsbawm, and African scholars Germano Mwabu from Kenya and Ibrahim Lipumba, a presidential candidate from Tanzania.

In a new book, written again with Jean Dreze, *An Uncertain Glory: India and Its Contradictions* (2013), Amartya Sen argues as before that economic growth is not enough to take care of the problems related to social and health sectors, expenditure on special programs for them is a necessity. *Time* reports how another renowned Indian economist at Harvard, Jagdish Bhagwati, criticizes Sen and believes that market reforms, which liberalized the economy of India in 1991, will generate the growth needed to bring people out of poverty.

Not only Sen, but also his more radical economics colleague from Harvard, Stephen A. Marglin and his anthropologist wife Frédérique Apffel-Marglin, who were in WIDER at the same time, represented the critique of the domination of mainline economics in development. They were closer to my line of thought based on the communal concept of economy, which they had developed while doing studies in India. The Marglins discovered that my research was akin to theirs and the cooperation with them became a relationship continuing for twenty years. It became significant for my professional development and above all gave me confidence as a scholar and convinced me that the line I was developing was of academic and social value. Research conferences with the Marglins and Tariq Banuri, another significant Harvard scholar in WIDER, originally from Pakistan, were held in Amherst, Massachusetts, in Karachi in Pakistan, in Bellagio in Italy and later three times in another composition in Manchester, New Hampshire. On Frédérique Apffel-Marglin's intervention, Zenya Wild rewrote my book *Ritual and Symbol*, in plain language. This more readable version was entitled *Blood, Milk and Death Body Symbols and the Power of Regeneration* and included personal additions by Salome Mjema, a Tanzanian student studying at the time in Finland; she was a close Zaramo friend's daughter whose maturity rituals I had attended (Swantz, Mjema, Wild, 1995; Apffel-Marglin and Marglin 1990, 1996; Swantz and Tripp 1993). I refer to the scientific input of the Marglins and Tariq Banuri in different chapters, especially to Stephen Marglin's division of thought to *epistemic* and *techne,* knowledge based on practical life. In his later book *Dismal Science: How Thinking Like an Economist Undermines Community* (2008), the critique of the domination of sole economistic rule in the societies is indeed dismal science and *epistemic* knowledge was replaced with *algorithmic* knowledge. The names of the books the Marglins edited and contributed express their line of argument, *Dominating Knowledge* (1990) and *Decolonizing Knowledge* (1998), the latter to which my daughter, Aili Mari Tripp and I contributed, our focus being on the fishing communities. I return to these theoretical aspects within the chapters that describe the different research projects.

Frédérique Apffel-Marglin saw to it that the role of women came to the fore in all the research. We organized two international women's camping seminars for the exchange of innovative ideas in Lohja, southern Finland, in the 1990s. Of significance at the seminar was the attendance of Signe Arnfred. She put me in touch with her women studies study group at Roskilde University in Denmark, and included my chapter on "The place of people's own knowledge in theorizing about the economies of the poor" in their Occasional papers (M-L. Swantz, 1995)· The contact continued when Signe Arnfred led the program on African gender studies for many years at the Nordic Africa Institute (NAI) in Uppsala (Arnfred 2011). NAI continued to be a significant contact throughout the years; I also served as the Finnish representative and was, as an elder, appointed to the distinguished category of Associate. Many of our writings were published by NAI.

Whilst at WIDER during the first period, the Academy of Finland accepted a project, *Grassroots Dynamics and Directed Development*, in which Benno Ndulu, then Professor of Economics at the University of Dar es Salaam, now the Governor of the Bank of Tanzania, and Aili Mari Tripp, were involved (Swantz and Tripp 1996).

In between my engagement for two periods in WIDER, I was the research director of IDS at the University of Helsinki for three years 1990-1993. During that period, we were engaged in a project *Local Actors in Development* in Mwanga district, Kilimanjaro region in cooperation with Professor Cuthbert Omari. William Mjema also became involved in the project as a local expert. It initiated his, and Salome his wife's, contact with the University of Tampere where they completed their Master's degrees and have worked far with their doctorate. Two other researchers were later to become professors, Joe Lugalla in the United States, who coordinated Tanzania Studies at the African Studies Association, ASA, and Bertha Koda, for many years the Director of the Institute of Development Studies in UDSM.

The Society for International Development, SID, joined in a Mutual Learning program, and in a seminar held in Mwanga, in Kilimanjaro region, at the time of the above research project. The project included the study of fishing in Nyumba ya Mungu lake and the women's engagement in employing fishermen, but also mainly in marketing the fish. Another project on entrepreneurship was also carried out during these years. In 1992 the Entrepreneurial Institute of Kauhava in Finland invited nine entrepreneurial candidates from Mwanga to learn the skills of entrepreneurship; seminars related to the subject were held in Mwanga. The participants started an organization of local entrepreneurs, UWAMWA. Further opportunity was given for participatory research; the women exchanged visits between Mtwara in the South and Mwanga, and a seminar was run in Moshi in which women from the North and South participated. The chapters within this book on women reflect some of these experiences. Before writing this I had the opportunity to meet fisherwoman Mwanashulu, one of the participants in the seminar and the women's group in Mtwara. Her excitement about our meeting twenty years after was beyond description.

Employed by the Norwegian development agency NORAD, I was involved in an evaluation of the fishing sector in different places along the Indian Ocean. I also spent one week at the lakeside of Lake Victoria. Maria, wife of President Nyerere, invited me to stay in their home while in the area, but the transport would have made it difficult for the whole week. I did have the privilege of spending one day and night with the Presidential couple. It happened to be the day when Vice President Kawawa and his convoy were visiting the President and I had the opportunity of listening to their discussions with the local elders. I was particularly impressed by the family's big library in a round room.

My second period as a visiting professor in WIDER (1993-1998) took place when Mihaly Simai was the director. He involved me in the program to change the nature of Global Employment, The Future of Work (M-L. Swantz 1995), which benefitted me as it involved looking into the economic issues related to women. At the same time, over the course of six years I spent half of my time acting as a sociologist in the Finnish development project RIPS in Mtwara and Lindi regions. This gave me the opportunity to apply my PAR in practice while I acquainted myself with the use of Participatory Rural Appraisal as a training program for development planning in villages. I have made use of some of the data gathered during that period in the extensive articles written at the time, which have not been fully utilized. The RIPS experience is reflected in the relevant chapters of this book. Two articles I wrote over this period at WIDER are "*Women Entrepreneurs in Tanzania, A Path to Sustainable Livelihood*" (M-L. Swantz 1995) and *Community and Village-Based Provision of Key Social Services* (M-L. Swantz 1997).

I have had additional research experience in Sri Lanka, Kenya, Zambia and Namibia and numerous academic contacts with other countries and continents but in this book I follow the historical progression of the way participatory approach was realized in Tanzania, not only in research but also in the implementation and planning of development.

CHAPTER 2

Anthropology and Knowledge Production

Introductory reflections

Participatory research approach as developed in this chapter brings forth the more general question of the involvement of the anthropologist in the studied peoples' lives and the role of the latter in the anthropological knowledge production. I reflect on some aspects of the role of the researcher and the researched as it has developed over the years. The discussion touches on some aspects on the anthropologists' engagement in the issues and problems of the researched community and the role of the "informants" in the knowledge production since the early years of the discipline. Participatory action research is frequently equated with applied research, which calls for clarification, differentiating participatory research (PR) and participatory action research (PAR) from participant observation and applied anthropology, and also different from the use of participatory rural appraisal (PRA) tools for village development, later applied in research in different ways.

Anthropologists adopted initially the terminology of going to the "field" and doing "field work" from the natural scientists, but the anthropological research was regarded as communication and creating relationships because the researchers related personally with people whose knowledge they appropriated. Anthropologists have encountered people in obvious need of some form of assistance requiring deeper engagement on the part of the scientists beyond what the scientific approach had anticipated or even permitted. Anthropologists have responded in differing ways not allowing the occasional interference to influence the research component. Leaving aside such human encounters the issue raised here relates to the roles the cooperating participants have in the production of knowledge in which the studied communities have a central role as recognized actors in research.

The historical review of the anthropologists' relation to the researched people introduces theoretical concerns of what Johannes Fabian has called "coevalness of the Other," whether the studied community remains the Other or whether there is a way of cohabiting the same space (Fabian 1983).

The written anthropological work is meant for the academic public, as it seldom has been readable by the "informants" or the studied communities themselves. But that situation is changing with the increasing global education and research being done in communities closer to home. The question is asked, should the roles of the participants continue to be so differentiated when the studied societies no longer are culturally distanced from learning and more participants interfere with the approach of the scholar. The ethical concerns have been raised within the situations in which the researcher seemingly appropriates key knowledge of a community in regard to the ownership of that knowledge. The awareness of the potential exploitation of the "field," the researched, has gained renewed significance (Caplan 2012). I refer to Pat Caplan's edited book and to the discussions held on the ethical questions within the American Anthropological Association (AAA), when anthropologists become involved in practical life, often because of the lack of academic employment opportunities (Caplan 2008). The issue relates also to the domination of the Western epistemologies brought out in the context of the Indigenous Knowledge Systems (IKS) and the demand made explicit in that context that knowledge should be carried out with the participation of the communities with reference to "epistemological justice" (Mazonde and Thomas 2007).

Western domination of anthropology

The engagement in problems of development has drawn anthropologists anew into the questions of terminology, which has troubled them since the beginning of the discipline. The discussion on the vocabulary used, the conceptualization of other cultures and the nature of participation have obtained new nuances, but have also brought up the old problems as newcomers to development go back to the phases long ago passed in main line anthropology. It has prompted attention to the old problems in a new light as the normative, pro-development, even if critical approach to development research is often not acceptable to the academic requirements in anthropology.

The question how anthropological knowledge is created goes deeper than the methodology used. The critique of the Western domination has for most of the history of the discipline been part of the self-search in anthropology, but it has become more pointed after the cultures earlier differentiated as "primitive" and later "less" or "least developed" have produced their own critical anthropologists and social science scholars.

Edward Said's *Orientalism* (1979) is a frequently quoted early attack on the ways the other cultures are presented by Western writers, but as Marcus and Fischer pointed out a critique is easier to present than to correct the way of writing (1986, 1-2). Said did not present an alternative mode for the representation of other voices as his voice was of an uprooted member of a dominated Palestine coming from a Western university. An often referred critical voice from Africa is to Ngugi wa Thiong'o of Kenya, whose use of indigenous Kikuyu language in his novels provided an alternative attempt to break the pattern of writing for the foreign readers and for the learned of his own country. Peter Rigby, anthropologist with a career in Uganda and Tanzania and married to an African, before moving to the USA, Pennsylvania toward the end of his life, was another critical voice. He tried to break off from the customary way of creating anthropological knowledge, particularly with the Parakuyo Maasai pastoralists (Rigby 1996). To his writings I return in other contexts.

Stanley Diamond wanted also pointedly to break the western domination in the discipline in his book *The Search of the Primitive* (1974). He challenged the concept of development and went as far as to say that humanity is going backward and losing some essential values which he found in what he called "the primitive," pointing out that to set the societies in order of the degree of development is based on wrong values. To him technically developed society was retreating rather than making progress in social relations and humanity. This was different from the prevailing social science conception of Emil Durkheim who defined the sociality of the less developed societies to be based on mechanical solidarity while the solidarity prevailing in an organic industrial society was based on multiple organized social relations. I was criticized for suggesting that the organic unity of the Zaramo society symbolized as a living organism was not in line with Durkheim's generalizing arguments, which to me devalued the organic symbolic view to life of such a society as the Zaramo (Durkheim 1933; Swantz, 1985).

According to Diamond we cannot reject what we consider primitive, we can grow out of it only by allowing it to grow within us in dialectical relationship between western civilization and the experience of the primitive in us. In pointing out that human poetic qualities bring out many aspects of the positive in the concept "primitive" Diamond referred to T.S. Eliot stating, "Primitive modes of cognition persist in civilized men but become available only through the poet." Diamond, as also Rigby, with many other contemporary anthropologists, applied simultaneously Marxist critique on the capitalist invasion of the studied societies, yet I found in Diamond's way of referring to the potentiality of human qualities some correlation with my own conceptualization of the symbolic qualities of the Zaramo. However, the terminology utilizing the prejudiced concept "primitive," is in itself questionable and distorts the discussion (Diamond 1992).

Johannes Fabian as a defender of hermeneutic approach to the way anthropology makes its object found my sympathy already when I was writing the results of Jipemoyo research in 1979 (Fabian 1971, 9-47). Fabian's questioning relates more to the theoretical weakness since the beginning of anthropology when scholars engaged in ethnography conceived the societies as the Other. He goes back to the beginnings of social science and its relation to philosophy of Hegel. This study benefits from his call for *praxis* and his references to hermeneutic frame in which the epistemological significance of lived experience of knowledge is rooted in the author's autobiography (Fabian 1983, 88-89). I respond to Fabian's thoughts in my search for the alternatives, albeit I find him going too deep and wide with the concept of Time in his search for the Other in his book *Time and the Other* (1983), but I agree with him that language and communication to "should be understood as a kind of praxis in which the Knower cannot claim ascendancy over the Known." In his view "the anthropologist and his interlocutors only "know" when they meet each other in one and the same contemporality" (Fabian 1979a; Fabian 1983, 164).

In the discussion in African Studies Association (ASA) conference in Philadelphia 2012 the sessions "Decolonizing Research Practices" Anne Waliaula, Faith Ngujiri and Nampumpelelo Radebe spoke on the theme "Identity as black women in a transnational situation in Kenya and US," utilizing the concept "collaborative auto-ethnography" as a method studying African life as African co-researchers with others. It means self-focused consciously critical dialogue resulting in being multi-vocal and thus democratizing inquiry and reducing power differentials. Domination in anthropology is not the case only in cross-national and cross racial contexts, it relates also to the long enduring male domination in anthropological studies and the prevalent use of male informants, even if well known women anthropologists have played a central role in the discipline.

Stanley Jeyaraja Tambiah, originally Sri Lankan Tamil of a Christian family, is a well-known anthropologist, who did his initial anthropological research on Buddhist communities in Thailand. In *Magic, science, religion, and the scope of rationality* (Tambiah, 1990) he identifies himself as a western scholar with a career in the western universities, in Cambridge, Chicago and Harvard. At the same time, his analysis of the non-western cultures, while comparing mystical and logical knowledge systems, has made it possible for him to feel deep identity with them. For him "This idea of the relevance of contexts of thought and action, which apply to all human beings in all societies" was a seminal idea he was pursuing in his book, initially based on Frazer lectures given in honour of Sir James Frazer (1854-1938) and his famous Golden Bough. Tambiah found it to have "compelling contemporary significance," especially referring to Wittgenstein's encounter with Frazer, who met other cultures only "in print." The great philosopher had also been stimulated by ritual and religious phenomena to search for a different meaning of them.

The western domination of scientific logic creates ambivalence in which the scholars find themselves after making their research on cultures different from their own. As Tambiah is a scientist in the western scientific context he starts his interpretation what he calls "from Western baseline" as we do also as Western anthropologists. At the same time it is a task of translating cultures "in their terms...in our language" which is the "grand problem at the heart of the anthropological enterprise."

Tambiah presents Wittgenstein's interesting response to Frazer's description of the "worship of oak tree," which with reaching into the human condition evoking religious mysteries seeks emotional solace. It makes the description more meaningful than search for explanation would be. As a religious symbol is not based upon opinion, you do not look for an error, as "error is relevant to opinion only" and "magic always depends on the idea of symbolism and of language" and "error only arises when magic is interpreted scientifically." This reminds me of my rejection of the term "magical," after I had used it in the title of my first study on the women's rituals "Magical and religious rites." Also Tambiah replaces magic with ritual. Tambiah is critical of Horton, who had approved my interpretation of aspects of rationality in the ritual performance, but with satisfaction I find Tambiah bringing up the significance of Susanne Langer, whose privileging symbol before rational thought was for me a key find in my analysis of symbols. Tambiah quotes Langer at length and links up with her differentiation between discursive and presentational forms of thought. He refers to Levy-Bruhl's and Langer's imaginative, holistic and configurative grasping of totalities as integral to aesthetic and mystic awareness.

Of interest here is the significance of participation in Tambiah's reference to anthropologist Maurice Leenhardt who before becoming a professor had been a missionary in Melanesia for 24 years. Through his long experience he refined participation as "a central feature of mystical sensibility of the New Caledonians" ... and "infused the participation with a realism and intensity and gave it body and substance" (Tambiah 1990, 95-105).

Tambiah refers also to a different woman's voice of Carol Gilligan, sub-ordinate, suppressed ideology based on gender but participation and connectedness of persons gives a sense of being a part of ensemble of relations and bridges to the reality of experiential and symbolizing qualities of life. Participation and causality like religion and science are complementary orientations two modes of ordering the world and different cultures experience them in different ways.

The western dominance becomes especially notable in the researchers' involvement in development studies as the concept of development originates in western ideology. When dealing with development anthropology one needs to do serious self-analysis of the way in which the studies have looked at development in other cultures. It reveals the western dress of the approach and the need to listen attentively how the people involved look at the analyses of anthropologists.

Development anthropology as a discipline has taken a large section of anthropological engagement, even if anthropological departments have avoided it. It has often analysed critically the approach of the agency rather than penetrating to the social scene in the changing conditions of the people while there are also such people-centred studies as Daivi Rodima-Taylor's study of the Kuria in Tanzania and as part of the series *Development and Culture*, Helena Jerman's study of the concept of ethnicity to mention a few (Rodima-Taylor 2010; Jerman 1997). Anthropologists have often separated themselves from the development scene not wanting to engage in science which – right or wrong - could be classified "applied" and which has not given the time needed for the research engagement. The leading Finnish anthropologist Jukka Siikala's studies of the Polynesian cultures could serve as an example of such a case (Siikala 1990, 5-24). An interesting contribution of Finnish anthropology is Timo Kaartinen's portrait of a small potentially isolated community with links outside, yet not looked at from the development point of view (Kaartinen 2010).

One of the strongly critical voices of the western domination in anthropology is Peter Rigby's last book, and the authors he refers to in it (Rigby 1996). They have not represented the main stream in anthropology.

Engaged anthropologists

The engagement of anthropologists in the issues and problems of the researched community has become problematic when they have encountered situations of special needs with potential for interference. It leads to the question of the role of the anthropologists in relation to the people they study and the nature of their involvement in the problems people face. Anthropologists have responded to such challenges in differing ways, often not recording fully the degree of their involvement in people's affairs nor permitting such occasions to influence their scientific writing. The terms "engaged," "activist," "collaborative," "community-based" anthropology are used openly, whereby the researchers become colleagues with former informants or collaborators in one way or another.

Anthropologists' engagement and the role of the former informants in the whole setting of research was interestingly discussed in Wenner-Gren Symposium, the presentations of which were published in *Current Anthropology* October 2010. The symposium dealt with the issues

"... from basic commitment to our informants, to sharing and support with the communities with which we work, to teaching and public education, to social critique in academic and public forums, to more commonly understood forms of engagement such as collaboration, advocacy, and activism" (Low and Merry 2010).

It is of interest that already in 1950s at the start of the Wenner-Gren Foundation the first symposium was on environment as the theme *"Man's Role in Changing the Face of the Earth* (Thomas 1956). This was a pioneering anthropological initiative on environmental issues involving 70 international and interdisciplinary scholars who were selected for their common interest and curiosity about the human impact on the earth. I quote further reasons, which have led to engaging anthropology utilizing "the capacity of the discipline through basic research to make important interventions in public issues through a specific focus on heritage." A symposium was held in May 19–22, 2005, with the theme "Anthropology Put to Work/ Anthropology That Works?" It focused on the ways in which global forces, structural changes in academia and in the labour market, and the anthropologists' engagement in the world, have led to a transformation in the discipline (Field and Fox 2007). The authors hoped to clarify the actual ways the discipline was contributing and adapting to global realities and demonstrate how younger scholars were already putting anthropology to work. This kind of application of the knowledge would come close to applied anthropology, but its point is to recognize the role of anthropology in the practical world.

Among the dilemmas taken up in the symposium in 2010, which were considered to have so far remained unresolved and not sufficiently dealt with, were the ethics of intervention, the appropriateness of critique brought up by anthropologists given their position, and the hazards of working with powerful government and military organizations. The history of anthropology has an inexcusable experience in the so called Camelot project in Latin America with US governmental involvement for ultimate military purposes, which was interfered before it was carried through (Beals 1982).

The issue of engagement relates closely to applied anthropology, which is brought up below. It has been the concern of sensitive anthropologists who realized that the key informants were the actual producers of the basic knowledge. The role of the anthropologist was to put the information into an academically acceptable theoretical frame, which brings up a further problem beyond the ethics. It relates to the concern whose themes the anthropologist chooses to deal with in her or his writings and whether the concentration on the academic theoretical concerns solely determines the choice or does the research arise also and perhaps principally from the problems of the studied communities of former informants. The problematic is bound to turn to theoretical problems for the academics, which the co-researchers seldom read.

The positive exceptions are likely to be more numerous than what the authors record. The study directed by Taimi Sitari thirty years after she had been engaged in the Jipemoyo research in Tanzania deserves to be quoted as it produced its main research results first in Swahili and not in English and the research team held meetings about the results with the village leaders and the Ministry officers responsible for the implementation that the land the government had surveyed was submitted to its owners. As producers they should have also had their share of the payments made. They also pointed out that the payment for the cut trees for burning into coals were not given monetary value. The individual researchers wrote later their personal articles in English (Sokoni 2010).

The emphasis of the anthropologists' engagement in the issues brought out by people as their own concerns leads to the common solving of problems and changes the role of the former "informants." Gender studies have brought up the involvement of women in research as the actors in a different light from the traditional practice. The wider concerns in anthropology have led also to the indigenous anthropology, which has exploded when people from formerly studied groups have become scholars of their own societies and critics of the scholarship approaching issues from outside (Fahim 1982).

It has been commonly assumed that the anthropologists come to their research situation with the basic principle of non-involvement. The ethical question is nevertheless frequently raised of the nature and role of the "informants" involved in the research process and in knowledge production. When the informants are taken as co-researchers we ask how they have benefited from their participation, how aware have the "informants" been of their role, how well had it been explained to them, had the issue of compensation been considered and had they received any (Writers in Caplan, footnote 2)

The professional anthropologists are nowadays frequently employed outside the academy and they produce knowledge for the employer for payment, as is the case in frequent evaluative tasks on development issues. It has its effects on the result even when the employer gives freedom to treat the subject beyond the requirements of the situation. The question is open should part of the payment go to the people acting as informants and how would it distort the knowledge and the anthropological ideals. This brings up the need to call research participatory recognizing the collaborators as partners.

The involvement of anthropologists in the affairs of the studied communities has come in waves. I review briefly some of the implications. The main issue in this book is not, however, the applied use of anthropology even if in this chapter the different ways of using it are brought up and its relation to engaged and participatory research is brought up. The question is ultimately about greater involvement of the studied people themselves in the analysis of their own societies and the role of the knowledge and analysis of the studied people in the end result of the work of the anthropologists.

James Clifford discussed the balance between subjectivity and objectivity in field research in the introduction to the book he edited with George Marcus *Writing Culture. The Poetic and Policies of Ethnography* (1986). The author pointed out that the convention of retaining impersonal standards cracked in writing up "field work." It did not mean only recording the field experiences in a self-reflective manner, but the ideal of participant observation was also shown to be problematic. The subject of research became alive. It transformed the "cultural" text "into a speaking subject, who sees as well as is seen who evades, argues, probes back." It meant that in place of the one voice, which had earlier an authorial function whereby the voices of the "informants" were paraphrased, many voices of the observed were recorded, as the "informants" had also a voice (Clifford and Marcus 1986, 13-15). In spite of the efforts made the anthropologists continue to represent the cultures they study, albeit often with the self-critique and awareness of the weaknesses of such positioning of knowledge.

In Clifford's introduction as in the whole book the hierarchical positioning of anthropology is called to question. Even in Godfrey Lienhardt's *Divinity and Experience. The Religion of the Dinka* (1961) in Sudan, which in Clifford's opinion was "among the most finely argued ethnographies," the people's true voices are men's voices with the exception of one weak case. The scholar decides what and how he presents the case (Clifford and Marcus 1986, 17). Later, women probably are in majority and the pioneering women in American anthropology are well recognized, but the authors must have a case to defend when they do not set women to the same line of recognition. Anthropologists do not obviously only write "reports of field-work," they interpret and find meanings in what they study in relation to other sources of knowledge. Yet the issue of the role of the researched requires further discussion, as it relates also to their motivation for making studies of their own cultures. The result might be that the ethnographer becomes only a scribe if the voices of the described culture are given the forefront. Fabian in his book *Time and the Other* gives examples of that extent of identification with the subjects of research.

The question of anthropologists' employment as researchers for practical purposes became acute when the western world was challenged with the issue of development of the Third World after the WWII, but their involvement for the benefit of the researched had started during the colonial time. The threat of Europeanization of the African cultures was seen as the problem to be studied by the British and South African anthropologists in Central and South Africa especially through the people's employment in mining industry in what then was North Rhodesia and after independence Zambia. The colonizers needed to know the conditions on which they could employ the local people, as thereby their lives would be changed. The sensitivity toward not destroying people's culture juxtaposed the anthropologists as also missionaries with people's awakened aspirations for modernizing change.

American anthropological ancestors faced such questions with their involvement with groups of Indians, later they were employed to characterize the enemy cultures during the WWII. After the war the field of development opened up and engaged and challenged anthropologists to different degrees. In all these cases a deeper knowledge of the societies was politically and economically opportune.

The basic question was then, as it has been since, how anthropology is equipped to deal with the problems of change, but also and above all, what effect such external interests have on the discipline as science. How did anthropology develop as independent science when it was charged with externally imposed tasks and how appropriate has it been to face these challenges? Was anthropology able to shake the reputation of colonialism from its shoulders? How colonialist, European or Western is anthropological thinking for African readers? How tainted is the discipline in trying to accommodate development and have those scientists who have kept themselves apart from such employments fared better? A brief look at the historical development of the discipline and its tools raises a number of questions.

Since the beginning there has been a tug of war between those who considered it their natural duty to work for the good of the people they studied and those who considered it an assault on the objectivity of scientific work. The sociology of knowledge has provided tools for analysing the social roots of scientific knowledge and exposed the falseness of objectivity on the grounds of non-interference. Before going further to the role of the researched in the research process the issue of anthropology as an applied science now and in the earlier phases of anthropology needs to be discussed briefly.

Anthropology as an applied science

According to AAA, the American Association of Anthropologists, today fifty per cent of anthropologists are employed outside the academy. The article recognizes a growing need for unified anthropology where academics inform practice and practice informs academics. On the other hand, in the discussion in 2010 the criticism was raised about the removal of the concept "science" from the new AAA stated principles. The governing committee later informed that the Association had made a change on that score indicating science as the base of the AAA, but the word science was avoided (*Chronicle of Higher Education* 8.11. 2010).

At the inception of anthropology the pioneers took a stand in the evolution of society. Edwin B. Tylor writing in the 1870s discussed the science of culture as the science of reformists, for transformation in the British society. Lois H. Morgan wrote memoranda to the United States Congress in defence of the Tonawanda Seneca Indians' rights. The more intimate the anthropologists became with the studied people, the more concern they had for them. By the mid-70s the aid agency USAID had at least 50 anthropologists employed on loan from universities. "The young applied anthropologists suddenly found themselves to be respectable." The author Beals had been one of them. At the time of writing in 1982 he had a different view, "If anthropology is to claim any scientific integrity, some of us strive for a detached critical viewpoint (even though I know complete objectivity is impossible, it should remain a goal…)" (Beals 1982).

Roger Bastide in his book *Applied Anthropology* (1973) went through the history of the discipline starting from the Cartesian Discourse on Method through to Karl Marx as two antithetical models. The method of hard sciences applied to human and social sciences meant that science was to be done first before its application. The anthropologist was caught up in this historical current whereby the softer communality was changing to individualistic society, *Gemeinschaft* to *Gesellschaft*, credited to Ferdinand Tönnies. The passage from "communities" to "societies," from the affective to the rational, has then become the topic of the anthropologists in regard to development. According to Richard Appelbaum "Toennies did not feel that *Gemeinschaft* was necessarily doomed to extinction." He had expressed the hope that even if it would not survive as such through the development of new institutions communality could be adapted in some form even into the urban culture (Appelbaum 1970).

Max Weber spotlighted in politics the rationalization of action, substituting bureaucratic authority for charismatic or traditional authority. According to Bastide the anthropologist differentiated between the role as a coeval researcher with the people s/he worked with and the role of the anthropologist as a scientist, moving from community to society (Bastide 1973, 1-5).

Anthropologists as social scientists – and to add, also development scholars - were called to study "communities" in the process of becoming "societies" by means of urbanization, by programming rationalization of the traditional economy or with projects, as it is today. But Bastide pointed out that although anthropologists were asked to work within the context of the prevailing model, first the research then application, they were free and could counter determinism, while nature submitted to it.

Bastide quoted Berque whose words sound uncomfortably real, "The world obeys processes of uniformity, which weigh not only on the young, independent (nations) but equally on the established countries" (Berque 1968). This is the world the anthropologists as well as the other scholars face. The globalization is the overarching trend, which the peoples in different parts of the world rise against in different ways, yet the Western rationality tries to govern it. Bastide wrote at the time when he with many other scholars saw the solution in Marx's *praxis*:

… theoretical knowledge develops at the same time as practical knowledge, in and of the same movement of praxis. Human interaction in social reality is both action and science at once, since it permits us at the same time to change the world, and in changing, to discover it. (Bastide 1971, 6)

I did not follow the Marxist praxis even if I was influenced by it as a teacher and leader of research in the 1970s and 1980s when it dominated the field of social sciences. In a way Bastide presented some essential points of participatory action research, PAR. Thereby theoretical knowledge develops at the same time as practical knowledge. The person in the society, which the researcher studies, is both actor and research subject. According to this theory, applied anthropology can only be formed in a struggle in which it risks being lost while in the process of formation. In spite of the name of Bastide's book *Applied Anthropology* he is striving to something different from mere application of anthropological theory to practice (Bastide 1971).

In most of the described cases even applied anthropology takes its topics from its own interests and viewpoints. Researchers apply their own methodology and study topics applying their tools to practical subjects. The projects the aim of which was to do some service in the communities which they studied took a step toward participation, such as Sol Tax did with his students, but they separated action from research of which more below.

What directs the control of social forces remained the question to be answered. Today one would say that market forces do it. Development and education as motivating forces patterned by Western models have refashioned indigenous cultures and have raised varied counter forces. Such influences are pictured in the works of Jean and John Comaroff and the other writers of *Modernity and its Malcontents* and Maia Green (2003) on the witchcraft cleansers. As counter forces at work are the variety of non-western prophetic and charismatic movements, which have spread in the name of Christianity in Africa and elsewhere and of the study of which Bengt Sundkler was the pioneer.

Anthropology as a critique and critique of anthropology

It is not surprising that the post-colonial and post-war anthropologists reacted against application, until the development aid programs gave another attraction and challenge. It is obvious that the context in which research is conducted and the social background of the scholars determine the mode and content of research, even when the scholar claims neutrality. Striving to retain objectivity does not mean neutrality or non-involvement, as solely by withdrawing from responsibility one is not thereby apolitical. It makes a difference who benefit from the scholarship but the outcome cannot be presaged in the fluctuations of the world politics and economics.

In anthropology as in other social studies specific socio-economic and historical contexts produce a particular theory, applicable also in other situations. Structural, functional and modernization theories, theories of economic and technological determinism as well as the wave of Marxist foundational anthropology were at the root of the later need to promote neutrality and objectivity in the research approach. A scholar engages in development research employed by a development agent for economic reasons or has an interest in solving political or social problems rather than out of theoretical and scholarly interests. Even anthropology engaged in the critique or for betterment of development is mostly done under government funding, which defines the topic even when allowing freedom of treatment (Gould and Ojanen 2005).

The author has experienced freedom on behalf of the development agency whereby funding has not limited the critique toward the role of the agency, but the research context limits the extent to which scientific discussion is carried out. The funds relate to aid-receiving developing countries and are tied to development agency interests, which limit the scope and time of research. Consequently, not only are the development studies separate from the anthropology departments, as in the University of Helsinki, but the topics relating to development are also avoided. Even in the mentioned discussions of AAA and the Current Anthropology Supplement on anthropologists' engagement outside the academy no reference was made to development studies.

James Ferguson is often quoted as an anthropologist, who writes on development issues, for one because it seems that his research on Lesotho was not bound to development funding. As many others he looks at the dominating role of the state as binding the studied people from independent action (Hirschman 1967; Robertson 1984). Ferguson's anthropological analysis of a development program is of the World Bank supported operation in Lesotho (Ferguson 1990). The analysis sets the conceptual apparatus, constitutes the object, "development" as the base for the analysis of the specific development project as a target, in Lesotho case financed with the assistance of the World Bank. Ferguson's analysis serves here as a reference point even if this study moves on less theoretical lines.

Ferguson does not try to do "value-free social science," nor does he try to rectify what he takes as the object of his analysis. That in turn is not a sign of indifference or neutrality. He recognizes that development ideology depoliticizes "everything it touches whisking political realities out of sight" yet performs unnoticed "pre-eminently political operation of expanding bureaucratic state power." He does not present his argument as a critique of development ideology refuting development or showing it is false, even when many ideas are false. Institutional production of ideas has important effects, as they play a role in producing a degree of structural change with no identified political goal. Consequently development apparatus can potentially be an "anti-politics" machine.

Ferguson puts his finger on a central feature about development discourse. It has a non-political face, it is carried out not regarding who sets the tune or which political and economic factors play the game, because money is needed and always welcome for "development." That development is carried out as if apart from the political interests of the funders is not taken into account but it has its consequences. It is not sufficiently considered even now when the new Asian economic forces attract material and financial support.

This brings us to the initial argument, which the politicians and President Nyerere presented when the independence was fought for: "We do not have the educated people to carry out the technical tasks, but we take care of the political and managerial tasks and call for the expertise from outside."

Viewing development assistance or cooperation merely as technical aid did not take into consideration that "whisking the political considerations out of sight" meant from the start going against the charter of the TANU Party and even the ideology, which initially drew the democratic Nordic countries to Tanzania as faithful supporters. The entanglement with the cultural, political and economic forces was not recognized in the beginning decades, but the realization of it and the continuing insistence of the initial political line led eventually to President Nyerere's resignation.

Even when the emphasis has turned to good governance, the hands of the local government are tied, the direction comes from above and the ministries play the tune of the donors, the WB and IMF setting the direction and using the NGOs as mediators, as Gould and Ojanen have shown (1993, 49-72). Also the core of the book by Hyden and Mmuya deals with the role of power of the so-called donors, even when the assistance is given as budget support, and it summarizes the results and analyses numerous evaluations (Hyden and Mmuya 2008). Can anthropology divorce itself from such power, even when it divorces itself from the development discourse, requires continuing consideration.

Ferguson's task was not to correct nor to criticize, but to produce ideas and knowledge. Ideas and discourses have social consequences, not only analysing for truth-value, but recognizing that what ideas do has social effect, it resembles vivisection rather than critique. It matters "what effects ideas bring about in larger processes." Foucault suggests, as many aspects of my analysis also indicate, that a discourse is an "elaborate contraption," which "does" something. Thinking is a real activity. This gives also hope to the role of anthropology, while it is also a warning.

The African research community is aware of the need for interaction between the researchers and the decision makers and development actors. This is repeatedly expressed in the literature produced by CODESRIA, the research society of African scholars closely linked with OECD development arm in Paris (Mazonde and Thomas 2007).

Akhil Gupta has together with James Ferguson edited *Anthropological Locations, Boundaries and Grounds of a Field Science* (1997), which articulates a critique of the American mainstream use of anthropological concepts and methods, containing voices of anthropologists, who have worked in close contact with practical life with different theoretical approaches. The editors' critique accords with the thoughts of this author questioning the anthropological use of the "field" and the role given to the "other." The radical separation of the "field" from the "home" valorises certain kinds of knowledge and constructs a normative subject setting "self" against "others." The authors describe early attempts of experiments with "field methods" in US by anthropologists, who were students of Franz Boas, Edward Sapin, Robert Lowie and Paul Radin (1935). The latter preferred to employ working class unemployed as assistants rather than PhD students, by virtue of their "direct and immediate contacts" with the studied community. Such large-scale studies required big numbers of investigators.

It is obvious that Ferguson's practice in knowledge creation is valuable, particularly if it does not stop at the critique but can also show the way forward. The effect of the traditional anthropological study on the studied society remains an unanswered question. Furthermore, how many of the decision-makers get the benefit of the research and the ideas presented if there is little interaction with them and the subjects of research are onlookers in the process. These factors are returned to in the chapters on participatory research.

Going back in history, the research of the North American anthropologists on the Indian groups challenged Sol Tax to do work with his students among the Meskwaki Indians in Iowa in 1948. In his words "... people are not rats and not to be treated like them ... Community research is thus justifiable only to the degree that the results are imminently useful to the researched community and easily outweigh the disturbance of it" (Tax 1952 Cited in Reason and Bradbury 2001, 37). Gupta and Ferguson refer to Sol Tax on action anthropology in 1975 as "a catalyst, organizer, broker for the local people," who "called into question ... taken for granted conventions." According to the authors during that period there was "vigorous disciplinary discussion of anthropology's political commitments" in relation to imperialism and colonialism as also witnessed by the author of this. Sol Tax's effort belonged clearly to the category of applied anthropology.

In reviewing the experience of Sol Tax's research, the reviewer Mertens asked the question, "Are the researchers in a position to know what is useful to the research community? Can the doctoral thesis as the academic outcome be considered commonly researched results?" Mertens voiced a central problem, which has prevented the academic teachers from proposing Participatory Action Research, for the doctoral students (Mertens 2004, 34). The reason given is the needed distance for the sake of objectivity, not taking sides with subjective views, even if being aware that true objectivity cannot be achieved. The development as a concept is in itself a preconceived notion from which anthropologists have often shied away.

The fear that anthropology no longer would be considered science prompted a heated discussion within the American Anthropological Association, AAA. The professionals majored in anthropology have been in demand in museums, hospitals, Federal government agencies, factory floors and over a longer period in the field of development. The scholars engaged in practical life adhere to the discipline continuing the learning process and hoping to influence the discipline. They question what the discipline can offer to practical life if it narrows its framework and the members of AAA no longer consider the members involved with practice as fellow anthropologists.

In the annual conference of AAA in 2010 with its four-field structure and 6000 participants the discussion was carried out whether the association is sustainable. In that context Mr. Baillie suggested that "five-field" model at times supplements the four traditional fields *by input from members of human communities studied*. Baillie as an archaeologist referred with the fifth component to Egyptian citizens who had cooperated in a site in Egypt (*Chronicle of Higher Education*, 21.11. 2010). That the participation of "human communities studied" needed special mention as a fifth field indicates the predisposed attitude to the research process, even more so if the citizens of the country in which the research was carried out were considered to belong to the fifth category, being external.

In Social Anthropology in Britain and France, where the four fields combination of the American Cultural Anthropology does not exist, the debate continues about the "culture" as a concept. In Helsinki University with professorships for Social and Cultural Anthropology, one originating in Sociology and the other in Ethnology, the issue is discussed how far anthropology as a discipline can engage in practice and still be counted science and be accepted in the family of sciences.

The relation to practice is debated also in ethnography, as the discipline stays close to the knowledge articulated by the studied communities. The main editor Paul Willis of the *Ethnography* journal with the co-author professor Mats Trondman from Sweden bring out in the "Manifesto for Ethnography," quoting Bourdieu, the corporeal character of knowledge "that provides a practical comprehension of the world quite different from the act of conscious decoding that is normally designated by the idea of comprehension" (Bourdieu 1999, 135). The authors give theory a high place but they also emphasize that "Ethnography and theory should be conjoined to produce a concrete sense of the social as internally sprung and dialectically produced" (Willis and Trondman 2002, 395). They do not specify what kind of dialectical production, but while the ethnographic study is to be "theoretically informed" they also recognize that the ethnographic practice and writing have to be aware of their relatedness to the world and to "the contribution they can make both to the critique of overfunctionalist, overstructuralist, and overtheorized views … allowing a voice to those who live their conditions of existence" (Willis and Trondman 2002, 395). While the authors do not promote actor based methodology and guard the limits of ethnography they indicate the potential role it can have in developing conscious and evocative policy forms "that help to make explicit embedded logics, so that social actors become more agents of their own" within a sociological frame, using "information that social actors use to understand their own positions and the likely consequences of particular courses of action" (Willis and Trondman 2002, 398). The careful wording is far from promoting Participatory Action Research Part III, but the need to get out more substantially the social actors' voices is a matter of cultural life scenes as much as it is in theorizing the scientific modes of expression. The authors defend also "culture" as a crucial concept. While I use culture concept I have also adopted the concept "lived world" as the scene of the common study.

From observation and applied anthropology to participation

For too long anthropologists have used *participant observation* as the research method, they have continued to go to the *field* and made use of *informants* as their assistants regardless what line of participation they have adopted. Participative research and participatory action research have called to question these three concepts, which many anthropologists have not in fact followed in practice. The fear of departing from the basic requirements of science appears to be the reason, why it has been important to stick to "participant observation" and not participation, keeping the supposed distance and not getting too involved with the studied practical life. When anthropologists have actually participated in the life of the "informants," and when the latter have also participated in the formation of the knowledge, they have not included it in their theoretical framework and as part of their scientific way of working. This is probably also the reason why among the authors of *The Sage Handbook of Action Research, Participative Inquiry and Practice,* Parts I and II, edited by Peter Reason and Hilary Bradbury (2001, 2008 and 2015 by Hilary Bradbury alone), as well as the earlier book *Human Inquiry, A Sourcebook of New Paradigm Research* edited by Peter Reason (1988), there are only three or four anthropologists or ethnographers in each volume among 61 and 80 writers respectively. I have a chapter in all three of them. Anthropologist Davydd Greenwood and Morten Levin (2001) in the chapter "Pragmatic Action Research and the Struggle to Transform Universities into Learning Communities" blame the conventional universities to be dysfunctional, dominated by the model of the one-way communication process, built into the Cartesian separation of thought and action. They call "for reconstruction of universities so that they would function as critical reflective training centres for new generations of social actors" (Greenwood 2001). Greenwood returns to the same topic in his lengthy article in 2012 in which with the experience of four decades he criticizes the divorcing of the academic system from practical life and knowledge (Greenwood 2012).

The decisive difference is which role the research partners are given and how recognized their role is in the research process, whether they are partners and co-researchers, informants or subjects of research. Participative or participatory action research, as also research which Greenwood calls simply action research, is a form of "inquiry where participants and researchers co-generate knowledge through collaborative communicative processes in which all participants' contributions are taken seriously" (Greenwood 2012, 105). Greenwood refers to John Dewey (1927), who after the WWI focused on participative democracy and linked the ethics of participation into knowledge creating processes. The criteria of scientific validity of such participative research rests on the knowledge negotiated by the involved parties and "the knowledge must also pass the test of creating workable solutions to real life problems" (Greenwood 2012, 105). The issues were different in Dewey's pragmatism and do not as such correspond with the arguments I am making.

The action research, which the authors above describe, does not follow the forms of the same practical application as the participant action research of this book but the arguments rest on the same logic and practical experience as also many of the other articles in the three volumes of *Action Research.* I return in the other chapters to the discussions on what in the beginning was called "new paradigm" following Thomas Kühn's introduction of the theme. Some years after I personally first introduced participative research with students as assistants in 1972-1975 I discovered that I was part of a stream, which brought together many small brooks, often being initiated in corresponding situations of a need to change the direction or at least not to be rejected by the mainstream. The connections and the initial impetus between these streams were not always recognized when they were being developed until the new stream had enough substance and later multiplied hundredfold, with little connection with anthropology. For example Rajesh Tandon, who initiated the Participatory Research Institute in Asia in India, PRIA, in 1982, attended one of the initial PAR seminars in Finland in 1981 after Jipemoyo project was finished, even if he does not refer to what he learned there in his writings. He has continued as an active researcher and is now the second holder of the UNESCO chair for Community-Based Research and Academic Learning. It was a stream running in the same direction, as was the development scene in India and in Sri Lanka and later in numerous other educational centres, with no specific connection with anthropology as a line of science. It has led to new kinds of openings in research.

The discussion relating to the participative action research concerns academic work in broader terms and it has been a part of the discussion as long as universities have been the centres of knowledge creation and learning. Both theoretical and practical issues arise in connection of action research. Theoretically they concern validity and objectivity of science as well as the basic task of academies of creating and further developing knowledge, which requires highly developed theoretical capacity and hardly can be done together with unlearned ordinary folk. In analysing the theoretical aspects of action research in the social sciences in 1970s I was helped by Heinz Moser's analysis (Moser, 1975, 1978). The second issue is meritocratic. The competition for academic excellence and jobs, which give both merit and economic benefits, does not permit messing with practical life unless it is part of the job market.

The new world situation and especially the universal concerns of poverty, development, peace, climate change and dire health problems have brought to the fore issues which require social scientists' knowledge as well as the specialists in the fields. It has become evident that there is a need to engage in practical life already during the learning process and necessity of interdisciplinary research. The issue presents itself whether the people should continue to be involved in the research process as informants or subjects of research, to remain mere informants and interviewees or recognized as partners in the knowledge creation. This does not concern only social scientists, its is a central matter with even greater practical consequences in technical and natural sciences, as we had a chance to discover when we were evaluating a water project in Tanzania.

The second editor and writer of *Human Inquiry* John Rowan discusses a dialectical paradigm for research and replaces the alienation in work as analysed by Karl Marx with the similar research setting. Rowan found four concepts relevant for the alienation a researcher experiences if the methods s/he uses separate her or him from the research subject. Alienation is relevant from the product, from work, from other people and from self when for 'the worker' we substitute the "experimental subject" or the "respondent" (Rowan 1981). More questionable than the alienation of the researcher is the marginalization of the research subjects and their role and contribution. When the research subjects were uneducated and illiterate their treatment was comparable to the colonial mode of engagement (Gupta and Ferguson 1997). The question remained open how they benefited from the long time use that the researcher made of them.

The briefly presented case studies in this book bring up the role of the people's knowledge in the field of health, the knowledge of practicing artisans and agriculturalists as well as in the technical fields. In development projects the missing capacity of the intellectuals to incorporate the studied people's knowledge and to recognize the skills of those involved become evident in different phases of experts' work. The attitudes adopted during the scientific learning phase were transferred to professional work, the mode of directing and the mode of governing. These issues have related to my early research projects, to Jipemoyo, the health training and village development projects and they become evident in research on and with women.

Since 1970s and 1980s questioning of the role of the former informants and people involved in the research process has become common. Clifford and Marcus in *Writing Culture* (1986) refer to subaltern voices and participation of studied people. In Hill (1996) the reference is made to informants, who became collaborators and co-researchers rather than subjects. Jean and Stephen Schensul write of collaboration as a research model (1992) and Luke Eric

Lassiter (2002, 2005) writes collaborative ethnography writing texts with those he studies, criticizing Dell Hymes (1974) and other engaged anthropologists in *Reinventing Anthropology* for direct action with communities being yet hierarchical.

Further methodological and theoretical issues come up with the experiences in different research projects, which required participatory action. The key concepts of *interpretation* and *meaning* have in my mind required a wider perspective than what the knowledge creation on the theoretical level solely permit. One questions the logic of the theoretician Habermas when he argues that praxis can be conceived with no contact with practice. It undermines the level of ordinary scholars' work but it also undermines the need for human contacts with the actors themselves, which touch dimensions of life in human interaction, which cannot be taken care of by recording thoughts in net.

Concluding thoughts

In this chapter I have shown that research has in many ways taken its direction from the need to recognize the research partners for truly grasping the reality of them and of the changing world. The chapter reviewed some historical situations, which have led to applied anthropology and to such writers as Bastide whose analysis has approached the need of greater involvement of the researched in the research process, yet retaining the interactive level and making room for common knowledge formation. While developing participatory research in its varied forms it has become clear from the start that the informant becomes a recognized subject in the research process and often such involvement has required action, which could not be separated from the research process itself. Another obvious fact noted is that such research properly carried out requires time, which has made it troublesome to include in academic programs and still less in assessing the development research and programs. Furthermore, studies, which deal with development, require an interdisciplinary approach, in which different disciplines adopt the participatory way of working together initially following the example of anthropologists. Action research is often participatory but it does not necessarily conceive the other actors as active participants in the research process as Participatory Action Research does. Participation is the word used today in practical life everywhere from schools to business, but strangely anthropology has shied away from PAR, even when engagement and collaboration of the former subjects have become accepted concepts.

True interdisciplinary work is difficult to realize and for that reason it is rarely carried out in an integrated way of sharing the leading ideas and the epistemological and theoretical underpinnings, acquainting team members to each other's methodological ways of working. In recording the interdisciplinary team research on transfer of Finnish technology to Tanzania and Zambia in TECO project I referred to Rossini and his associates' organizational characteristics. I recognized that for many practical reasons we had failed in several aspects to follow them. The same points pertained also to PAR team organization in Jipemoyo, in which the practical action brought the research team together even when the researchers could not always agree in the theoretical underpinnings (Rossini et al. 1981, M-L. Swantz 1989, 37-39).

Research in which participation with a variety of people from different levels of expertise and different disciplines are working together need to be modified according to the varied circumstances. Recognizing the obstacles in implementation as a proponent of PAR the author is convinced that the human and social research methodology needs to include the possibility of incorporating the researched as partners and actors in the research process. The research community needs to be broadened to include community-based research.

My starting point has been anthropological, but I have worked in interdisciplinary teams realizing that my approach was given direction from my first experience in research with people in Bunju. I quote from an article of mine,

I faced a situation in which you could not start from a scientific scheme, start working from some pre-conceived theoretical construct, with which you faced the people. That has influenced my total work ... I had faced many different situations, but the reality was always different from what you would think it theoretically to be. I had to reject the concepts "culture" and "development" and face only "life situations" and work with people in their life situations, how they could defend and stand against all the forces thrusting on them from all over. Someone would say you were not fitted for scientific work, and that might have been so. (M-L. Swantz 1996)

CHAPTER 3

Paths to Participation in Development Research

Introductory thoughts

Participatory and action oriented research approaches were developed in the 1970s in different parts of the world as a critique of the modernization theory, but also as a tool to support political and development action. Since the latter part of 1970s, participation as a concept has been used but also criticised in development research and action. In this chapter, I clarify the ways in which I have defined and applied participatory research throughout my career. But first a few words about the terminology.

Participatory research has been referred to using various terms. In her recent book, Dorothy Hodgson describes her anthropological research with the Maasai as "participatory problem-posing" (Hodgson 2012). Budd Hall, my former colleague from the early years of participatory research in Tanzania, is engaged in "community-based research." Helena Jerman reports that "engaged research" was referred to in a conference in Ireland under a topic "Making sense together, the role of participant research." I return to the use of different terms, but start by analysing the varieties of participatory research or participatory action research (PAR), both of which I have used. Second, I differentiate participatory research from development tools. The scholarly critique has treated PR and PAR as the same as what was first known as Rapid Rural Appraisal (RRA) and later as Participatory Rural Appraisal (PRA), or Participatory Learning and Action (PLA). These are used as practical tools in planning local development. To contrast, in PAR participation stands as a way of engaging the subjects in the research process without immediate application. While the insights and data gained through PRA have, for instance, been used in village planning in Mtwara and Lindi regions, I differentiate PAR from PRA, with the realization that the latter has also been turned to tools of research. I will bring up the criticism toward such use in a later section (Chambers 2008). To conclude, I realize that the multiplication of different terms for participation as a concept is confusing.

The participatory approach in research offers one answer to the crucial question whose knowledge anthropology produces and how the researcher relates to the researched as research partners (M-L. Swantz 2008). As long as anthropologists have studied cultures different from their own, they have recognized the need of being also of some service to the people they have studied. Yet, applied anthropology has been differentiated from research in which "observation" has been the recognized method. Anthropologists have faced the sensitive ethical question, well articulated by Pat Caplan and other authors in the book she has edited, of studying people who had not asked to be researched, whose names can be quoted, or only archived in the field notes but are then avoided in the scientific texts (Caplan 2010).

Participatory Action Research

Participatory research indicates that the researcher does not only observe, but comes as a participant who cooperates in the research with the researched community. The actors in the community do not only provide their information and knowledge, but recognize themselves as partakers and begin to share and formulate the problems together with the researcher. The research becomes a shared process, as the participants' knowledge does not only provide the researcher with information for her analysis. Even if that happens, there *often are* recorded results and practical action that occur prior to the formulation of the theoretical findings of the research process. The former "informant" becomes an initiator and ideally a co-researcher in the process of problematizing and solving problems, even formulating them, thus becoming a recognized subject in the research.

Participants *involved in the process in different roles* proceed to identify problems, which are often of a political, but also of a social, cultural or developmental nature. The process has differing phases and outcomes and cannot be expected to work out as ideally as intended. It also requires more time than ordinary participant observation or research. This further development in research methodology occurs because development research takes as its departure point normative science, if development is considered a goal to strive for. This kind of participation also differentiates between what from the point of view of the former informers, now partakers, are the goals they strive for and what they see as harmful for their social or personal life.

The setting described here presupposes that the participants from both sides are aware they are partakers in a research setting. Participatory Action Research is often an on-going process that requires long periods of time as traditional anthropological studies also often have done. In it the researcher becomes part of the concerned people's life situation in different degrees so that the differentiated roles no longer pertain to it during the process. What matters, is confidence in each other's intentions with the ultimate aim that the shared knowledge becomes part of what could be described as everyday life.

With regard to methodology, PR and PAR need to be differentiated from applied *anthropology*. Anthropologists, wanting to remain respected scholars within their discipline, have avoided becoming *actively involved in the studied people's lives*. Yet, it is likely that in many cases the anthropological knowledge gained has been obtained collaboratively, i.e., bringing the actors and researchers consciously together in the process of analysing the different aspects of community life, although the rules of anthropology have not generally acknowledged collaboration as a methodology. While an anthropologist can recognize the commonly achieved knowledge by mentioning the names of some collaborators, the scientific knowledge created has been the scientist's production.

Dorothy Hodgson has written a good review about the role of an involved anthropologist by reflecting on her own research of the indigenization process among the East African Maasai. Her article, "Critical Interventions: Dilemmas of Accountability in Contemporary Ethnographic Research," (1999) expresses the core of the issue a researcher *faces* when s/he becomes involved in the problematic of the society s/he studies. In her case, the researched people were not invited to participate in research. Alas, they knew she became involved as an anthropologist in the efforts of the East African Maasai to have themselves recognized as locally based communities with the claims of being "indigenous." The term had been initially applied to people claiming to be the original inhabitants of the area where they lived in. In her later work, Hodgson expresses the research as a "participatory problem-posing method to encourage dialogue, critical awareness and self-defined development among communities" (2011). In my interpretation, this statement describes a key aspect of what I hold as PAR, although my initial participatory research did not have development as its stated aim.

Hodgson uses the freedom of an anthropologist to be critical of all the groups involved in her research and to be able to defend the stand she takes to all sides, while creating personalized relations with people, not establishing herself as an "objective" researcher and retaining the customary distance. When research contacts are no longer research objects and the issues treated as not only of external research concern, the balance between the conflicting parties requires a degree of distancing from personal relationships. An anthropologist can see the power hierarchies within the societies from a different perspective than the people themselves. In Hodgson's case, this meant observing the status of women who had been sidelined. The role of the researcher is then to find the ways of creating links and new ways of networking between the parties with differing interests and approaches to the issue at hand. Dorothy Hodgson describes the three significant steps she worked out for a situation, which demands the intervention of the scholar. She intervened but avoided taking a political stand, yet she recognized that her intervention was on behalf of the women. I quote:

The alternative – not to intervene - also has political consequences ... There is no neutral position in ethnographic research and writing (or other kinds of research and writing); to be neutral is to side with the structures of domination, be they global, capitalism, imperialism, or patriarchy. The process of research, however objective and detached some might pretend it to be, is always interwoven with other processes of domination and webs of power relations. (Hodgson 1999, 215)

Hodgson makes reference to Rajesh Tandon of the Society for Participatory Research in Action in India (PRIA), who claimed that research in social settings is always political. Hodgson quotes him on the role of politics in social studies: "... research in social science has always been political and either maintains, explains or justifies the status quo or provides data to those who want to question, examine or transform it."

A path to participation

I had been working on participatory research in Tanzania in the 1960s and 1970s. At the same time, the South-American sociologists had forcefully put forth similar arguments, when they raised the critique against the positivist theories of the American social scientists. Many of them had been educated in North America and had been imbued with theories of modernization, against which they developed the politicized dependency theories and engaged with oppressed communities. They had a dominant role in bringing together the theoretical, political and practical aspects together as Action Research (Fals Borda and Rahman 1991). The coming together of the AR and PR took place initially through the contacts of the Latin Americans with the Tanzanian researchers in the international and often politically loaded conferences. Both sides adopted participatory action research (PAR) as distinct from the common research tool of participatory observation. Action Research continued in a broader perspective not related to specific political situations, but many using it had also the participatory component in their research.

Neither the action research of Latin America, nor the participatory research we were developing in Tanzania had a connection with the Rapid Rural Appraisal or Participatory Rural Appraisal developed by the team of Robert Chambers from the Sussex Institute of Development Studies. Orlando Fals Borda openly criticized Chambers' approach as a method used for development. For Fals Borda, PAR meant cooperating in people's struggle for their political rights. He organized and led two conferences in Carthagena, Colombia, for practitioners of participatory and action research, which gathered researchers and political activists together. Through the conferences, participatory research gained more space as it was becoming an internationally practiced approach. The first conference on Action Research was held in 1978 with 78 participants in Cartagena, Colombia. The second conference on Participatory Action Research was held twenty years later in 1997 and was more extensive and less radical. It included some 1800 participants of which most were South Americans. Two researchers from the Tanzanian *Jipemoyo* participated in the first one, while the second one was attended by Colonel K. Nsa Kaisi, the politically active Regional Commissioner of Mtwara region, Julie Adkins, the director of the participatory development program Regional Integrated Project Support (RIPS), its skilled Participatory Rural Appraisal trainer Mwajuma Masaiganah and the author, working at the time as a social scientist in Regional Integrate Project Support (RIPS), a development programme supported by Finland for twenty years within which the PRA was applied as a development approach, not a research tool. The dominating role of men at the common sessions was brought up, so to correct the gender imbalance Mwajuma was called on the spot to direct a general session. She showed a great skill in covering the topics and involving the hall full of participants. Professor Chambers attended the conference and wrote a research paper, which Fals Borda, in spite of his initial strong critique of the PRA, included in the publication of the conference papers, which he edited.

Between the two conferences, the PAR practitioners had met on many occasions, supported often by international and European adult education organizations. The discussion on PAR was activated and sponsored internationally by the International Council for Adult Education (ICAE), based in Toronto, Canada, where Budd Hall worked after returning to Canada from Tanzania. It played a central role in developing the participatory approach further, getting initial impetus from the Latin American, Paulo Freire, whose thoughts of engaging education and conscientisation had reached the adult educators as far as Finland. The Finnish leader in international Peace Education, Helena Kekkonen, attended the World Adult Education Conference supported by ICAE in Dar es Salaam in 1976. Her role in the world level adult education received attention because she had actively involved groups of prisoners in participatory learning and analysis (Kekkonen 1977). Two Latin American scholars visited the Jipemoyo research area in Western Bagamoyo and found commonness in the approach. As a result, Jipemoyo researchers agreed to use participatory action research and the Latin Americans similarly added participation to their action research.

The World Conference of the International Sociological Association (ISA) had its meeting in Mexico in 1982, for which Orlando Fals Borda had initiated a Research Committee for Social Renewal. It formed the 9th committee in the Association, consisting of social scientists active in politically oriented action research. Fals Borda presented a paper "How to do research so that it changes reality" and the committee members carried out discussion on Action Research and Participatory Action Research, where the pros and cons of the related theoretical problems were debated, many finding common ground in Marxist theories. My paper dealt with the PR research experiences in Tanzania. Professor Ulf Himmelstrand from Sweden, who had been the opponent in my doctoral disputation in Uppsala in 1970, was at the time the President of the ISA and presented a mediating view in the 9th Committee meeting. Heinz Moser, a Swiss educationist and specialist in Action Research working in West Germany was one of the participants in the ISA meeting and in other international conferences on PAR. He and Helmut Ornauer had edited a German volume of the first International Conference of the Committee on Action Research. He became interested in participatory research and his writings were useful in analysing the history and different methodological aspects of Action Research (Moser and Ornauer 1978). Moser was invited to be the chief evaluator of my work as leader of the Jipemoyo research project at the evaluation conference in Helsinki in the autumn of 1979. From the 1970s to the late 1980s, much of the mainline sociology was engaged in theories of radical social change, being involved in revolutionary transformation of societies. It influenced also the approach taken by many researchers engaged in participatory and action research, with participators from Hungary, Poland and Yugoslavia.

The author attended Participatory Research conferences in Europe, which suggested the fast spread of this approach. An international conference was held in Ljubliana, Slovenia, in 1981, which at the time was part of Yugoslavia. It was organized by the Yugoslavian Federation of Adult Education in cooperation with ICAE, UNESCO and the International Centre for Public Enterprises in Developing Countries. Fifty participants represented 23 countries from Africa, Asia, North America, Latin America and Europe. Adult education was at its peak in popularity in different European countries as well as in countries, which aimed to quickly increase literacy among adults and children. In this way there were people who readily found participatory research or action research, in the case of Latin America, to be a useful tool. The conference was reported in a volume *Research for the People, Research by the People* (1981) with a foreword by Budd Hall, Thord Erasmie from University of Lindköping, Sweden, and Jan de Vries from the Netherlands Study and Development Centre for Adult Education. Soon after this conference, de Vries organized an Adult Education Research Conference in Oest Geist in May 1977 and the same year a larger European conference in Amersfoort, Holland. The introduction of the above book recognizes the beginnings of the spreading interest in participatory research, started in Tanzania (1981, Preface), without specifically mentioning my work or the Jipemoyo project:

This meeting was the culmination of a stream of activity in participatory research, which can be identified concretely as having begun in Tanzania in the early 1970s with the work of a group of researchers who began to experiment with research which consciously involved the community in the entire process. It bears mentioning that the European assistance to adult education in different parts of the world was notable at that time, not only in developing countries. For instance Swedes cooperated with Portugal, which had not kept up with the same development in reading skills as the northern Lutheran countries.

Coming together of the African, European and Latin American Action researchers resulted in networking across the continents. The South American researchers were main line sociologists whereas anthropologist Arturo Escobar started his research some years later and remained within the anthropological discipline with his critique of development anthropology (Escobar1991, 658-682). It needs to be noted that the political situation of Tanzania was only nominally revolutionary, even after the ruling party, Tanganyika African Union (TANU) changed its name to Chama Cha Mapinduzi or Revolutionary Party (CCM) when joining with the Zanzibari Afro-Shirazi Party. In spite of the name, the political atmosphere in Tanzania was more focused on development problems than radical politics, although the North Korean influence grew in time and was visible in the way in which the Independence celebrations were organized at the Stadium. The political difference between the Latin American and Tanzanian action research was evident at a meeting held in Helsinki, in which the Minister of Finance of Tanzania Amir Jamal and South American politically engaged representatives joined the discussion in the context of International Group of Grassroots Initiatives (IGGRI), of which the author was one of the initial members. IGGRI was a non-governmental international group of activists who found each other initially branching out from Society for International Development (SID) with headquarters in Rome, initiated by its former secretary Ponna Wignaraja. Martti Ahtisaari, who at the time headed the Development Department of FINNIDA, cooperated with the aims of IGGRI, taking part in one session at the international conference of the activist groups in Hanasaari. Even when he became the President of Finland and the IGGRI group was meeting in Finland, they were invited to the Presidential Palace for an informal visit.

Participation as a tool for development and planning

Beyond being a research approach, participatory tools have also been used for development planning, such as Rapid Rural Appraisal (RRA), a one-week exercise with villagers, later expanded to Participatory Rural Appraisal (PRA) consisting of 15 instruments (Laitinen 2002). These tools have developed into Participation, Reflection and Action (PRA) and Participatory Learning and Action (PLA). A journal was started initially for six years as *Rapid Rural Appraisal Notes* and for 47 issues as *Participatory Learning and Action,* published since 1988 until 2013 under the IIED, International Institute of Environment and Development. Robert Chambers was one of the initiators and the IIED Resource Centre, which has been housed at the Institute of Development Studies, University of Sussex, Brighton. I have been a member on the International Editorial Advisory Board.

Participation was to be the key concept in a 12-year development program known Regional Integrated Project Support (RIPS) taking place in eleven districts of Mtwara and Lindi regions of Tanzania since 1992. The program was sponsored by the development agency of Finland, known as FINNIDA. RIPS had experienced four years of largely failed efforts, after which the implementing agent Finnagro employed me as a member of the team to utilise the participation concept for the preparatory phase of a year and a half and after that interchangeably I served during another four years with Timo Voipio (2011). Prior to RIPS, I had been the director in conducting evaluative research for FINNIDA on development projects using partly participatory approach (M-L. Swantz, 1989). Yet, Lars Johansson, the Swedish director of the preparatory RIPS project had participated in the training using PRA tools by the Robert Chambers' team, in a UNICEF program in Shinyanga and he was determined that the same team should be invited to train the RIPS facilitators in participatory tools. This would overrule the participatory approach with which we had started the cooperation with the villagers and district officers in Magumchila and Samora villages in Newala District. After some tight discussions I gave in as I saw some benefit in the use of specific tools for the guidance of the civil servants.

Using the PRA tools for administrative purposes in RIPS gave the villagers an opportunity to think of their situation concretely with some officers and to know what the Party politics demanded or proposed from them. Such tools would not have been utilized in the earlier *Jipemoyo* project or in participatory research in general, even if they had been available, as the starting point was intended to be in the discussions with the cooperating people and in their questions and problems. Chambers strove for the same goal by "giving the stick" to the locals signifying giving the leadership over to the participants, but the use of a defined set of fifteen tools were not fitting research tools as such, even if some data could be made available that way.

Starting in 1998, the local government was being reorganized by transferring operational responsibilities from the regions to the districts. In 2000 the Government invited the Finnish team leader Tor Lundström, Dr. J. Wembah-Rashid and the author from the RIPS programme to take on a mission to identify how institutional partners were utilizing participatory planning and to suggest linkages to other initiatives and institutions with the use of PRA. As a social scientist I was asked to recommend the organizational body to be responsible for the participatory planning programme. Our work resulted in a document FNFPP, Formulation of a National Framework for Participatory Planning. We visited the headquarters of the Ministry of Local Government in Dodoma and consulted other aid agencies and listed potential institutional possibilities. We ended up recommending the Ministry of Regional Administration and Local Government as the organizing body, but we also indicated that it would need reorganization and trained personnel. The use of PRA could be continued and its use encouraged if other approaches had not been established. The important point was to make the basic concepts clear and to include the participatory planning in the educational system, including participatory methods at the academic level.

In 2004, the first of the closing seminars of RIPS, to which leaders were invited as representatives from many other regions, was chaired by the Permanent Secretary for Rural Development and the second by the Chief Secretary of State. They declared that the government will implement the countrywide participatory village planning and the use of it would be continued and it would be started where it had not been used yet. As it commonly happens after some time, the new officer in charge of local government sent around a statement that ordered the Opportunities and Obstacles to Development, O and OD, for village development planning for general use but the planning officers versed in PRA continued the modified use of them as they gave the villagers more guidance for the analysis. O and OD followed the four square method generally known, in which the conditions and benefits for successful planning are listed but the potential for obstacles with their consequences are similarly indicated. The planning thus is prepared for both consequences and their conditions.

Nevertheless, the participation of the villagers became incorporated into the planning, especially after the World Bank began promoting it in 1994. It was also the time when the RRA and PRA instruments began to spread. The PRA tools consisted of 15 tools to be used in cooperation with district officers for analysing the needs and resources of the people. The experience of 12 years of participatory development in the southern regions led the country to adopt the participatory program for village planning (Freling 1998). How faithfully it is followed depends on the officers and villagers responsible for planning as everything else in implementation of development. The plans were supposed to be reviewed every three years.

With an array of participatory projects, it is no wonder that "participation" has gained multiple understandings in Tanzania. First of all, the Swahili wording used for PRA in village planning is a causative form. *Kuwashirikisha watu,* and *vyombo shirikishi* include the meaning "making people to participate" and "tools (of making) to participate." In the same way in Finnish the words, *osallistava tutkimus,* indicate "making to take part in research," which the English term *participatory research* does not have. *Kushirikiana,* "to participate together," would be the better translation, which in itself indicates the inner intent of the actors doing it together, not someone making them to act together.

Michael Jennings uses the term in the title of his article "The Very Real War: Popular Participation in Development in Tanzania During the 1950s and 1960s." He refers first to the colonial time and then to the book by President Nyerere, *Freedom and Unity – Uhuru na Umoja* (1967), which includes Nyerere's speeches and writings from the time when he was a student in Edinburgh in 1952 until 1966 (Jennings, 2007). However, the word "participation" as such was not used in the speeches of Nyerere in the recorded two first books of his speeches published in Oxford University Press in 1966 and 1968, nor in the article of Jennings, but since the Party policy was built on the concept of people's participation in development the idea of people implementing their own development was contained in his speeches. However, self-help became eventually more of an order than participation in something, which was planned together. Jennings shows how the first decade was of national excitement expressed in self-help and in numerous small projects, which were in some way related to Village and District development. In the early 1970s, the planning was transferred from districts to the regional level and people's planning was distanced from such planning. Jennings' article shows that self-help was the dominating concept in the Tanzanian politics and he returns to the term "participation" only in the end. I quote President Nyerere's statement from 1974, which mentions participation:

Development brings freedom, provided it is development *of people* … development of people can be effected *by the people.* . . . The components of this are: *conscious participation,* decision making, doing, increasing understanding of doings, increasing knowledge and ability. (Nyerere 1974, italics added)

The wording "conscious" is significant, as participation was in the beginning years of great hope in people's voluntary efforts. When the Tanzanian government exhorted people to work in the 1970s, conscious participation was unfortunately not included in the analysis and in village planning. Rather than engaging people in development measures of their own planning, the exhortations became more of a command such as planned cultivation of commonly owned village fields under the Ujamaa concept. When the President read my paper "Participation in Development Planning" after he had retired, he remarked that he wished they had understood participation in that way, according to his personal assistant, Joan Wicken, who gave the paper to him.

Responding to the critique of participatory research

The differentiation between the participation as the research tool and as a tool for local village planning was often not seen and thus not made, when the critique by the academic community against the use of PRA and RRA in research expanded. The critics presented the view that the tools as methodological techniques would make participation lose its meaning in the fight against neo-liberal policies and they would become tools directed from above. Orlando Fals Borda had resisted and criticized the PRA as a technique, which to him missed the counter-hegemonic process for grassroots resistance and transformation emerging through PAR. Similarly, for Pablo Alexandro Leal, participation had "gained legitimacy within the institutional development world to the extent of achieving buzzword status." It needed "to be re-articulated within broader processes of social and political struggle" because when reduced to a "methodological package of techniques" it loses its "philosophical and ideological meaning" (Leal 2007). Interestingly, such critique of participation as a set of tools with the clear aim of development ignored the use of the concept in Latin America, where it had been a part of the political struggle with radical roots founded by Paulo Freire.

Another strong voice was of Majid Rahnema (1990), whose article "Participatory action research: the Last Temptation of Saint Development" left no doubt how, in his opinion, people's lives in developing countries were manipulated. His critique was more general even of the development concept itself. However, Robert Chambers defended PRA as fitting also for participatory research. In my understanding, the interpretation of the use of PRA for more technically oriented agricultural research does not pertain as well to more humanistic, social or anthropological research (Chambers 2008, 297-319).

Anthropologist Maia Green was asked by the Policy Research for Development (REPOA) institute in Dar es Salaam to review of 41 NGOs implementing participatory action research as a means to community empowerment. Furthermore, she had been asked to evaluate the use of participatory planning in the southern regions after RIPS had been discontinued. She wrote an extensive criticism of the use of PAR for village development using the PRA tools in development planning in villages. On the basis of these experiences, her views of participatory research were mainly negative. From her report of the evaluation it becomes clear that the REPOA had used the PRA tools as the method for the research. PRA could be used as tools for getting some information but to learn research in two weeks, as appears to have been the case, undermined participatory action research (PAR) as a research approach.

As a further response, it seems that REPOA was cutting corners by training 30 representatives from 41 Community Based Organizations (CBOs) in participatory action research. Green wrote an extensive criticism of the use of PAR for village development using the PRA tools in development planning in villages engaged in village development in coastal and northern districts. Two representatives from selected villages were accepted for a course of two weeks in which the research was taught utilizing the PRA tools as the operative method. The villagers' analysis of their own situation and participatory planning by use of PRA tools was neither intended to be a research method nor was it meant to be for work implemented by NGOs, even if volunteers could have been instigators and guides in the effort. Green's critique is rightly directed at stakeholders, which use participation as a "boundary object," enabling the "stakeholders" to align temporarily around a common project in implementing development. As such, her critique rather than being directed against participation is about the misuse of the concept (Green 2000; 2010).

A further criticism by Green concerns the problem of power. Instead of being empowering, using PRA might lead to a situation in which people are victims of external powers. The use of PRA by the World Bank is considered to be questionable, as people become dependent on the order set for them from above. Government directives may limit people's own capacity for enterprise. In my personal experience, all the methods used in development can be turned to their opposite, when they become tools of the leaders in charge using their power and authority. Yet, power is not inherent in the concept of participation, nor the reason for negating the use of it. The people in Mtwara region rose in 2013 to defend their rights to the gas produced for electric power in their otherwise neglected region and waters. This was the case after the Government announced the transfer of the developed power to Bagamoyo harbour area where the Chinese Prime Minister, during his visit to the place, promised development of the harbour and industry. It has been suggested that people's violent reaction against the plans had its roots in the extensive use of people's learning of action from below in the region. Thus giving voice to the people during RIPS would have ended up in violent action.

Author Caitlin Cahill brings an interesting and constructive analysis of the use of PAR in a personalized context related to six young women of color in New York, which shows "how a participatory praxis can inform post-structural theory and practice." She refers the issue to Foucault's term of "subjectifying social sciences" by bringing attention to research practices which "mask realities of tokenism, reinforce social hierarchies, emphasize consensus and reproduce the dominant hegemonic agenda." I agree with Cahill when she proceeds from the quotes of several familiar critics to concede that despite the critiques "… participatory research, and PAR in particular, represent viable, vital alternatives to the exclusionary domains of academic research. … especially appealing to social researchers working in an activist tradition" (Cahill 2007, 209).

The tendency in development evaluations and research is to put an emphasis on negative aspects. It is undeniable that all efforts to pursue development deserve critique, and equally so participation as an approach can become corrupted. Opinions differ whether the use of PRA has empowered people. Jeremy Gould and Ojanen's analysis of the role of the NGOs in Masasi in Mtwara region is a general critique of the NGO's dominating role in the local development, also covering the use of PRA. Granting the potential of the power hidden in the methodology left in the hands of the people, yet being directed from above, which Gould and Ojanen suggest, the general understanding in the southern regions at the end of RIPS was that empowerment had taken place. The two books written by the empowered people are evidence of this. Generalized conclusions are questionable in either direction. I am reminded of the words of President Nyerere, when I complained to him that the officers were not working with the people as intended. His response was, "Not all." Yet the difference has to be made between research and implementation of development using PRA.

It is also inevitable that implementing such a shared research can be done in different ways. For instance, Heinz Moser, the evaluator of the director's part in Jipemoyo project, who in general accepted the use of PR, was of the opinion that the participating researcher should not become an actor in practical implementation after the common line of thinking has been reached. In my view one cannot always differentiate when the researcher's role in development research becomes that of an actor. In a similar vein, it has turned out to be risky to advise students to incorporate participatory action research into their degree by adopting the role of a community actor. Some have had their doctoral work rejected, when an external examiner has not been acquainted with the researcher's participating role. Action Research has been rejected by the scientific world over the last four decades, as brought out by anthropologist Davydd J. Greenwood of Cornell University, an established user of action research for all those years and an editor in the forth coming third edition in the series of Action Research volumes (Greenwood 2012).

The difficulties in integrating PAR and AR into the standard human and social sciences relates to the lack of institutional academic centres in which contacts with the studied communities could be kept alive. Much progress has, however, been made, but more as the mediating practice between the scientific research and different forms of application. Professor Budd Hall, director of Community-Based Research Institute in the Canadian University of Victoria in British Columbia, holds the UNESCO Chair in Community-Based Research and Social Responsibility in Higher Education together with Rajesh Tandon of the Society for Participatory Research in Action (PRIA) in India. They have continued to institutionalize PAR further not only in the ways the participatory research methodology was initiated in Dar es Salaam. Initially Budd Hall adopted participation as a mode of research while he was the director of adult education development in the University of Dar es Salaam at the time I started the first participatory research projects. He received a Canadian visitor, whom he sent to follow the sessions in which I trained the students for the first research project in which they would act as research assistants, telling the visitor that I was the only one doing the kind of participatory research involving the people in it. He saw the way I defined participatory research to be in line with the approach taken by Paulo Freire from Brazil, who was influenced by his visit to the University of Dar es Salaam, before I had come and started developing what I then called Participatory Research Approach as a Senior Research Fellow in the university (Freire 1970, 1973).

Kerry Strand has developed and institutionalized the Community-Based research in San Francisco University and has published on it extensively (Strand 2003). The number of institutions has grown using participatory research in different ways in development context, and the difference between the research and practice is not easy to maintain. Budd Hall recognizes this multiplicity of institutions applying participation to different degrees in his article together with Lise Berube "Towards a New Architecture of Knowledge: The Office of the Community-Based Research in University of Victoria, Canada."

Nevertheless, none of the names above carry the term *participation* in them. It appears that the terminology of *engaged and community-based* research has taken over from participatory research, because it is difficult to differentiate PRA from scientifically engaged research. Similarly, Community-Based research includes research done outside the academic circles as part of community action. In these situations, the distinction between scientific research and community action becomes difficult to maintain.

A reason for this might be that the use of these practical tools for research has blurred the difference between the participatory tools for development work and PR/PAR, the main subjects of this book. For instance, the title of the final issue in a series of publications on PRA by the International Institute for Environment and Development (IIED) is *Tools for supporting sustainable natural resource management and livelihoods* (No 66, 2013). The journal was "seeking to test out new ways of learning and understanding how to engage a more bottom-up process of decision-making and development." The intention has been to publish results of projects in which the analysis of the methods and approach were firmly rooted "at the level of the people who actually plan and manage fields and landscapes on the day to day basis." I personally differentiate between Participatory Action Research as a research approach and Participatory Rural Appraisal as the tools for development practice and I retain that position. My main argument is that for the research to be called PAR the researched people should be involved in the research process itself, not only in practical development, even if their role in the research is not theory but rather understanding the problems and the ways in which solutions to them can be found. This approach does not exclude practical application of what is studied nor does it always anticipate practical solutions.

Concluding reflections

Experience with concrete development situations has taught me that scientific work relating to people cannot be separate from people's practical life. The political and social situation of a newly independent country aspiring to achieve national unity was bound to influence the way the research was carried out in Tanzania. Development research derived its basic methodology from anthropology, which had from its inception as a science been close to people. Development research had to be related to the aspirations of the society and to move from the objectifying concept of science to interpretative, phenomenological and hermeneutic search for meanings in the new and changing situation. Research had to engage in this task, which the decision makers missed. I understood that participatory research was necessary for gaining *deepened understanding* of the society and social processes in action, and theory should grow out of it.

Participatory research, PR, later joined with action, PAR, became for me a personal response in the political direction that the country had taken but was not implementing in practice. People would need to understand the situation they were in and learn to participate in the analysis and decision-making. If they learned to participate in formulating their thoughts, which in cooperation with a researcher would develop into further questioning and research, they would also express problems relating to their own lives and realize that such a search was significant. As an anthropologist, the researcher understands that she is indeed a learner and cannot all the time direct the discussion with questions, which are formulated by her thought structure and intentions. PR could then become Participatory *Action* Research and potentially equip some people to participatory planning as part of the political process.

CHAPTER 4

On Whose Culture is Development Built?

Introductory thoughts

The problematic in this chapter deals with the concepts of culture and development in the social context as they relate to the theme on participatory and engaged research. The use of culture as a concept both for anthropology and development has been questioned and criticized by leading anthropologists, and side-lined by development scholars. Culture and development are both general problematic concepts, when applied in specific contexts and meanings amidst the baffling changes people are experiencing in every part of the world. The chapter views critically different ways the concepts are applied and the potential strengths that cultural resources could bring to people's self esteem and social life, and encourage action while creating cultural identity.

Well-known anthropologists and social scientists replace the "culture" concept with "society." The division occurred initially between the scholars in the United States, who built their anthropology on "culture," and the French and English who based their analysis on the concept of "society." This chapter first deals with the difficulties in translating the concepts relating to culture and development into the Swahili language and goes on to the general use of the concepts in the political parlance. The linguistic difficulties hide differences in interpretation also in practical life. The concept "development" brings up the problematic of its historical interpretation and meaning. The concept leads to the problem of market and donor domination also in relation to the citizen's organizations and their potential role as the voice of the people in creation of space for sociality at the heart of culture. It is ideological to think that cultural and social forces can mitigate the power and the rule of the market forces and make room for the cultural specificities in society, yet the pitfalls in the world economy necessitate strengthening of social and cultural forces of society.

The problem relating to the concepts culture, society and development is not only in the use of language but rather in the foreign cultural and economic domination, which plays its role when the development paths are externally ruled and controlled. The conceptualization of development solely in politico-economic terms with its negative implications is taken up in this and other chapters. The discussion leads to the role of the knowledge production and the potential of the participatory research to deal with the problem, when the former objects of research are given roles as subjects and partners in research and action. When the concept of culture is taken in a broad sense, it then leads also into the meanings that sociality and social relationships play in the non-western societies. They in turn are central in conceptions of development. Participatory research makes their scholarly use relevant to the participating communities and gives them an active role in the formulation of the problems and the follow up of the study results. The chapter refers to the broadening field of community-based research, and touches on the issue of the control of knowledge on which development is built and the space left for the indigenous knowledge.

The negative connotations and the hidden fears often related to traditional meanings of cultural concepts lead to the secret use of the assumed powers by the practitioners multiplied in countryside but even more in cities. Such fears and negative connotations have prevented seeing the wealth of indigenous culture as a potential source of inspiration.

Linguistic roots of culture and power of concepts

Culture and related concepts do not cause difficulties only for scholars but also for common people needing translations in their native languages. Tanzania faced it in looking for a fitting Swahili word for the abstract concept and then interpreting its meaning. As the Eskimos had any number of words for snow of different qualities and colours but no general name for it so the indigenous Tanzanian languages have different names for each aspect of their cultural features, but lack an indigenous general concept. The search for the word to make an abstract concept understandable demonstrates a key development problem in human and social history, which today with the fast developing technology brings along a need for new comprehensible terms in every language. The words for culture in many languages are derivatives from the Latin word *cultura,* which is derived from meanings relating to the cultivation of land. In English you cultivate when you still land by prefixing the word with *agri* meaning land, thus following the original meaning of the words, yet noticing that both words originate in Latin. In Finnish *kulttuuri* is the same as culture and has no trace of its agricultural roots. The meaning is dependent on the interpretation in different contexts. This was the case also in Swahili when a translation was sought for, but the word was sought from Arabic, not Latin.

Initially the word "culture" has in Europe referred to "high culture" and the same is reflected in the history of the concept in Swahili. The word *ustaarabu,* adopted during the colonial rule, originated from the time when the Oman Arabs had made their abode in Zanzibar and on the coast of Tanganyika and brought with them features of a foreign "higher" Arabic culture. A man wearing a white gown, *kanzu* and a cap, adopting Arabic customs and Islam as religion had then *ustaarabu,* "Arabicization." The colonialists adopted the word to mean culture, then "civilized way of life." The Arab derivation was contrasted with *ushenzi,* translated as "savage way of life." People use still the word *kustaarabika* (*ku-sta-arab-ika*) translating it "to become cultured, civilized," not realizing that it carries the meaning of becoming "Arabicized."

When Tanganyika became independent and sought greater self-identity, *ustaarabu* with reference to Arabs was no longer fitting. Paradoxically the coastal experts of the Swahili language suggested another word of Arabic origin, *utamaduni,* which then was adopted regardless being a derivative from Arabic. But unknowingly the meaning u-ta-madu tied even closer to Arabia and Islam. The root of the word *madan* signifies the centre of an Arabic city, *medina,* with urban connotation. Furthermore it is of the same root as Medina, the city to which Mohammed with his people escaped. The origin is not traced in the dictionaries, but it implies Islamic origin in linguistic terms.

The Swahili-English Dictionary, *Kamusi ya Kiswahili-Kiingereza* (2001) of the Swahili Institute in the University of Dar es Salaam, translates *utamaduni* as "culture." The new Swahili-Swahili *Kamusi ya Swahili Sanifu* of 2004 (printed in 2008) gives the word *utamaduni* the meanings *mila, asili, jadi na desturi za kundi la jamii fulani* in the meanings of "tradition(s), origin," "inheritance and customs of any communal group," avoiding the word tribe or ethnic group. The translations in the Kiswahili-Kiingereza dictionary are *mila,* "traditions, customs"; *asili,* "origin"; *jadi,* "tradition, origin, lineage, pedigree, ancestry"; *desturi,* "custom, tradition, norms." All the given words refer to the past tradition, thus not to "high culture."

Utamaduni commonly came to mean such features as *ngoma* dances performed in public events or school students standing and singing in horizontal lines facing the dignitaries, thus rejecting the meaningful circular or square forms of traditional dances. Rituals arranged in the home yards in Bunju or any village, where they are still performed as part of the village or family tradition, are not ordinarily called *utamaduni,* except when they are performed in public events for visitors and dignitaries or when replaced with modern instruments. In the Lugoba area of the Jipemoyo research project the people told the researchers that the *ngoma* were *utamaduni.* They were proud that there was now a Ministry for their *ngoma,* as they knew that our research team was under the Ministry of Culture, *Wizara ya Utamaduni* (Jerman 1989). They had heard it from Israel Katoke, the director of research in the Ministry of Culture and Youth in mid-seventies who had made a visit to Lugoba in Western Bagamoyo District to familiarize himself with he location of the proposed research project. The modern loudspeakers and new instruments have changed such occasions, but drums still play their role.

The word *ngoma* refers to drums and dancing, but the word narrows the meaning when used for a ritual. In the English-Swahili dictionary the meanings for ritual are "*mapokeo, fikira, mila, desturi kutoka kizazi kimoja hadi kingine,*" "things inherited, thoughts, customs passed from one generation to another." In ethnic languages the rituals have their own names but no general name. In Swahili *unyago* and *jando* are used for the ethnic female and male initiation rituals, but in a guidebook for the maturing youth these terms are used with no reference to customary dances or instructions (Mamuya 1972).

The *Standard Daily* newspaper recorded that the 15th TANU Biennial Conference charged "the Party to actively take a leading role in all cultural activities in the country." The Cultural and Political Division of TANU was to submit the proposals via the sub-committee on culture for acceptance of the

Central Committee of Culture. "The Party's role is just to ensure that people are in full control of their day to day life, without anyone doing it for them" were the words of the Party spokesman who foresaw that "TANU branches and TANU Youth League members would play a vital role as they are the base institutions close to the people." It resulted in the TANU Youth League defining the kind of clothes people could wear and its members arresting young women wearing short skirts and young men with thick-soled shoes, taking them to the police station and making them sweep streets as a punitive measure. For the pastoralists, the TANU policy on culture meant wearing pants instead of their traditional wraps, as they were seen not to cover the body fully. Barabaig men came to the American missionary couple Faust living among them near Balangida-lake to borrow short pants to wear under their wraps when they made a trip to Singida or Arusha towns.

Similarly some party leaders assumed to be "closest to the people" faced difficulties in defining the meaning of the concept "development." It was conceived that development, *maendeleo*, from the verb *kuendelea*, "to continue, move on, move forward," was an overarching category understood by everyone. In the Swahili-Swahili dictionary of 2004, the meaning is extended to *hali ya kufanikiwa, kwa kijamii, kiuchumi, au kisiasa*, "the state of succeeding (or prospering), socially, economically or politically." When the women in Bunju first saw me wearing their traditional *kanga*-wrap in 1965, their reaction was, "*Maendeleo haya!*" This is development! The concept of politics, *siasa,* had the same difficulties in interpretation. A leader of the Lutheran women in Dar es Salam asked me what *siasa* meant when it had become a word in everyday speech on everyone's lips.

Society, culture and development

Giving meanings to the basic terms reveals the deeper cultural differences, which the anthropologic analysis interprets and combines with globally comprehensible lines of thought. Anthropologists have been divided about the usefulness of "culture" as a concept for analytical purposes while "society," social relations and values determine people's way of living. This chapter analyses these concepts contextually as they relate to the dominating "development" concept, which is generally taken as an overarching category acceptable everywhere yet generally dealt with in the terms that the Western development theorists and implementers have conceived it. The question needs to be faced whether development can be pursued with a social group or internationally while eclipsing and ignoring the indigenous cultures with their hidden convolutions. The anthropologists have not been helpful with their scholarly language for those engaged in practical development efforts. The problem is not only of language. In the words of Alfred Schütz (1953), they have not come out of their "scientific situation," and the anthropologist "has not made himself understandable to the actor ... in terms of common sense interpretation of every day life."

Maendeleo, development, has dominated the parlance as the magic term. It was assumed to be capable of overriding the old customs and to bring good standard of living for people once poverty was reduced and finally eradicated. I refer to my short article on the subject "What is development?" in another context (M-L. Swantz 2009). A significant treatment of the subject of development is James Ferguson's analysis of Lesotho as a less developed country. It has drawn much attention as an anthropological analysis of the factors affecting the development scene, in his case focusing on a project supported by the World Bank. The author emphasizes the influence of the formulation of the discourses, which deepen the analysis of linguistic terms. In the book *The Anti-Politics Machine* (1990) James Ferguson does not write an ordinary critique of truth or fallacy of the development problematic. Rather, he shows that thinking is a real activity and the ideas and discourses have real social consequences. He discusses the main tone of the bureaucratic powers and the influence of the development agents such as the World Bank. Their influence could determine not only the way a project was run, but the expansion and entrenchment of the bureaucratic state power in such a way that there was no room left for the state's own political decision making, and even less room for the people's political action or their own conception of developmental solutions. For Ferguson what ideas do and what consequences they have is more interesting as an anthropological approach than the ordinary run of development analyses. Ferguson's anthropological opus does not take people only as objects, but analyses structures as multi-layered, polyvalent, and contradictory, located in other encompassing structures invisible to the people who inhabit them. An anthropologist gives the powerful forces the status of an interesting problem, as structures can overtake intentional practices. Ferguson uses Foucault's ideas of "discourse of practice" and a decentred conception of power and shows how key discourses work as, and turn to, the means of power.

This is what I see happening with the generalizing concepts, which have taken over external development assistance, such as the overarching conceptualization of poverty and the dominating Millennium Development Goals referred to in all the documents as MDGs. Ferguson's book gives another angle to treating development from the point of view of concepts and discourses (Ferguson 1994).

It is relevant here to refer to Stephen Marglin, emeritus professor of economics in Harvard, whose influence in my research career was significant for over twenty years starting with his and his wife Frédérique Apffel-Marglin's time at the World Institute for Economics Research (WIDER) in Helsinki. He classified people's knowledge into *techne* practical knowledge, T-knowledge, and more theoretical *epistemic,* E-knowledge. In his later book *Dismal Science* (2008) he calls the latter *algorithmic* instead of epistemic knowledge and *experiential* instead of *techne* knowledge (Marglin 1990, 231-246; 1996, 226-243; 2008, 128-152). I add the *realm of symbols* as another pervasive category, essential in the African culture even when it is losing significance. I return to this later in the chapter in the section on culture. In *Dismal Science*, Marglin suggests that no categories are "pure," "… one knows with and through one's hands and eyes as well as with one's head." He also refers to Martha Nussbaum and Amartya Sen's notion of "cognitive role of the emotions" (1989). African knowledge is traditionally practical T-knowledge but the richly endowed symbolic interpretation of life suffers loss under development measures, which means neglect of a rich resource base, imagination and inspiration for development. Stephen Marglin brings the issue of cultural differences to a broad perspective in his book in the chapter "From Imperialism to Globalization by Way of Development." He uses "culture" in the way anthropologists understand the term "to mean the totality of patterns of behaviour and belief that characterize a specific society." Culture is "sustained by and through community," which binds people economically, socially and spiritually. Marglin's point is that the market as the organizing principle undermines traditional communities. According to him, individualism can be also in the Western culture decoupled from the commitment to the market. He quotes St. Mark (8:36) "What shall it profit a man, if he shall gain the whole world, and lose his own soul?" In the West, the price paid by material gain is breaking of ties of community. Marglin's view of community brings out the significance of it in situations in which outsiders see only scarcity, i.e. poverty. The Western confidence in the market economy is well described in the section of "Economics as Cultural Theory" of the quoted book. He challenges the Western readers to reflect on the ethical implications of the kind of development, which destroys the ways of being different from our own culture and ways of living (Marglin 1998; 2008, 245-248)

My close cooperation with Frédérique Apffel-Marglin was another significant influence on me, especially in deepening the understanding of the women's central role in enriching the cultural significance in development (Apffel-Marglin 1996; 1998).Together with her we organized two seminars on the lake in Lohja, Finland, bringing together other significant women with whom the contact continued over years. One of them was Signe Arnfred, who invited us to continue the thinking and cooperation in Roskilde, Denmark (Arnfred 1995; 2011; Ahmed, Salokoski, and Swantz 1995). I also continued to maintain contact since the time of WIDER with Sheila Rowbotham, whose writings on histories of working women and their inventiveness have inspired my imagination in analysing their situation (Rowbotham 1992; 2010; 2011).

It is difficult for the feminists today to fathom that we were pioneers in developing women's role in research and in international feminism in the North, starting in the 1970s getting our inspiration from the first conference in 1975 in Mexico, in which women's position was for the first time strengthened in international conferences, even if women had worked for women's rights in different countries since the past century. Helvi Sipilä was the first Assistant Secretary General of the United Nations and had a decisive influence in bringing up the women's role in human and social affairs. Hilkka Pietilä was another Finnish feminist pioneer as the long time secretary of the UN organization in Finland (H. Pietilä, 2013). While I was teaching anthropology at the University of Helsinki and had written my doctoral thesis "with special reference to women," the Secretary of the Human Studies Department of the Academy of Finland sent me to Norway to meet with the Nordic feminists, who had been inspired by Berit Ås, another pioneer in fight for women's rights. Together with selected women and some men representatives from Finland, I attended the first Nordic feminist research seminar in Sweden, where I gave a lecture in Swedish. Some Finnish participants initially expressed doubts of the necessity of a feminist movement, including Lea Virtanen, who had written on the different roles of girls and boys. I return to the women's issue further below.

In Tanzania, President Nyerere had paid special attention to women, recognizing that their position need special attention in the Ujamaa policy text. The country has not forgotten its first president whose teachings until the present time have formed part of the daily after news program in TV. The *Ujamaa* policy, which was primarily his creation, was based on the traditional idea of enlarged family, communality. It was the foundation of the Arusha Declaration on which the TANU policy was built. The *Ujamaa* politics have been almost totally forgotten and proved to be based on an idealistic conceptualization of kinship based society, but President Nyerere had also a broader view of culture. He translated Shakespeare's *Merchant of Venice* into Swahili and he transformed all the Gospels and the Acts of the Apostles of the Bible into the *utenzi* Swahili poetry form. He called a traditional singer to entertain himself when he spent time in his village house. He agreed to have a *halubadili* read with his Muslim brothers to show that he was not hiding anything from them.

The academic community in Dar es Salaam were highly critical of President Nyerere's ideology and the very core of Ujamaa in the 1970s and 1980s. The Marxist critics attacked the basic ideas of building on the ideology of traditional culture instead of building on the historical materialist conceptualization of production patterns to prevent the creation of a class society. The dominance of the leftist scholarship based on economistic class formation was changed since the time of President Mwinyi toward liberal market economy, which has dictated the politics and left little room for indigenous interpretation of social life and culture, apart from looking at its market value and subjecting the historical sites to the tourist interests under the Ministry of Tourism.

President Nyerere was acutely afraid of the control and power of the global market forces and opposed the power of the IMF and its influential monetary system. Edwin Mtei as the Minister of Finance at the time has in his autobiography recorded the conflict into which he ran with Nyerere, when both of them simultaneously discovered that they could not continue their cooperation while they differed about the direction to which the nation's finances were heading (Mtei 2009). In the President's mind, the struggle was not only monetary but the social and cultural grounding he was building did not fail to satisfy only the market economists but also the Marxist politicians and theorists. Eventually the Father of the Nation, as he is still today called, chose to resign from his position as the President in 1985, not wanting to be responsible for the takeover of the market. The way of building economy on the basic African communal mode was not feasible, not at least in the way it was implemented.

My research in Rufiji in the first half of the 1970s, in which I was engaged with University of Dar es Salaam students, indicated that even when the communal possession of fields seemed to work out, as in the model Nyambili village in Rufiji, the common field was former clan land of the one or two dominating clans in the village and commonness was based on clan ownership. At present, the total change away from the *Ujamaa* politics is most evident in the new land policies, which have permitted the private control of land and in practice ownership of land (Ylhäissi, 2003). With this process, the inequality increases and diminishes the possibility of looking for cultural roots in building up the social cohesion and integrity. The "communal" concept had its limitations as clan and lineage rights limited the general communal possession and even the ethnic identification limited the sense of commonness. The lesson learned was that communities cannot be created if there is no initiative coming from the people themselves who could potentially have reformed their communal experience and the role of kinship in it. It is notable that in the societies such as the Chagga of Kilimanjaro and the Haya in Kagera region, the kin-based ownership has continued, while new relationships have been formed through work, creating new meanings in social life.

When doing the study of the Zaramo in Bunju village in 1965-70 I was more in line with the changes taking place in anthropological analysis than the critics at that time realized, when they missed the kinship analysis, which had its place in all anthropological case studies. The society I shared life with in Bunju consisted of people who had come from inland Zaramo country moving there via Bagamoyo or Dar es Salaam and looking for land to cultivate and engage in small-scale fishing. Gradually they had formed a concentration of Zaramo on the hills a few miles up from the sea. Their ancestors' graves and spirit shrines were left in what was the heartland of the Zaramo around and beyond Maneromango and Ubena Zomozi. This meant that they had to put up small shrines in which they made their offerings and prayers, remembering the same spirits whom their ancestors had honoured. Instead of analysing the kinship structure, I turned to interpretation of the changes taking place in the society and was surprised to learn about the rich ritual life in which people were engaged. It led me looking for the meanings of the ritual symbols, which kept the Zaramo identity alive. When I was looking into the kin relations, the wife of my adopted medicine man (*mganga*) father secretly told me that her closest woman friend was not among the kin and the people building the spirit hut in her husband Salum's yard were his partners, adherents in his ritual practice, or his patients. The rituals and symbols became central in holding to the identity. The patients who needed the spirit rituals, some coming from the city, together with the kin and neighbours, formed the community.

Another close friend, famous diviner Mwawila, had hardly any of her kin relations around her, even the brother living not far away, kept hardly any contact with her, and her divorced husband, father of her daughter, had been Nyaturu from Singida while she too lived in Dar es Salaam. From there she had settled to cultivate in Bunju. She practised raising *rungu* spirits while my father Salum raised the widely known female spirits, *kinyamkera* and male *mwenembago*. When the social situation changed and the land holdings were no longer held onto in the coast, new social relations and new meanings and interpretations to the diseases were bound to influence the meanings of the social relations.

Of interest here is the changing substance in ethnological research as it appeared in the *New Departures in Anthropology* series. The central anthropological topic of kinship in Janet Carsten's study *After Kinship* (2004) was notably of special interest to readers with its three reprints in 2005, 2006, and 2007. Even if the book looks at relatedness in the West, it presents a critical challenge in kinship studies relating to the African situation, as it reminds us that the changing concept of kinship is universally relevant. There are "modern" Tanzanians who find the kinship rules binding and others who tend to separate themselves from binding relationships and get into quarrels with the older generation's claims. Carsten refers to her own earlier book *Culture of Relatedness* (2000) and to the influence of anthropologists Stephen Gudeman, Maurice Bloch and Marilyn Strathern, whose initial research was based on three different continents, in Panama, Madagascar and Melanesia, yet have special relevance amid global changes. Godelier also needs to be mentioned here, as the kinship base of societies he studied formed for him the basic problem in relating to Marxist interpretations (Carsten 2004; Gudeman 1976; Bloch 1993; Maurice Godelier 1987).

The scientific and technological development would find more creative paths if people's rituals with symbolic forms of thought and action would give more space for the rich sources of creativity to flourish in new ways. Now the spirit practices influenced by Islam are no longer based on the traditional symbolic forms and development models pave the way for sheer imitation and offered in the name of modern and scientific. People turn the search for meanings into fears and forms of witchcraft in the process of modernization as suggested by Comaroffs (1993) and Geschiere (1997). The prevailing image of development leaves little room for people's imagination and positive creative change. Fortunately some of that creativity is bursting out in different forms of art and music, as is shown in the new doctoral dissertation in Swahili by Method Samwel with collections of wordings for songs from several ethnic groups (Samwel 2012).

Recent studies look also for possibilities of building on the still existing sense of cooperation that links the urban clan members with their places of origin. Such is the sense of belonging related to the continuing custom of burying the deceased family members in their villages of origin. The power attached to the graves and the role of the elders in guarding the graves is still recognized when in times of trouble the kin members return to make offerings on the graves, as shown by Fraterline Kashaga in his research on the Haya elders in Bukoba district. The custom of burying the dead in the land of origin is still in general use among the city people (Kashaga 2013). The link to the place of origin also sets conditions for the urban relatives toward the needs of the elders in the home area, as the city people send their contributions to the members of the family for burials even when they cannot attend the burials of related kin members in their villages.

Such burial customs have drawn the interest of anthropologist Peter Geschiere who in his book *The Perils of Belonging, Autochthony, Citizenship, and Exclusion in Africa and Europe* (2009) uses *autochthony* in the context of identity and sees that the prevalence of relating one's identity to the "roots" becomes evident in the burial customs. Geschiere relates it into the custom also in his homeland, the Netherlands, and calls "The Funerals as a Final Test for Belonging." The urban people I have interviewed in Dar es Salaam have even given the burial in the home village as the explanation why the urban folk build an urban type of house in the home village regardless whether they intend to live in it or not. There has to be a respectable house to accommodate the related city people who come for the funeral.

It can be argued that such continuity has cultural roots, which prevail after the tradition-based ties weaken and no longer have the significance they have had before. The social continuity and the significance of social ties in the maintenance of family based economy can continue only if the cultural understanding of the meanings animates them.

Music and dance have the central effect in communal gatherings directed toward inherited or newly gained spiritual values. The most notable practice of communal sharing evidenced in studies in Iramba and in the southern regions is the women's ways of working in groups not only for saving but also serving in need, of which more in the chapter on "Women's Ways of Sustaining Life." Such communal or social experiences are in one way or another selective as are also the custom of the educated city folk who are prepared to spend large sums of money to organize their friends' weddings or birthday and other celebrations with selected kin based or social and professional acquaintances.

These derivatives of past practices lead us to ask how culture relates to social development. Culture was given prominence anew in the Tanzanian Government system when since 2010 The Ministry of Culture and Sports was again separated from the Ministry of Education of which it has been a part from time to time. Culture gained its contents from the activities of the Ministry, which besides carrying out cultural events and providing cultural programs included a section for research. Helena Jerman has elaborated this aspect and has clarified it further in her later research paper (Jerman 1989). To rectify the purely economic view of development United Nations under the leadership of UNESCO brought culture to the centre stage as part of the World Decade of Cultural Development (1988-1997). It set up the World Commission on Culture and Development under the chairmanship of the former UN General Secretary Javier Pérez de Cuéllar de la Guerra to clarify culture as a concept in relation to development. In the Report of the Commission the definition of culture is taken in the comprehensive anthropological terms. The Report states clearly what the place of culture in relation to development in the Commission's terms is:

Development divorced from its human or cultural context is growth without soul. Economic development in its full flowering is part of people's culture. This is not a view commonly held. A more common view regards culture either as a help or a hindrance to economic development, leading to the call to take 'cultural factors into account in development.'

Culture, therefore, however important it may be as an instrument of development (or an obstacle of development), cannot ultimately be reduced to a subsidiary position as a mere promoter (or/and impediment to) economic growth. Culture's role is not exhausted as a servant of ends - though in a narrower sense of the concept this is one of its roles - but is the social basis of the ends themselves. Development and the economy are part of a people's culture (1995, 15).

Symbolic and religious elements of culture

It can be argued that the time has passed when you could derive cultural meanings from the way the traditions offered symbolic understanding of life, but even if the cultural meanings have less significance to people they can derive from them intellectual and artistic inspiration if their value is made explicit to them. My essay on the Zaramo, *Human body as a symbol of resistance* (1992), shows that symbolism reflecting the organic unity had great significance to the people on the coast until the 1980s, when the understanding of life was retained in unity with the surrounding environment and nature. Fresh understanding of the richness of the past cultural features would open up new forms of expression and use of imagination instead of people fearing their vaguely known past, conceived as utilization of witchcraft or spirits *(jinni)*. Inherited cultural components are not integrated into the present education program in Tanzania and the references to the local histories depend on the teachers' interests. *Ngoma* music and dance troupes are used for public performance, for visiting leaders and at national events. *Ngoma* groups are paid for private celebrations, but the meanings of different drums and music are not in the teaching program.

To illustrate, a specific drum was needed when at an exorcism a man was in deep trance and could not be awakened from it because of the absence of the instrument needed for releasing him from the spirit that empowered him. The Zaramo used a specific big drum accompanied with a small drum for sending the spirit of a dead relative to the nether world, and the same drums were used when the *mkema kumbi*, the organizer of the circumcision, awakened the boys in the morning in the male *kumbi* camp, where the boys stayed after their circumcision. The small drum represented the female element. Such cultural features broaden the significance of the meanings they have in their customary culture still available in local experts' explanations.

Having studied the symbolic aspects of the coastal Zaramo culture and learned their central social role still in the 1960s and 1970s in the coastal areas, the question arises how the development programmes could better make use of the capability of the people whose ritual life centred on the symbolic conceptualization of life and whose social relations were close to the organic environment from which the symbols grew out. The Zaramo knew the denotations and connotations of symbols and to varying degrees they existentially experienced their meanings still in the 1970s. *Denotation* here signifies the concrete object in comparison to *connotation,* which refers to the symbolic meaning. The basic unity of experience related to organic modes of life and found its expression in social symbols in various rituals. The human body had been the microcosm in which both the society and cosmos were reflected. The use of "organic" in the social context was criticized as according to Durkheim's reference to the modern organized society was far from that of the Zaramo. To quote Durkheim:

... we propose to call this type of solidarity mechanical ... by analogy to their cohesion which unites the elements of an inanimate body, as opposed to that which makes a unity out of the elements of a living body. ... Thus in these social types, personal rights are not yet distinguished from real rights. ... It is quite otherwise with the solidarity, which the division of labor produces. ... The first is possible only in so far as the individual personality is absorbed into the collective personality; the second is possible only if each one has a sphere of action, which is peculiar to him; that is a personality. (Durkheim 1984, 130-131)

Thus in Durkheim's commonly adopted organic society, individuals are personalities capable of forming an organic collective. It is evident that society becomes organic in such interpretation when individual personalities become individualistic and the cohesion in the society comes about in the end through deadening bureaucracy as Weber also predicted. I claimed that the symbolic view of life had its groundings in the common psychobiological experience of the community with its strengths and weaknesses, which made it organic. I argued further that the shared existential experience in unity with nature, which is acted out and put into the perception of senses through words and music, required also reasoned conception of the phenomena of life in song and words of explanation given as teachings to the young. It required the capacity to wonder before the unknown while giving the symbols both universal and particular meanings. The dominating symbolism connoting death corresponded with the crisis the society was experiencing (M-L. Swantz 1986; 1992; 1993).

The interpretation of the symbolic elements relating to varied aspects of life, and distancing them from their former *existential meanings* could lead to the reasoned understanding of their significance in human development. This leads in turn to the concepts of *awareness* and conscious adaptation to the changes that take place. Jean Comaroff writes in her chapter "The Forms of Tshidi Consciousness":

... what does appear to be distinctive about precolonial Tswana culture ... is the absence of an awareness of the process of objectification itself. With the exception of the unevenly systematized repertoire of norms that governed rank, succession, and legal procedure (*mekgwa le melao*), and the even less explicit body of ritual technique of the specialist (*bongaka*), there was no indigenous notion of formal knowledge, of "myth," "tradition," "history," or "belief." Established cultural forms were conveyed largely through participation in everyday practice, and involved a mode of communication, which, as Bourdieu (1977,120) has pointed out, seldom attains the level of open discourse. (Jean Comaroff 1985, 125)

Comaroff continues further with a reference to Horton (1967), who represented the view that also the people's symbolic consciousness relates to rationality. The question is whether the meaning of rational here meant "self-conscious, critical discourse," which Comaroff on the other hand credited to the Tshidi when they "experienced and sought to reconcile conflicts generated by the social system that encompassed them." This would indicate that there was rationality in social action but not in the symbolic sphere of the ritual. The Comaroffs have in their volumes of *Of Revelation and Revolution* analysed the role of the Wesleyan Methodist influence in South Africa as the colonization of consciousness and how consciousness was made and remade (Comaroff, J. and J. 1991, xi).

I have suggested that thinking follows its logic also in the use of some symbolic forms by the leading ritual practitioners even if the partakers do not rationally work out what they go through. They believe that through the ritual the spirits are appeased and they retain health as they prevent vengeance of the spirits with their veneration. When one of the oldest and most veneered ritual performers, Ndamba, explained his experience of being taken into the depth of water and how he was raised from the underground world, it was not a rational story, but he was telling the "myth" which he believed and had experienced. He did not explain how it was possible to be kept under water and listen the mother spirit talk with the father spirit, it was irrational, but he had experienced it. The experience was alive in his consciousness.

Philosophers want to reserve the term rationality for use in scientific terms. Religious beliefs of any religion are not in the final analysis explained rationally, yet the philosophers deal with them rationally. In discussing this matter with the well-known Finnish philosopher George Henrik von Wright, he suggested the use of "reasonable" in place of "rational" when such "reasoning" of the Zaramo wise women and men were in question.

The interpretation of the ritual and its symbolic conceptualization relates to the issue of development and whose consciousness and interpretation of ritual practice defines it. There are at least two reasons why the topic requires discussion. We need to ask whether the capacity for imagination and thinking in metaphors and symbols does not indicate creative capacity, which is totally missing in today's development discussion. Development means a greater consciousness of the on-going process by different sectors of the society and within different aspects of consciousness. Every society has different levels of reasoning and the significance of understanding the changing mode of consciousness within the development process is at the heart of it. Secondly, today's national development experts need to know the richness of their cultural heritage and not to limit it solely to *ngoma* performances, and in some cases with veneration of the deceased elders as described among others by Päivi Hasu and Sally Falk Moore about the rituals of the Chagga in East Kilimanjaro and Fraterline Kashaga in Bukoba District (Hasu 1999; Falk Moore 1986; Kashaga 2013).

There is a tendency to describe and analyse the traditional culture in negative terms related to fears of spirits and witchcraft or dance troupes are made use of for entertainment such as *madogoli* drummers and dancers performing in public places. The listeners and viewers rarely connect such performance with its actual meanings as in a *spirit exorcism* in which the client is exorcised in a weekend long ritual with a variety of songs and intense drumming, with every drum having its own role and the rhythm varying according to the requirements of the phases in exorcism. The spirit exorcism with no connection with the ritual meanings has also spread as a makeshift tool of fake spirit healers to cities and communities with slight contact with original practices, as has been the case among the Chaggas (T. Pietilä 1999, Hasu 1998)

The second edition of *Ritual and Symbol in Transitional Zaramo Society* (1986) has an introductory section in which the development potential of the rituals is discussed, basing it on the closing sections in both prints. This raised the interest of professors Terence Ranger, Ulf Himmelstrand, and Robert Horton who commented on the thoughts. Ranger wrote about the role of ritual:

African religious beliefs can often constitute a force opposing development. But there is a counter argument – namely that in the past change has been mediated through ritual and sanctioned by religious authority and that if we wish modernising change on a communitarian basis we need to understand these rhythms of innovation. This is the importance in this context of the work of Marja-Liisa Swantz. Her massive book on the Zaramo of the Tanzanian coastal hinterland is of interest to historians of religion in other ways also… But in many ways the most provocative pages in the book are those which seem to promise a demonstration of the relevance of all this to development. (Ranger 1972, 46)

Ranger quoted from the book at length, referring to the contention that the development agents had failed to understand the symbolic unity and to respect the basic integrity of the representatives of that tradition. The potential for a constructive transition from presentational and communicative symbols to discursive forms of symbols was lost, quoting my book:

If presentational symbolism can be taken not as something pre-rational, which does not belong to the sphere of science but as symbolic material with its own forms of conception and as such pointing to the sources of knowledge, this would mean that a study of presentational symbolism can be taken as a serious attempt to analyse the human mind and experience. (M-L. Swantz 1986, 52)

In my analysis the terms presentational and discursive symbolism were used following Susan Langer (1956) with the contention that the meaning of the presentational symbolism, which was acted out and made understandable to the participants in the cohesive rituals, could be interpreted and put into words by the participating actors and the anthropologist. The symbolic expression of the experience other than language had its own experiential message about the human mind and being. The message was interpreted in individual and corporate terms. I made reference to Mircea Eliade (1958), who initially had led me to thinking in terms of the universal symbols. I argued that because large parts of the human experience were kept outside the rational sphere and conceived as not susceptible to logical mediation, there was no total universal building on basic human experience.

Because of the spreading individuation, which was induced by the coming of literacy, the corporate understanding of symbols diminished. Also Comaroffs referred to this effect of literacy, which the institution of the school has further strengthened. I suggested that presentational symbolism could be moved from conceiving of it solely in terms of feelings and metaphysics to the sphere of inner interpretation of meaning. To quote Langer, "Rationality is the essence of mind and symbolic transformation its elementary process." But symbolic expression does not need to be rationally interpreted in order to be meaningful to people, as subjective feelings and inner conception touch the core of the person as an individual and profoundly influence human life.. I return to these thoughts in referring to Stanley Tambiah who analyses the philosophers' differing views on the rationality in cultures generally interpreted in operational terms (Tambiah 1990). I had put the same thought into the following words:

It is not only because man has lacked scientific language that s/he has used symbolism. It is also because a symbol contains a different mode of expression and interpretation on a different level of human experience. (M-L. Swantz, 1986, 52-53)

According to the Comaroffs, as a result with the encounter "with Christianity, colonialism and the money economy," the Tshidi obtained "identification with the symbols of these global forms and a concern with the coherence of 'belief' and practice in the face of cultural syncretism..." It meant being "self-consciousness about knowledge, its absolute 'truth', and its systematicity..." and "colonization of Tswana consciousness" in the chapter, "Meaning of Conversion" (1991; 199, 248-251). The book deals with the concept of "meaning" in multiple ways, but in the conclusion of the chapter the difference of the meanings of the new faith diverged between the missionaries and the Tswana. The pioneering missionaries often had a weak understanding of the indigenous beliefs and symbols, nor did they commonly think of their faith in terms of symbols. They came from a society, which had found a new way of learning through literacy both about faith and other forms of existence. In the Protestant mode, the attraction to interpretations of belief through the word and in the Calvinist tradition even the Christian symbols of the crucifix were avoided. Faith based on the written and spoken word required a degree of awareness, consciousness and even rational understanding of meanings, which led to faith. According to the Comaroffs this prevented the Tshidi from taking in what the preaching and the plain form of service, which the Methodist missionaries introduced, was composed of. This interpretation does not take into consideration the possibility of "believing in," a critique Joel Robbins made of the way the Comaroffs interpreted Christian faith. Robbins's extensive study of the Urapmin in New Guinea had given him deeper understanding of the people's belief in the meanings based on the Bible, which they had acquired without missionary influence (Robbins 2004).

The different forms of consciousness had caused differentiation within the Tshidi community. But one should not throw out the baby with the bathwater. Apart from the Comaroffs' biased view of Christianity, the reader gets the impression that in the context of the adopted religion, self-consciousness and being systematic were also negative attributes. One questions whether the acquisition of literacy and learning would not have caused differentiation in any manner of its appropriation. As in all societies, the people who first have gained literary skills have also gained different positions in society. The Comaroffs list literacy in several places as a negative when it came with the nonconformists. It is obvious that the change would have come in any case. By bringing literacy, missionaries expedited the process but also general development, with its negative and positive consequences. All societies have experienced and continue to experience the negative consequences of increased and misused knowledge, but the greater self-awareness could ameliorate the process. The societies with Lutheran heritage have become "readers" as they were required to read the Bible, which has meant building the societies on a more rational basis than partaking mainly in the ritual, especially when performed in Latin, with no literary interpretation. Even the President Kikwete in Tanzania, when laying the cornerstone of the new Lutheran university in Bukoba West of lake Victoria in 2012, made a remark, wondering why they, known to be "readers," *wasomi*, had not established the university there earlier.

I looked for some elements of rational interpretation and saw some potential aspects of them for application in terms of development. In the transition from the ritual conception of life, which united people into a social group with a common understanding of life, there were traditional leaders who had a deep understanding of the traditional life forms but were also adopting a new concept as members of society and were finding a new avenue for learning and activity in political engagement. They were the wise men and women, whose understanding, or what Horton calls "common sense" I tried to lift out and interpret to the modernizers. I found them also in my mentor Bengt Sundkler's interpretation of the wise Haya men, who moved from honouring the inherited local spirits to the universal Christian spirit belief (Sundkler 1948, 1961; Swantz, M-L. 1986, 19-29, 377-302; 2004, 378-390). A Zaramo man versed in the ritual practices had a rational concept of the symbols, which he expressed in explaining to me the difference between the Islamic and their own ritual symbolism. He said, "For a Muslim when he wears a white gown the white is just white, it does not have another meaning, for us all the colours have meanings." Any women as well as men as actors in rituals could reason and interpret the meaning of the symbols to me when I became interested in them. A birth delivery ritual was performed with a woman seven months pregnant, to secure the birth of a normal child. When I found a trained midwife going through the same rituals, she remarked that she wanted to follow the custom so the child would be accepted by her community. Ritual continues but its interpretation changes over the course of time.

Even if I do not agree with Robert Horton's main cognitive interpretations in the discussion on culture and its meanings, I return to Horton, who elevated the "primitive thought" to meaning when he found in the explanations of the diviner understandings of the causes of mental disturbance or depression. He, along with many others, regretted that Western medicine had been so enthused about the germ theories that it neglected the human potential of seeing, as the Africans did through divination, the significance of human relations when looking for the causes of illnesses and meanings of treatment (Horton 1967).

In the introduction to the second print of *Ritual and Symbol* I have reinterpreted the diviner friend Mwawila's way of telling the causes of events for which people came to her. Following numerous divining sessions of hers it became clear to me that she had an inner understanding what caused problems between people in the societies she was familiar with. She had the comprehension similar to the interpretation of a social scientist who finds causes to problems in specific social relations, even if she might have also agreed with her customers' beliefs of the more eccentric causes (M-L. Swantz, 1986,14-29).

The understanding of the wholesome healing and positive aspects of psychological treatment could be consciously developed as part of the healing systems. I have made reference to the interest that Finnish psychiatrist Martti Siirala showed in traditional healing because in his own psychiatric practice he had seen the significance of social sharing as a cause of illness in an individual and the significance of social sharing in healing. When the majority of an ethnic group adopted Christianity, the rituals related to the inherited spirits were pushed to the background even if honouring them was not totally rejected, but Christianity offered another community with its own meanings.

The story of the initiation rituals is different from the rites related to the spirits. Terence Ranger came across the spread of the Beni dance in Tanganyika and it took him to study the meeting of two cultures and the different ways of conforming to the modernization as it was shown in the adoption of the Beni dance in Eastern Africa. One way was to find how the British missionaries in southern Tanganyika tried to adopt and modify African customs getting into conflict with the educated Africans. The effort of the Anglican Bishop Vincent Lucas' efforts to perpetuate African customary clothing and "to Africanize the Christian rites" in the 1930s failed when the "trousered people" were attracted to Beni dance with modernizing trends in music and clothing that was spreading in East Africa. Ranger brings out the basic problem relevant in all intercultural relations, especially if there is a sense of inequality in the social relations, in this case interpreted as hindrance to modernizing the lifestyle (Ranger 1975). The ritual practice has been perpetuated in the southern regions. German Lutheran missionary Bruno Gutman in Kilimanjaro was ready to continue the Chagga male rites but found the Christians rejecting the perpetuation of the boys' traditional ritual. On the other hand, stopping the girls' circumcision was not successful. The custom continued until after WWII, when it was gradually stopped within the Lutheran areas. The Zaramo have not practiced girls' circumcision but have continued the maturity ritual. As the Christians formed a small minority they continued the practice and only added some Christian teaching in the instruction given as part of it (M-L. Swantz 1986). Generalizing cultural practices requires caution, as the varied forms introduced or practiced at present include beliefs in spirits and the different forms of expelling or pacifying them have attracted thousands of followers also among the groups which have not had them before (Hasu 1998).

Within the coastal societies Islam as the dominating religion had served as an umbrella for the continuation of traditional rituals, but the Islamic traditions for pacification of fears have also brought the negative aspects of power, which do not have any meaningful symbolic backing. The coastal people call the practice *elimu ya dunia*, earthly learning, opposite to *elimu ya ahera*, paradise learning and the *waalimu*, local teachers of religion, divide themselves according to the kind and degree of teaching they have had in Islam as religion. The practitioners of *elimu ya dunia* serve as the *waganga*, medicine men, for the earthly problems as evidenced in the study of the *Medicine Men in Dar es Salaam* by Lloyd Swantz (1991). Attending the Islamic religious functions has been strengthened with new foreign influences. In the 1980s at least in some of the *mwali* rituals *maulidi* reading of the birth of the Prophet, written by Maulid Barzanji, in place of *hitima*, reading of the whole of Koran, had been added to some of the female rituals as reported by two female students, who had done their final study for bachelor's degree on the Zaramo female rites and had acquainted themselves with the author's study of the Zaramo (M-L. Swantz 1986, 100).

The ethnic content in the formation of individual self-image is consciously no longer recognized for the sake of national unification and the cultural differences are minimized in the frequent intermarriages between the ethnic groups in growing urban circumstances. Only little scratching of the surface is needed for exposing the significance of the differences. The way Salome, living in Finland with her family, describes her Zaramo ethnic group as "being very, very friendly, very sociable and sharing is almost touchable" while the husband belongs to an industrious Pare group, which cannot share the time for unnecessary social contacts. According to Salome this difference is clearly discernable between their two girls. One has taken after her father's Pare group, while the other is a Zaramo ready to share everything with everybody, very social. Salome tells that the Zaramo living on the fertile hills in the hinterland of the city have not needed to farm as much and so become industrious as the Pare have had to do.

The boys' circumcision had not been the custom in the coastal Bantu groups. The boys' circumcision ritual *jando* had spread on the coast with Islam. When it was introduced it incorporated and elaborated the older rituals. The Zaramo had adopted some Yao customs in their *jando*, singing even some Yao songs. I could not detect any Islamic religious features in the way the Zaramo performed *jando* at the time I observed it in the 1960s, a full description of which is available in the Research Report in the Sociology Department and now on line in the University of Helsinki (M-L. Swantz, 1973). A Kwere scholar Sengo, found it to be similar to the *jando* he had gone through as the Kwere had adopted the initially Islamic *jando* from the Zaramo. A local former Zaramo chief Simsim Selasela Kaambwa in Miembe Saba told the author while demonstrating his paraphernalia of chief's hat, gown and sword that he had brought the circumcision of boys to the Zigua in Miono in Bagamoyo district (M-L. Swantz 1986; 186-193).

According to Ulla Vuorela and also to my own communication with the Kwere in recent years the elders continued the performance of the traditional ritual *chikulege* (in Zaramo pronounced *kikulege*) for their grandsons, even if *jando* was performed for the circumcision, as according to an elder the traditional cultural instruction was not given in *jando*, which a Kwere man confirmed to me during my recent visit to Msoga in 2013 (Vuorela 1986, 117-118). The Kwere language is closely related to the Zaramo and their girls' *mwali* rituals were the same as those of the Zaramo with the same variations and signifying bead decorations between the clan or lineage customs. For instance lineages used a gourd or a carved doll, which the *mwali* held with her or him, while she was sitting in or during his time of induction. The Kwere had continued wearing the bead ornaments, which they made for themselves, and only for want of imported beads the renewing them gradually ended during independence, as evidenced during the Jipemoyo research (M-L. Swantz 1969).

One needs only to look at the basket weaving and pot making of women to realize that before the products were commercialized the colours and shapes of pots and baskets, even broken pots, had a commonly shared symbolic significance. Do the youth of today know what symbolic significance a broken pot had when they see one placed on the grave in the woods? Do the Zaramo or the Kwere female students know why the young girls sat inside not being allowed to go into the sun, so that their skins would become whiter? Do they know the basic significance of the white-red-black colours? Do they know the significance of *mwiko,* taboo? Do men know the meaning if they as boys still jumped over the *kungwi* or *shoari,* who was covered with a burial cloth *sanda,* when they came out of the camp *kumbi,* where they had been healing their wounds of circumcision? Do they know why the circumciser *ngariba* had to cool with cold water the day after the coming out of the camp? (M-L. Swantz 1973). Many women and men have still gone through the rites but they have been less meaningfully passed on to new generations. Symbols lose their wider connotations and thus their communicative significance disappears, but learning to understand the general symbolic significance would enrich life.

In the groups in which the changes have been the fastest and people have had early education there are third, fourth even fifth generation Christians, who as young critics have accused their elders for discarding the rituals. They have the advantage of the historical and social distance from the scene. The criticism is justified when looked at from a distance of time, the choices made were different at the early times, but to learn about the lost culture from a different perspective could be treated with greater interest.

In the Singida region in Central Tanzania the symbolism attached to the Nyaturu young girls' bead covered *imaa* gourds have still meaning to some who still have gone through the girls' maturity rituals (Mdachi 1991), but central symbolic features of Nyaturu homesteads were destroyed in the big movements of people when they were settled in concentrated village formations. A case of this is the former ground plan of the Nyaturu kraals where the young mothers with breastfed children, the newly born domestic animals and the grain that fed the families with the stones that ground the grain were placed in *tembe-* houses in the back part of the kraal facing the life affirming rising sun, which was greeted with a beautiful prayer song in the morning. It was the source of life, a symbolic feature, which was disturbed when traditional village structures were broken down. Another feature was the grave of the family elders in the middle of the kraal with the stone cover, a reminder of the symbolic grinding stone. A sacrificial place is still intact in Puma cave. Also the other structures we found in place when I had an opportunity to witness these structures and visit the cave with the Swedish opera dancer and dance teacher Birgit Åkesson, who gave some courses even in the Theatre Arts department in the University of Dar es Salaam. She visited them with me and has recorded them in her book *Kvällvattnets mask, Om dans i Africa* (1983).

I suggest that certain characteristics of *tembe* structures are retained in people's minds, even when they build new brick houses, but the modern Mnyaturu or Mnyiramba villager might no longer recognize their hidden meaning. That even the new houses are kept dark, leaving only small openings for air or light to come in, indicates that unrecognized fears of spirits and witches linger. As the reminder of the old house structures in the new brick houses spaces are left for windows but they are stuffed in with a variety of materials, even with bricks, leaving only small openings for light but little for air. The reason given is the lack of money but it has been available for costly metal sheeting for the roofs. The shape and the roofs of old *tembe* houses had a symbolic function as did the flat stone covering the grave of the elder in the middle of the kraal.

Anthropologist Marguerite Jellicoe and social worker Frida Chale were the first community development officers in rural Singida in the 1950s. Jellicoe described the rituals they observed and the symbolic structure of the Nyaturu kraal. In a letter (16.09.1968) she told the author that she saw the harvest dances, circumcision ceremonies and the various women's secret societies' and secular singing and dancing during the months June-August.

An example of a positive adaptation to an inherited cultural feature in public use in Tanzania today is the recital of a long poem, *risala*, to honour a person in a public meeting. This was done when the President Mwinyi was honoured at a farewell gathering at the Stadium of Mtwara, when leaving his presidency he was making his farewell rounds. Another modified tradition is *ngonjera*, a form of public debate, initially in a poetry form, between two parties in singing or reciting, which has been introduced in some schools and social gatherings. The initiator of the Chadema party, the first Governor of the Bank of Tanzania, the Minister of Finance and a Director of IMF, Edwin Mtei tells in his autobiography of a debate he conducted successfully when he in his youth respectfully beat the British Rector of the Senior Secondary School in Tabora (Mtei, 2003). Such debates customary in the British colonial secondary schools are also reminiscent of a debate in traditional court proceedings, in which the side, which could present its case more skilfully in singing, won the court case. An example of such was *kitala cha kutagusa* of the Kwere ethnic group, that of President Jakaya Kikwete. He told the author that he was still familiar with some form of it. The Zaramo had earlier had the same practice, the existence of which they could tell about and so were also the Luguru according to information from Father Vermunt (M-L. Swantz 1986, 421).

Many parts of Africa are experiencing the rise of the old tunes and rhythms interwoven into new styles of musical performances. It no doubt is the best-known form of modern culture globally recognized as originating in Africa. The treasures of traditional poetry and songs have not been widely collected in Tanzania as it was done in Finland starting from the early years of 19th century. The vast collections in Finland have inspired professor Mulokozi and his students in Swahili and linguistics in UDSM, first to collect the local Swahili newspapers in a corner of a room separated for the purpose, as in the daily paper discussion and debates are carried out in a poetry form. Films and varied collections from small ethnic groups are being collected. Africa needs to wake up to the task, which still is possible to take on.

The Tanzanian policy of making Swahili the national language prevented the study and collection of texts and songs in ethnic languages until the start of the new millennium. The interest in them has now grown, even by some Finnish linguists. It offers rich opportunities for linguistic work and cultural preservation. Concentration on the national language united the nation and avoided ethnic skirmishes, but now the cultural variety of ethnic inheritance can be brought forth. After Swahili has been established as the first official language it no longer is in danger of being slighted. Even the Father of the Nation, President Nyerere invited a local singer to sing to him in his local language when he went on a leave to his home village.

The assumption here is that if the growing youth, the artists and writers would learn of the riches of the past culture, their creative capabilities would flourish and it in turn would strengthen people's sense of meaning in the communal culture they have inherited. Culture would not mean only alienation and imitation of the foreign modernity but would bring forth new creativity. Tradition has no permanency. Tradition continues to change constantly, what today is everyday practice is tomorrow tradition in the usual meaning of the word. The intention here is not to promote the continuity of tradition in the ways it has been so far retained, but rather that it would serve as a positive source for renewed cultural imagination. The better word for tradition is "lived world," which Frédérique Apffel-Marglin used in the discussion, as it "recognizes the dynamic, changing, shifting and contradictory nature of reality" when T-knowledge and E-knowledge intertwine (Apffel-Marglin 1989, 1996). They feed one another and are dependent on each other, but they could also be in an important way complemented with elements from the symbolic ritual and art forms. Something on this line is perhaps behind the intentions in the Aalto University in Helsinki, in which the Technological and Commercial Science Universities were merged with Technical Arts College for enriching the Industrial and Economic knowledge creation with the Arts.

Historical glimpses in conceptualizing development

This book is an effort to view development and its relation to culture in a time perspective by a person who has physically lived through the development efforts starting from the colonial time when the author discussed with the future women teachers each new development project started by the colonial government as part of the subject taught as *Current events* (In Ashira Teacher Training College 1952-1956).

The effects of the failed groundnut scheme after the WWII were still acutely felt. The most gigantic failure ever to bring development to Africa was the post war colonial undertaking by the Labour Party of Great Britain to start two groundnut schemes, one in Nachingwea in southern Lindi region and the other in Kongwa along the railway in Central Tanganyika in 1946 (Wood 1950). The colonial government cancelled the project in January 1951. The 49 million pounds expended turned out to be a total loss, mainly for failure of poor preliminary planning. Huge construction works were done before the agricultural experiments, which ended up as big failure. British consumers had anticipated additional food oil for their tax money and the scheme was to beat the French similar but a more successful project of ground nut oil production in Senegal, later continued in Burkina Faso, former Upper Volta. The hope of a green revolution was lost but while on the slopes of Kilimanjaro I witnessed that some of the recruits to south had learned there skills which they made use of after returning to their home area. The hope of exporting groundnuts required building a deep-sea harbour in Mtwara and a railway from there to Nachingwea. The independent government picked up the rails, as running the railway there seemed useless. The houses built for the staff were later utilized for district staff and the warehouses for the anticipated groundnuts served the military during the independence war in the neighbouring Mozambique and afterwards for military training.

The past has its consequences also today. The Mtwara deep-sea harbour is being resuscitated when rich findings of gas and oil in the sea and in the dry land have drawn international companies to the area. The southern regions have been connected with Dar es Salaam with the new all weather road, leaving so far 50 miles of old road in the middle. A solid bridge over Rufiji River, and further south over the Ruvuma River anticipate time when the road leads to South Africa. In spring 2013 the news told of demonstrations and burnings of government officers' and ministers' houses in opposition to government's intention to lead the developed power to Dar es Salaam and Bagamoyo, where the President of China on his visit in 2013 promised money for construction of the harbour instead of utilizing the deep sea harbour of Mtwara. During the author's visit to Mtwara in the end of October 2013 to the celebration of 40 years of Finnish development cooperation in the southern regions the tension between oppositional forces had calmed down but were felt in the discussions with some of the inhabitants. Of interest here was people's discussion about the political involvement of the former president Benjamin Mkapa, whose home region Mtwara is and who in his time had accomplished the developmental improvements in road and bridge building.

Before the WWII the anthropologists' problem was Europeanization as they studied social customs of the people from different ethnic backgrounds who yet were recruited to mining and industrial jobs. There was a debate whether the people they studied could be called primitives. Among others Mary Douglas defended the use of the term "primitive," becasue to her it gave the true interpretation. Diamond used the term in appreciation of the people's culture he studied, which the Europeans should learn to appreciate and be ashamed of their own ways.

Anthropologists have commonly felt uneasy with the "development" concept. Anthropologist J. Gus Liebenow studied the development as pursued in the colonial time in what he called Makonde District in Newala in southern Tanganyika in the 1950s. He drew a colourful picture of the erratic development efforts, which he called "White Man's Madness," each District Commissioner bringing along his own pet ideas staying in Newala average one year and a half, 26 men trying in 43 years to make their mark with paternalistic attitudes, constant interventions and detailed instructions (Liebenow 1971, 138-144).

After the WWII the western countries woke up to the concept of development. Harry Truman, who followed Roosevelt as the president of the United States in 1945, called the western countries to join in support of *development* in, what came to be called, the Third World in order to prevent the spread of communism by the Communist countries, which formed the Second World. This is considered to be the beginning of the concept of "Development Aid." After the publication of such books as Walter Rodney's *How Europe Underdeveloped Africa* (1974) the term "underdeveloped" countries gained currency as the book showed how the colonial and other developed countries had developed because they underdeveloped their colonies by subjugating and exploiting them. The development assistance was eventually changed to development cooperation with developing or less developed, even least developed countries. Today the aid receivers are commonly referred to simply as "poor countries" after the World Bank, UN Millennium Development Goals, and Paris Declaration have generalized the development goals and poverty eradication is the dominating theme.

The international theoretical analyses of development and underdevelopment and the policies, adjusted to the WB, IMF and OECD directives and the donor domination, have for long ruled the course of development. The local implementers and the people whom the measures concern, experience repeated changes, demands, and rules with disheartening consequences, when new people take leadership in aid agencies and repeated ever more exacting evaluations are imposed on the implementing agencies after one and half a year periods. Four NAI researchers in Uppsala have made a disturbing analysis of the internationally agreed policies, which are implemented to train the NGO actors mainly in finance management (Follér et al. 2013).

The situation requires existential urgency and a new awareness of the social and development processes, and re-evaluation of research methodologies and research structures. The foreign occupation of large sections of land in Tanzania, as also in other African countries, and the introduction of seemingly progressive business enterprises and numerous high rises in Dar es Salaam make a progressive story, which inspire the elites, but they also raise doubts. In addition to the increasing occupation of land by foreign governments and companies and their entrance into the commercial sector there are new channels and contacts with India and China. They have opened up unexpected opportunities in the field of health for clinical operations in India for those who can afford it and business and tourist visits to Hong Kong and China mainland. Much of the occupation of invading companies takes place unknown to local people who then suffer the consequences.

Engaged research and theoretical pathways

The changes that have taken place give a new role for the social sciences and anthropology with its epistemological foundations, whereby an intense search and exploration is taking place for extending the contextual disciplinary boundaries. Anthropologist Davydd Greenwood related to Cornell University has been engaged in Action Research over forty years and in his article in the *Action Research* journal (2012, 10, 115-124) he makes a suggestion that a separate faculty would be created for Action Research. He refers to a degree program in Action Research in the University of Science and Technology in Norway and University of Bath and Southern Cross University, which have included AR in their degree programs. It is in line with the department on Community Based Research and Academic Education department in Victoria University, Canada and similar institutional forms in other universities in the States, which connect with studies in other departments for degrees. Also Cornell University had experimented AR in Tanzania and had created Cornell Participatory Action Research Network (CPARN) and offered training in AR. Hartford University in Connecticut, which in 1950s published Practical Anthropology journal, has initiated again practice oriented courses. Numerous other similar efforts have been made not listed here.

Intermediary departments between the academic and community for research and planning need to be further developed and institutionalized, within which knowledge production can be conducted and written up in cooperation with the representatives of the formerly researched people. In development studies this would require placing units of such departments in the countries of cooperation (M-L. Swantz 2013). According to Greenwood Action Research is anti-Tayloristic, and at odds with the current direction and practices, as he points out (2012, 121):

AR is based on a holistic, systems understanding on the complexity and dynamism of society's problems and on the premise that all relevant actors have key knowledge and actions to contribute to the analysis and solutions to the problems.

The central concept in this is the phrase "that all relevant actors have key knowledge." This brings the discussion in development research to the crucial question on whose conditions the research is conducted. It is an issue, which is brought up in most of the chapters in this book. The development processes in the lands still extensively covered by external ethnologists and anthropologists require a new kind of indigenous and interdisciplinary research. The Community Based Research and Social Responsibility documents report statements about freeing the knowledge creation from the sole domination of the leading academies with financial resources.

The Global University Network for Innovation (GUNI) shows that much thinking and practical experimentation is already being done to bring the different levels of theoretical and practical research into interaction and to find new channels for the less privileged centres for science. Some quotes from the above net, "The struggle for global social justice will therefore be a struggle for global *cognitive justice*" a quote by Boaventura de Santos Sousa from Portugal. "As long as African intellectuals attempt to stand only on the shoulders of European thinkers, they will remain *pidgin intellectuals*," is a statement made by Paulo Wangoole, Uganda (Reference also to Marglins' writings on different knowledge systems.) I find *cognitive justice* specifically fitting, yet what it means in practice in today's world of empowering cultures is increasingly difficult to defend and even to know what it in individual cases mean.

The need for research by the indigenous people is relevant in Canada and South America, because indigenous communities live in the neighbourhood of the universities. The concept "indigenous" as used in Canada comes up also in Tanzania, when the indigenous groups are classified according to their original habitation. The Hadzabe live in Iramba, one of the areas covered in this book, and the Maasai have fought for being counted as indigenous as recorded by Dorothy Hodgson (Hodgson, 2012). However, the term is also used when referring to the people in Africa to differentiate them from usually racial groups as Indians and Europeans or Whites, depending who identify them. For instance in the World Bank book on indigenous technology and in general in parlance when the original African languages and ways of living are analysed the word indigenous is used.

The academic research on development suffers from disciplinary boundaries. The language of anthropology is not understandable to scholars from hard sciences, and often they do not consider the method of the discipline even scientific, yet the economists, agriculturalists and mining scholars would need the understanding that comes from the study of social and cultural specificities, local institutions and the relatively short history of "development."

Susan Wright's introduction to the book she edited in 1994 *Introduction to Anthropology of Organization* gives glimpses to the change that was taking place already in 1990s. She goes through the history of organizational anthropology during the decades since 1920s from the perspective of the British anthropology in Africa and its continuation as the Manchester School of Anthropology. Of interest is her observation that the anthropologists in 1960s "changed from participation in order to observe, to full time participation," she also refers to S. Cunnison's reference to "Custom and Conflict in British Society," by Ronald Frankenberg as the editor. In the study of organizations the anthropological methods were drawn to meanings, "... how the meanings people brought into the work situations were expressed, how these meanings were drawn into the work situations, and integrated into the production process" (Cunnison 1982, 135; Wright 1994, 14). The point was according to Wright that British "anthropology was moving away from a society made of structures toward a way people make meaning in a particular situation out of an available cultural repertoire." The authors in the quoted volume were moving within the context of Applied Anthropology, which bordered with the Participatory Action Research and Practical Anthropology, the latter term Malinowski already applied. The question here about the concept of "meanings" relates to the difference between the applied anthropology and PAR, of which there is more in other chapters. Development as the concept is normative and anticipates application even when during the process of research it remains on the theoretical level. Moving from structures to participation requires participating actors' conceptualization of meanings.

The interdisciplinary participatory Jipemoyo research described in Chapter 8 is an effort to cross the disciplinary boundaries needed in development. While planning before starting the research dealing with development in Western Bagamoyo there was freedom to experiment and shape the mode of research on the basis of contacts made with the people while engaged with UNICEF supported Child Study projects and the preliminary ILO supported study on people's level of education and skills. Participatory approach was already made use of while statistical information was also collected. For instance a student was staying in a home for the long three months holiday sharing life with a family and so having a deeper understanding how they and the surrounding community made and organized their living.

After the pioneering Jipemoyo project the Academy of Finland required research plans with minute details about the study areas and social situations. It prevented the necessary imaginative approach to research if details were formulated with only a preliminary touch with the area and its people. Ready thought out theories and methods in research plans do not allow the needed freedom of research, which would arise from the people and their situation itself. The dominating theoretical underpinnings at the heart of the study plans will also dominate the implementation and prevent establishing close contacts with the people. The initial research problems are supposed to be formulated from within the scientific tradition whereby the language gets harder even for the scientists from another discipline to interpret the written texts. The verbal specificity is the trademark of science and there are too few texts as interpretations of the findings of research. This pertains especially to the problems of development. The question remains, whose development and for whom is knowledge and interpretation of development ultimately sought, when it is created for the sake of intellectual exercise, for doctoral degrees and meritocratic purposes.

According to Pekka Seppälä (2013) and his many years of experience as a researcher in Tanzania and in practical development work in the government in Vietnam and in Nepal, there is a break between research and application and what is anticipated from the texts. How research aids the transformation of the studied societies needs continuing thought and engagement in the new kind of planning. The participatory action research purports to come close to the studied people and to have an outcome during the process, but it has often neglected aspects of culture studied from a developmental angle. Development planning has not considered the requirements of specific "lived worlds," incorporation of the involved people, yet the communicative ways between cultures are broadening and opening more space.

Further theoretical considerations

For the anthropologists, "development" followed social evolution as a purposeful human effort to change people's conditions of life, which in common understanding was equalled with "modernization." Research, which initially avoided interfering in people's life style, began to aim at purposeful altering their living conditions. At the early phase of development discussion Gunnar Myrdal (1968) gave a simple definition for development as "the movement upward of the entire social system." In practice it demanded as many added components from him as any other definition. Nyerere made an important point in specifying that development does not consist only of economic forces:

Development brings freedom, provided it is development *of people* ... development of people can be effected *by the people*. . . The components of this are: *conscious participation*, decision making, doing, increasing understanding of doings, increasing knowledge and ability. (Nyerere 1973, 60, italics added)

The wise words about "conscious participation" were not easy to bring about but in them the basic principles of participatory development were spelled out, even if Nyerere's intended meaning was not concretized in practice. People live out their culture, thus how they interpret it in terms of thought structures relates to the issue of *giving meanings* to one's experiences, which even Nyerere aimed at being *consciously* brought about.

Linking development to the cultural traditions brings into the picture the *rational* component of change from the given state to one, in which the members of a society have ability, power and space to influence it. The analysis of cultural change can become part of the self-analysis of the social group. This kind of a research approach was attempted in Jipemoyo in Bagamoyo district described in Chapter 8. In such research participating in purposeful development the ongoing process of villagization was combined with the meanings of the traditions with drums, dance and song and people's lived history, the maturity rituals and modes of reproduction, traditional methods of saving water were recovered in the areas of water shortage, narratives reflecting women's position were interpreted with women, gathering women officers and village women leaders to seminars, interacting with the village women, recovering pastoralists' indigenous ways of utilising and preserving best grazing specimens of grass, cooperating with them in counting the heads of cattle as an evidence against the order of ten per cent sales and collection of local histories were some of the ways to study together with the people their symbolic and pragmatist roots of traditions. Above all, opportunities were created for different groups to discuss between themselves and to present their thoughts publicly to decision makers in meetings and seminars.

Phenomenological support for such research approach was found in the critique of German philosopher Edmund Husserl of the objectivism of science. The ignoring of the commonsense world, in which the scientists also lived, made them blind to the guiding interests (*Interesselagen*) of the basic ways of life. Husserl called it "phenomenological description" and adopted a contemplative attitude towards the interests that guide the interconnections of ostensibly objective facts, equated with "pure theory" in the traditional sense. It brought about the dissolution of knowledge and interest, but it was not seen as transcending subjectivity, it recognized its connection with practical life and gave rise to education oriented towards action. This united the theoretical with the practical, which if taken seriously could lead to a new kind of praxis in improving humanity. According to Husserl this way the truth could be grasped on all levels and could bring people to greater self-responsibility, because of its theoretical insight.

Habermas criticized Husserl for not recognizing the link with praxis in the traditional "objective" and "pure" theory. The illusion of pure theory meant that the sciences in the traditional sense do not fail to define the praxis of their research, but rather the way they understand themselves, imperturbably ignoring their guiding interest (Habermas 1970, 51-52). Habermas presented a critique of phenomenology in his *Theory and Practice*. He ended up with the pessimistic view, which governed the everyday life of the scientists as well as the practitioners. An industrially advanced society had to "look after its survival on the escalating scale of a continually expanded technical control over nature and continually refined administration of human beings and their relations to each other by means of social organization." People encounter a limitation they cannot overcome, it can be altered by a state in the consciousness itself, by a practical effect of theory "which advances the interest of reason in human adulthood, in the autonomy of action and in the liberation of dogmatism." This is achieved according to Habermas by the means of the penetrating ideas of a persistent critique (Habermas 1974, 254, 256). The question remains, to which extent this can be realised in practice. Ferguson, to whom references are made in several chapters also points out that discourses have meanings, they change ideas and ideas change the practice (Ferguson 1990). The question remains how do the ideas come to people who make the changes.

Here we return to the role of participatory research. According to John Heron, one of the initiating members of the group cooperating with Peter Reason of Bath University, inquiry can have four sorts of outcomes: experiential, presentational, propositional, and practical. *Experiential* outcomes have to do with transformations, of being in the subjective-objective domain. *Presentational* outcomes disclose the subjective-objective reality in terms of non-discursive symbolism - sound, song, music, movement, composition, or in terms of metaphor and analogy via poetry, storytelling and drama. *Propositional* outcomes report the traditional form of research findings, *knowing that,* while *practical* outcomes have to do with *knowing how.* This way of looking at the rationale of research has obvious consequences on participatory research setting (Heron 1996).

In participatory action research *knowledge is formed in and for action*. This was so also in the co-operative research in which Reason and Heron had specialised. The main outcome in scientific work is writing books and articles for the scientific community, not for the researched community, although "often the knowledge that is really important for them is the practical knowledge of new skills and abilities" (Reason 1988, 13). Heron takes this idea further. He points out that there is a hierarchy of knowledge, which procedes from experiential knowledge, through presentational and propositional knowledge to practical knowledge, the realm of skills. "The deeper way to do participative research is to make skills in a domain, not statements about a domain, the primary intended outcome' (underlining mine; Heron 1996, 45). According to Heron practical knowing how, the active execution of skills, is the true consummation of an inquiry, not a paper or a book, even if these are also necessary as a secondary outcome:

After trying it both ways --- I now believe we get deeper information about the nature of our realities when our prime concern is to develop practical skills that change these realities than we do when our prime concern is to get information about them through the exercise of certain skills (Heron 1996, 45).

This brings us back to the discussion on the concepts of society and the cultural underpinnings and meanings of development. Robert Horton's contested thoughts elevated the "primitive thought" to a *meaning* when he found in the explanations of the diviner understanding of the causes of mental disturbance or depression and regrets that western medicine has been so enthused about the germ theories that it has neglected the human potential in seeing the significance of human relations for the causal meanings (1967, 10-71; 1993,197-258). The concept of "illness" is much broader than in the typical practice of medicine. It relates also to the people's concept of development. The human reason works in different ways in different cultures.

The Finnish psychiatrist Martti Siirala's article "Our Conception of Illness" and his theologian brother Aarne Siirala in his book *Voice of Illness* have described a holistic way of treating illnesses and Martti Siirala applied it also in his psychiatric practice. Illnesses are not only based on the suffering of an individual but they have also social causes, as is the case when an individual is suffering on behalf of the surrounding closely-knit society. Martti Siirala wrote about traditional healers who treated illness holistically, regarding individual suffering as tied to the ills of the closest social group (A. Siirala 1964). Such interpretations of illness lead Tanzanian people to traditional practitioners who do not distinguish between physical and social causes of ailments. In fact, they are not satisfied with mere physical causes, but look for human ill will behind them.

My research done together with a Finnish child psychiatrist Anja Forssén was also relevant on the subject. She did studies of the Bunju school children, modifying the tests used in Finland, some of them in cooperation with psychologist Elli Keinänen and other leading psychologists in Finland who interpreted the tests. One characteristic stood out: In one picture of the Wartegg test there was only one dot in the middle of the paper and you were supposed to make a drawing in the paper. None of the Bunju children used the dot as the starting point, interpreting it as the identification for the drawer as an individual, who then customarily drew circles around the given point, as did the Finnish children. The Bunju children ignored the point and made different drawings. Similarly when asked to draw a person, *mtu*, they always drew two, *watu*, as they were not alone in the society. When the same test was done with Tanzanian students who had more education and were studying in Finland to be airplane mechanics and pilots, they had become more individualistic and responded to the same test more like the Finns, making the dot the centre of circles around it, drawing one person and not two or more. They also joined the vertical lines of different lengths as steps climbing up indicating ambitious hopes for life (Forssén 1979, 1984).

Development cannot be pursued without paying attention to enduring local cultural characteristics. A Catholic nun with a long experience in Chalinze in Western Bagamoyo District told me of a typical occasion. The Regional Commissioner had come to speak to the villagers, reiterating to them their development duties. Their response was, "*Huyu mtu hawezi kutuelewa mazingira yetu,*" "This man cannot understand our circumstances." The sister's remark was, "They need someone who can understand them." The differences in people's thinking and the conditions of life in different parts of the country require *listening to* the people. People react on the basis of their social, material and environmental conditions, which require cultural understanding of people's potential for development. The opportunities in free discussions with individuals or in informal groups paying attention to the gender, age and means of sustenance, serve well the purpose whether for planning or for research, better than pre-formulated questionnaires or calling selected people together in focus groups.

Continuing participation in the process of planning and re-planning is part of the cultural pattern for development. Traditional planning takes place by stages in a ritual occasion when people attending arrive and take part in it. Similarly leaving out the representation of the implementers in evaluations of the development projects is incomprehensible to the parties involved, also because the "project," if rightly carried out, should be part of an ongoing process. The experience has shown that in research and development projects the theoretical planning is done long time ahead and too often out of touch of the context of the practical implementation requiring re-planning when the work unfolds. The development planning could consciously utilize the model of traditional planning in African countries like Tanzania, in which the participants agree on the general pattern of what is aimed at, but the practical planning is made stage by stage *together with those who are partakers in implementation.*

Preparing meetings or festivals with the mode of the customary ritual planning has been found to be a workable practice even in planning bigger festivals. A large advertisement across the road in Dar es Salaam invited public to a Culture Festival in the grounds of the Cultural Institute in Bagamoyo on certain days and time. Two Finns planned to attend the opening discovered that the given time meant starting the preparations and the actual opening was to be the following day. For personal feasts such as weddings or birthdays, invitees receive a program with exacting timetables, seldom followed as given. The guests decide their time of arrival knowing their role in the preplanned program. Instead of seeing this as a hindrance to development it could be taken as a lesson. Planning, preparations and implementation all require participants taking part in them stage by stage.

Negative aspects of the "lived world"

The "lived world," a concept for which the term "tradition" and even local culture is here used, also has negative connotations, which take hold of people in a mental state of uncertainty experienced in the midst of cultural change. When a person is in need of personal success s/he experiences fits of jealousy, envy and greed if a neighbour, relative or co-workers seem to succeed better. The vocabulary generalizing the old beliefs with negative connotations was invented and adopted under the early European influence utilizing indiscriminately words like witchdoctor, fetishism and magic. Less attention was paid to the conceptions related to people's understanding of natural phenomena, their detailed knowledge of nature around them, of the living habits of animals, birds and insects, the rich symbolic aspects related to them and their beliefs in God and prayers to God.

The traditional beliefs were often fathomed to be in conflict with the belief in one supreme God. Anthropologist Evans-Pritchard as an early scholar of the Nuer looked for what was common rather than what separated the religions and he saw also something valuable in the differences. He devoted three chapters in his book *Nuer Religion* on the elaboration of the concept of God relating it to the similarities with Christian God (Evans-Pritchard 1963). Today African theologians are looking anew for commonness instead of differences in beliefs, but many modern Africans miss the positive meanings of the old beliefs and face with fear the negative connotations of the old powers. To them they do not fit into the modern way of life, yet they exist in the background and arouse deep down fears or attract people secretly to try out their efficacy.

The hidden and unknown elements create also in the educated ambivalent feelings of uncertainty. A visit to the village of Mlingotini near Bagamoyo in 2010 was a reminder of this when a local fisherman showed the place where "persons in high government positions" park their cars when they come to see the local *waganga* who are believed to have powers to prevent or to cause evil. Mlingotini near Bagamoyo is often mentioned when people in Dar es Salaam speak about fellow Tanzanians consulting *waganga*. The locals tell that the big people come to acquire the means of self-protection against witchcraft practiced by others on them or for gaining lucky moves in life, often at the expense of harming others. Fears of witchcraft affect people's actions more than is openly acknowledged. Today the powers of *jinni* take the place of or are mixed with witchcraft. Such aspects of social life would require open public discussion also within the churches, which deny the efficacy of such powers, or who as new Christian actors claim to control such powers yet perpetuate fears. The methods they apply require open clarification. The resuscitation of the fears of witchcraft among the academics and parliamentarians, not to speak about the commoners, and the killing of albinos for acquisition of power, all call for cultural explanation. Rationalization is not a sufficient way out, but even the religious faith requires rational explanations combined with faith. I have dealt with some of these questions in the article *Pathways to the study of religion*, relating the significance of the topic for the sense of communality and the country's efforts for development.

An important question raised and legislated against in recent years is the mutilation of the girls' genitals in the groups which still practice it. The most radical form of it has not been done in Tanzania, but varieties of *clitoridectomy*, cutting of *labia* and/or *clitoris*, have been the custom in inland groups. I have witnessed the painful cutting of the clitoris of a Parakuyo girl as part of the initiation ritual. At one time I was invited to stay in a Parakuyo Maasai kraal for the night by the first wife of the elder. She wanted to spend the night with me in order to discuss and find out whether their custom of cutting the genital organs was harmful and could it cause infertility as she suspected had been the cause of her inability to bear a child. After a lengthy discussion she gained confirmation of her suspicion after which she did not stay for the night but rather went out to talk with other women waiting outside. I could hear them talking in the moonlight late into the night. According to a young Maasai man, men demanded the cutting of young women's genitals as a guarantee that they would not go to other men, as it was thought to affect the sexual desire, but the old women have also been the agitators of the custom. Dorothy Hodgson tells of a case among the Northern Maasai whereby the rite was nominally performed to fulfil the requirement, but no actual cutting was done. According to a Parakuyo Maasai elder, the same is said to occur among the Christian women in Bagamoyo District, but no woman was consulted.

There are examples of unwise choices of return to old customs such as a case recorded by an anthropologist from Meru in North Tanzania in which even some educated girls whose mothers no longer had gone through such a rite, had asked their grandmothers for the traditional circumcision. Such occurrences call for a reasonable explanation, which relates to other puzzling features within the clash of cultures. They indicate that the more educated young generation sense that they have missed something when they know so little of their cultural inheritance. In some cases, the custom of operating girls has spread to groups which have not earlier practised it. This was the case among the Nyiramba young women when the operation had been done to some of them having adopted it from the Nyaturu neighbors in Singida region in Central Tanzania most likely through intermarriage. The frequency is not known but it was referred to several times in my study of women in Iramba District. With the Nyaturu, the custom was connected with their *imaa* rituals in preparation for marriage and teaching woman's duties toward men and marriage. The belief was that it gave women power to personify a lion and to be able to use the lion power over men. The *imaa* was done in two phases, at the start of menstruation and after giving birth to the first child. The key aspects of the rites were a closely hidden secret from men and the belief that women had power to use men-lion power has not disappeared when the fear was recorded (Mdachi 1991).

The custom of *clitoridectomy* among the Singida ethnic groups had caused deaths in Iramba as it was reported in the newspaper in the early 1970s and was mentioned in a research paper by South African anthropologist, Archie Mafeje, who was a professor of sociology at University of Dar es Salaam (UDSM) in 1971. The opinions about the traditional customs were hotly debated in the 1970s at the UDSM both for and against. The operation was illegal, but it has not disappeared by legislation. Quoting Mafeje:

... recently, the second Vice-President did not hesitate to pass judgment and demand that 'those Singida culprits' be handed over, meaning some witchdoctors who had been insisting on the traditional right to perform thorough-going female circumcision rites thereby causing a number of deaths and creating a medical crisis, it does not make sense to avoid critical evaluations.

The paragraph shows the typical mistake when rituals are discussed in general terms. "Witchdoctor" is used as a generalized category of traditional practitioners, here even in relation to maturity rituals. It does injustice to the traditional practitioners and mixes the role of the healers, *waganga* with the negative forces practised as bewitching. The term "witchdoctor" was adopted by European observers early in history and is still commonly used inaccurately.

Professor Mafeje's critique addressed traditional "African religions" in general. According to him the failure of the Africans to reject the ritual in the past should be made apparent but he went on to pass a judgment over all the traditional beliefs, adding

They might have helped to hold together the people during the colonial disruption but they also perpetrated certain forms of oppression and mental enslavement, which should be judged as such for the benefit of present day society...

Ranger reported this reference in the same journal in which he quoted my thoughts on the Zaramo. Mafeje had extended his critique also to Ranger's research programme as the first professor of African history at the University of Dar es Salaam in the 1960s. Ranger considered that not knowing and understanding the wealth of one's past history with its positive and negative implications, one meets them unexpectedly in a deformed manner. The nation also misses the opportunity to build on its constructive past culture. For this reason the first decade of academic research on history largely consisted of movements such as Maji Maji rebellion and religious movements, which crossed the central and eastern African borders, drawn by the colonial powers. Ranger also made a study of the earliest Anglican mission in Masasi, Mtwara and the first efforts of Bishop Lucas and the missionaries to Christianize the maturity rituals.

An example of beliefs with serious consequences was the wave of murders and cutting of people's parts of the body of albinos, which took place in the first decade after the beginning of the new millennium. As a result, the Government and the churches took serious measures and helped to make arrangements for special care of the albino youth, but it was an indication of the beliefs that still arouse fears with sad consequences. It is another indication of the need to include the cultural elements in the concept of development and development research and planning. The research done by anthropologists Simon Mesiakini, Ray Abrahams and Harri Englund among others serve as references here for the study of the threat of witchcraft specifically in relation to the Nyamwezi and Sukuma in Tanzania and the neighbouring Malawi.

The social system in relation to the land issue

The necessity to know something about the lingering inherited social system has become evident, especially when the present situation of women has been studied. The country adopted the patrilineal inheritance system as the national policy in 1964, with the intention that the problems in traditional marriages should be solved on that basis. The decision gave no regard to the matrilineal tradition widely practiced by the coastal people and among the southeastern ethnic groups in Mtwara and Lindi regions but also in Iramba District among the Nyiramba, all of which have been groups in my research areas. In general, the established inheritance system with permanent rights to land allowed people to maintain their rights whereas those who were landless and villagers in areas where the land use was shifting because of the regulations made during the villagization resulted in the permanent loss of land and has affected especially women's rights to land. The matrilineal family system has no longer legal status, but it is followed when it is convenient, especially for men. According to this system, the father who conceives the children is not fully responsible for these children as the mother's brother is the main person in charge. Consequently the father has his interest in the children of his sister's homestead.

In Iramba, the sister is known to have taken her extra earnings to her brother's homestead for her children's future school fees or for a potential future need, should she be divorced. Thus the father's neglect of the children he begets is justified following the traditional system, yet officially the system is no longer operational. The situation in between the two systems frees the man from the responsibility on both sides. It is generally known that the traditional legal systems under Customary Law were formally abolished, but men can refer to whichever system is convenient for them. Women not only bring up the children, they also pay for their education through their earnings and through their savings organizations. This sometimes leads to their sending their daughters in search of work, which may result in prostitution. The Ministry of Labour was alerted to this and it involved the International Labour Organisation to organize support to take care of such girls, giving them training for self-employment.

Anthropologists have been keenly interested in kinship systems and their research co-operation would be of help in the present situation, when the old system is breaking up. Studies like Janet Carsten's *After Kinship* in a series of New Departures in Anthropology give perspectives to emerging themes in anthropology in changing societies and cultures. Even if the study relates to the kinship system in Europe, it gives new direction in the situation in which different forms of relatedness matter increasingly (Carsten, 2004).

According to the national policy "all land in Tanzania is public land vested in the President as trustee on behalf of all citizens." The land law was revised first in 1997 and again in 2007. The long-standing occupation of land is supposed to be ensured by the law and land distribution and access to land should be equitable. The expansion of land that any person or corporate body may occupy is regulated and "the right of every woman to acquire, hold, use and deal with, shall to the same extent and subject to the same restrictions be treated as a right of any man." Furthermore all citizens should be enabled to participate in decision-making on matters connected with occupation of land and compensation of land if its occupation is revoked (Iramba District Council, Strategic Plan 2006-2007, 2010-2011).

It is evident that a deeper analysis must penetrate to the changes taking place in the social system and comparisons need to be made with other ethnic groups, which did not traditionally follow the matrilineal family and inheritance mode. The attention to ethnic traditions was minimized when the country was building the unified nation, yet they play greater role than what is officially recognized. The Magistrate in charge of land issues for Iramba, at the time of the interview in 2010 located in Singida, told the author that many Iramba women came to him with problems of land inheritance regardless of the distance from Iramba to Singida, while the Nyaturu women living closer did not have such complaints, an indication that the matrilineal tradition caused the problems. When the wife could return to her brother and claim right to clan land she did not run into the same trouble if she was left alone. When the matrilineal system no longer had legal standing at the time of divorce the wife was left without any right to land. This was the main reason why women had to rent land for their cultivation as they most often were left with the responsibility to feed their children. Further research and analyses made in cooperation with the people, local committees and officers continue to need attention.

In general the question of land ownership is acute and it concerns especially women, who cultivate the food for their families. The implementation of the villagization program in 1973-1976 caused the nullification of clan land occupation in large parts of the country, when people's houses were broken down and land was reallocated in small two acres areas or less around the house. The cultivated land belonged to the village and the people had a share in it according to the expanse they cultivated. Villagers who did not need to move to another village were likely to keep their traditional land holdings after the villagization programme lost its grip. In Iramba it meant that such women could claim land as their heritage and after the one party system ended they could rent plots to landless women.

The issue of land holdings was brought up in many interviews with women during my research in Iramba district in 2004 and 2007 regardless of the ethnic background. The claims to the inherited land by the former owners, who did not need to move away from their land, have left the others at disadvantage when moving to the concentrated villages such as Msingi. Such was the case with the wives, who moved from their villages to their husband's place of residence or work, have divorced, or were initially given only small plots. The interviewed women in Msingi village said they rent land and quoted prices ranging from 2,000 to 20,000 shillings per acre. Women retained their right to their clan land only if they did not need to move during Operation Villagization. The landless women were not given land for cultivation even from the village land, as the Prime Minister Edward Lowassa assumed in 2007, when I brought the issue to him, informing him that some women rented and some had bought land. The District Commissioner Grace Messiaki confirmed the information when she received the Prime Minister's inquiry while I was in his office. The process of official village land surveying in Iramba started with external support from the Finnish Hartola project in Msingi village in 2011 and it was to be continued. At least 39 women had land surveyed but how many of the new landowners had their land certified has not yet been verified. The village community chose the beneficiaries among themselves and 71 people (32 widows and poor women along with 39 poor men) had their plots demarcated.

The cost of the surveying in the implementation of the Village Planning Ordinance in the district makes the process slow and favours those who can pay for it. Women as the villagers in general need to know which laws apply to them and which rights of ownership or usufruct they can claim. The women need to be aware that testaments have to be made to indicate their right to the land if the husband dies or divorces. The situation as it is today does not in practice follow the Government and the ruling Party policy, which is supposed to guarantee land for any villager wanting to cultivate, women and youth with equal rights to land with adult men. In the areas in which inherited clan lands were retained as in Karagwe and Kilimanjaro the situation is different from the areas where villagers lost their land during the villagization, as was the case in Iramba and in the coastal and southern districts.

The rights to land not equally retained in all parts of the country differed depending on the officials in charge, as the instructions given did not fit all the situations. The Chaggas on Kilimanjaro did not make big moves, but their land had become scarce with the increased population, which together with the advanced education resulted in the spreading of the Chaggas all over the country as entrepreneurs and civil servants. During villagization, the Kilimanjaro area produced its own directives taking into consideration the densely populated areas and created extensions in a few new villages on the planes, of which my study of Mtakuja *Ujamaa* village below the central part of the mountain is reported in Swantz (1985, 113-124) and in further studies (T. Pietilä 2007).

The present situation in the country does not offer citizens guarantees to what the law indicates. In a country in which salaries do not cover family expenses, most people need land for cultivating food or cash crops. The upper grade government workers acquire land for cultivation or for planting trees away from their inherited land areas to pay for their children's higher education and for their future security. The land study in Western Bagamoyo District indicated that in Kilosa District, formerly unused land had been rented or sold to outsiders. A Government Minister has had the power to sell or rent land to wealthy private foreigners or state powers for great lengths of time with a promise for some communal facilities in exchange, with no consultation with the people concerned. This happened with large stretches of Maasai, Sonjo and Hadzabe lands in the 1990s, where large areas have been allocated as hunting grounds to a citizen of United Arab Emirates and various foreign agencies as long time rented lands.

The land problem is different for the herders, hunters and gatherers from what it is to the cultivators, but the principal question is the same. The Tanzanian media has indicated that there are plans that the Hadzabe would be shown as objects for tourism, which brings into mind the Congolese villagers brought to Belgium by King Leopold to be shown to tourists! Sadly the Tanzanian Government has brought the Department of Antiquities under the Ministry of Tourism, which threatens the serious research on the numerous archaeological sites and makes the collection of local and oral histories subject to the interest of tourists leaving aside the opinions of local communities. The citizens of Kilwa Kiwinje and Sokoni were annoyed in the 1990s by the fact that their interests and knowledge in the culture of the island and the shore of the mainland had not been considered. They had their own stories to tell and an interest to dig further into the culture of the area.

The situation for village planning at the time of writing offers the opportunity to divide the land anew. The expense of the land surveying and the speed with which the land is being sold demands publicly shared information. The women, in particular, need to be alerted to their potential for gaining land rights when the village land planning and surveying is undertaken in the districts. The acute land problems have been accelerated when large stretches of land have been sold or rented to foreign companies and individuals for long periods of time. The legislation relating to the cattle keepers also affects the areas of this study. I refer here to the research thirty years after Jipemoyo (Ylhäissi 2003; Sokoni 2010)

The political decisions of the Government and the leaders of the country have led to situations which go beyond the local decision making and rights to land when natural resources are being discovered in unexpected scale and locations. This relates to the use of the concept of *space,* translated as opportunity *(nafasi, fursa)* available for the people, and the significance of their increasing awareness of their potential, thus also PAR as a research approach. If their opportunities are limited or out of their reach, they need to become *conscious* of the political and economic avenues, before they can politically act. Local level people experience the political problems when they affect their lives concretely. Their political action begins from learning to analyse that experience. Participatory research creates awareness of how the problems connect their potentialities within the political economy.

The people's uprisings in Mtwara during the writing of this book, which led to the burning of houses referred to earlier appears to follow models from the North African uprisings. Mtwara has a deep-sea harbor with the potential for the industrial development, but the issues go beyond the decision-making powers of local actors. These issues are connected with the issue of awareness.

Concluding thoughts on culture and development

Universities in Africa as academic institutions cling to the universal scientific epistemic system, which distinguishes itself from the local systems of knowledge. There is very little practical *techne* or experimental knowledge included in the courses of the academic institutions, some practical subjects and potentially anthropology making the exception. Furthermore the poor information about the land surveying and village land plans in making gives the upper strata of society the opportunity to deprive the land from the less informed villagers. They have the knowledge where the land is available and the means to purchase it and to take advantage of the villagers who do not know their rights or the actual value of the land. The utilization and encouragement of the use of Participatory Action Research as the channel of information and debate could potentially close this gap and bring a great improvement into the development discourse (M-L. Swantz 2001). Community Based Research is used in many academic institutes utilizing the Participatory Action Research and is referred to in this and other chapters.

Understanding of both the positive and negative significance of the inherited interpretation of life in relation to organic life and natural environment would greatly enhance the building of the society on the foundations of the cultural heritage and also relate it to the acute environmental issues. It could branch into flourishing economic measures when the reinterpretation of culture would increase self-determination and desire to look for originality in development efforts. Its wise use could even find meaningful patterns in the growing tourist industry. However, it presupposes that the researchers work closely with the people concerned using participatory and community based research to the extent that it is found to be possible and acquaint themselves with the social and cultural contexts from which the new societies emerge, translating the knowledge for the use of people themselves in their own development but also for Government workers, politicians and artists – in close cooperation with the development scholars, anthropologists, historians and academicians in general.

In development planning the significance of the inherited culture is brought up when certain sectors such as Antiquities or conservation of ancient sites are considered. They are now placed under the Ministry of Tourism which means that more planning is oriented toward the exterior sites rather than toward historical knowledge of antiquities and cultural self-understanding. The distance from the time when many rituals were considered to be a forbidden realm of life for Christians has potentially diminished the fears connected with the spirit powers, which earlier were an integrate part of many rituals. The symbolism can be studied and looked into without fearing that they conceal hidden negative forces. Many aspects of the maturity symbols, such as going through a period of symbolic death and emerging as new persons with new social status, would have been applicable to Christianity had they been better understood. It is obvious that the introduction to the Western Science with capital letters, often in its stale form, has further alienated the African scholar from her or his former "lived world." The negative image of anthropology as a colonial discipline, not initially included in the University curriculum in Tanzania, has affected the dearth of scholarship on the topics related to the inherited rituals and beliefs. The studies have been made on witchcraft instead on the positive meanings of ritual symbols beyond the skillful dancing and music. There is a new wave of interest in research on religious phenomena closely related to the spirit world, which often are falsely classified as being Pentecostal.

It is hoped that the time is ripe for the recreation of cultural treasures in the form of art, song and poetry relating to the disappearing cultural features. They could replace the poverty politics, which now captures the thoughts and stifles imagination. The domination of the power of capital imposed on people, works toward uniform lines of thought and scholarship. The international influence with the emphasis on human rights and gender equality have had their effect, but the global repetition of them also stifles the ingenuity of local thinking. When the lines of thought are created at the centres of power, hidden economic and political goals penetrate all the levels of the "lived world" with their seemingly noble goals. It is up to the local politicians and common people to differentiate what is applicable in each situation and where it is possible to create more space for local creative thought and art. I have suggested in this chapter that bringing out the inspirational cultural foundations of the society is necessary for overcoming the passive receptive spirit and dulling influence of the negative connotations that the poverty politics have brought along, dominating the concept of development and obscuring the positive impact of inherited culture.

CHAPTER 5

Women's Ways of Sustaining Life

Introduction

This chapter deals with rural women's livelihood in Tanzania. The perspective adopted reaches beyond statistics on poverty. I criticize the negative image that dwelling on the vocabulary of "living on one or two dollars a day" leaves in the minds of people so described and, specifically, on the self-image of women in their struggle for the subsistence and welfare of their families. The monetary understanding of poverty ignores how rural women as individuals, as family members, and as groups build a social economy to manage the welfare of their families. The women's central role in rural development in Tanzania has been dealt with only in the margins both in the former *Ujamaa* and in the later neoliberal politics. Women's work contribution in the production of maize and millet and other main food production is not counted in the figures of GDP and thus gives a distorted picture of the production and ignores women's central role.

I draw on studies conducted in Iramba District (2003-2004 and 2007-2008) by Professor Bertha Koda (2013) with the assistance of three students and my own cooperation in the first phase. The Iramba research was made as a part of the North-South Local Government Cooperation between Iramba District and Hartola, my home municipality. It included my frequent visits to women's groups in different parts of the district in 2001- 2012. Comparative material is included from studies on women in Kilimanjaro and from RIPS program in Mtwara and Lindi regions, where I represented participatory research in development work in 1992-98, while I was also part time on the staff of WIDER.

Theoretical background for social economy

Writers who have measured women's unpaid work point out the need for interdisciplinary studies, "because the household is the place where economics, social values and personal characteristics converge towards the very end of human activity: the transformation of natural and human resources into something capable of meeting human needs or wants" (Goldschmidt-Clermont 1992, 266-7). The emphasis needs to be shifted from the sole focus on the material base to respecting the broader spectrum of human, social, and regenerative values, and developing economies as the means of upholding life in its entirety.

Hilkka Pietilä has developed a way of separating the food production sector from the economic statistics. Her proposal for a framework of a Triangle of Human Economics consists of 1. household, 2. cultivation and 3. extraction/manufacturing components. Each has an internal logic of its own, instead of subjecting the household and cultivation economies to the framework of extraction/manufacturing economy. Placing household and cultivation economics into categories *sui generis* is fitting in the African context in which the two sectors form such a central part of economy. According to Pietilä, particularly food, essential for living, should not be subjected to vicissitudes of the market (H. Pietilä 1997).

Pietilä has worked out a model whereby the commodity economy should serve human needs and preserve natural resources. The cultivation economy through its interaction with human culture and living nature is essential for all human life. The triangular of productive, reproductive and market sectors emphasises the intrinsic value of each of those aspects of life, which sustain it (H. Pietilä 2006).

In the Iramba study as also in other research referred to in this chapter, I analyse the extent to which the women's economy could be described as a social economy, and whether it had similarities with "human economy" of Karl Polanyi (1944, 2001), the "moral economy" of pre-capitalist village societies as described by James C. Scott (1976) and the "economy of affection" of non-captured peasants in Tanzania by Goran Hyden (1980a, 1983). I refer also to other scholars who have analysed the rural economy and women's role in it as social economy referring to Maghimbi, Kimambo etc. (2011) and Kashaga (2013). Hyden has pointed out that in such an economy, upholding the motivation of mutual care is more than likely to become a hindrance to market based economic development. As the economy is progressing while writing this, such a development is unlikely to have an alternative, since the land ownership and traditional engagement in agriculturte have left room for manipulation of the situation by market forces. However, studies show that women can invest in relations of affection and engage in markets in a way that reinforces both activities (Swantz and Tripp 1996, 12-13; T. Pietilä 2007; Omari 1998). The chapter deals with what are the ways are in which women develop alternatives rather than being called "the poor living with a dollar or two per day."

Further, the premises in the Iramba studies go together with the "impersonality postulate" by Tariq Banuri, who criticized Western philosophy and economy on its alleged binary opposition between the personal and the impersonal (Banuri 1990, 29-101). Another line of thought was offered by economist Stephen Marglin, who developed a critique of liberal economy in his writings while attached to WIDER in Helsinki. He summarized his thinking in the book *The Dismal Science, How Thinking Like the Economist Undermines Community*. He criticizes the prevailing economics as a dismal science, which in its individualistic focus works against communal life essential to humans (Marglin 2008). Frédérique Apffel-Marglin has developed the same line from the perspective of Indian and South American peasants from a feminist perspective. I have had the privilege to join the group of scholars working on similar issues over the years in gatherings in different parts of the world (Apffel-Marglin and Marglin 1996; 1998).

Researchers have sought and found alternatives to mainstream economics in village economies designed to cope with contingencies and overt market penetration. Polanyi's self-regulating markets were resisted as a threat to co-operative ties. Anne Mayhew points out that the counter movement to the self-regulatory markets was inevitable: humans are social animals, which use their social relationships even in production and distribution (Mayhew 2000). Polanyi's book has been republished in 2001 and has received fresh interest. Platteau's review of the studies on traditional systems of social security provides a good comparative base for testing the assumption of the "service economy" on a wider scale, not only in pre-capitalist societies (Platteau 1991, 112-170).

Throughout the research history, men writers have looked on the households as units dominated by men. Several women economists have joined the critique of mainstream economics and have defended women's social and human departure in their economic pursuits centred on family welfare. They have also pointed out how family surveys use men as interviewees (Henderson1992; Mayhew 2000; Beneria 2003; Power 2004; H. Pietilä 2006, 2010).

Women's work in agriculture

In Iramba District and Tanzania in general, women are the main producers in an economy built on agriculture and livestock. Men have traditionally done the ploughing in Iramba, but you see also women behind the oxen. A fundamental reason for the lack of progress in agriculture in Central Tanzania is uncertainty caused by environmental fluctuations from drought to floods in alternate years. The region experienced severe drought in two years between 2002 and 2008. In 2007, the region suffered from floods and excessive rains, which continued throughout the cultivation season from November until March. The unfavourable conditions made the repayment of loans a burden and discouraged women who had optimistically joined in groups and applied for loans to increase the area of ploughing. Also banks shied away from giving loans for agricultural projects because of uncertainty. Irrigation has been introduced with assistance from the World Bank, but the continuity is not guaranteed.

Women's work for sustenance of the families has not been included in the production figures of the country, which gives a false picture of the Gross Domestic Products (GDP). Kenyan Professor of Economics Germano Mwabu, while working at the UNU-WIDER, estimated that 90 per cent of the maize production in Kenya was for domestic use and thus generally not calculated in the GDP figures (Evenson and Mwabu 1997). The same pertains to the situation in Tanzania. According to an IIED *Participatory Learning and Action* issue in 2009, around 80 per cent of Tanzanians grow maize, but with the gradual climatic change they have had to shift to cultivating other species, which tolerate the dry weather better. In Iramba, millet and cassava are grown in addition to maize, as well as non-recorded domestic grains, roots and bananas, none of which are counted in production figures, giving a different picture of poverty.

In Iramba oxen are used for ploughing the fields. This has traditionally been men's work but these days women are also taking part in ploughing. Women also own oxen together with other women. However, when meeting with women in groups and asking how they cultivate, only exceptional women reply that they have their fields ploughed by oxen. This is the case also when the women earn their cash for domestic needs by basket making and selling tomatoes or other garden products or handwork.

In Mtwara and Lindi, ordinary village women did their cultivation by hand hoes and the fields were smaller than in Iramba. Growing rice was more general than in dry land but in coastal parts of the region, men often sat in their chairs while the women did their work. Fishing attracted those who could afford nets and when that was the case they could afford to sit back and have their sons or hired younger men to do the work.

All generalizations are dangerous, but the surveys which have been done have the same weaknesses as observation and case studies as they do not give accurate results. One common reason to be doubtful is the custom of taking the information from men who appear as heads of the household but do not do most of the farmwork nor understand the multiplicity of the women's responsibilities. Two surveys were done in the same Mtwara rural villages in the first decade of the new millennium, which indicated people's weak economic situation. According to the statistics, the people on the coast and in the "southeastern parts of the country," meaning Mtwara district, were counted to be the poorest. But the concept of measuring the wealth in cash did not go together with the people's way of looking at their life pattern, as long as they lived from the land and/or the sea. The people who had to be employed by the wealthier people were measured to be poorer than those who managed with their own food production. The surveys showed that the people from the inland Mtwara district customarily went for work to the island where the fishermen employed workers during the farming season. For them employment was evidence of poverty. Had they managed with the food they grew throughout the year they would not have been called poor in their own vocabulary.

The economic policy of the World Bank aimed initially at people being employed in order to be part of the cash economy and paying for the services they received such as schools. People rather offered work directly for building the schools. But when the potential for new wealth in oil became evident in Mtwara whereby the local people would be robbed from the power taken to Dar es Salaam and Bagamoyo they were ready to rise up in arms. Remarks were made that people had learned from the participatory PRA, which had developed people's thinking about their possibilities, not however violence.

Customs affect women's economic lives

Women's chance of participating in the economy is affected by cultural factors. The Iramba inhabitants are Christians or Muslims, but there are also traditionalists. The last census in which religion was an item was done in Tanzania in 1968. Research done by the University of Dar es Salaam scholars to identify the numbers of people of different religions had selected Iramba district as a representative of traditionalists. This might be because there are both Barabaig pastoralists and Hadzabe hunters and gatherers, who have been counted as traditionalists, but there are also Christians among them. Using focus group methods, both the Christian and Muslim leaders interviewed by Bertha Koda emphasized that ideally assistance to women should not cause any divisions in the family. Both religions recognize men as the heads of the family, but it should not mean that men dominate or oppress the women. However, the opinions expressed in focus groups in which different categories of people, men and women are selectively called together for views, do not give the whole picture.

In Iramba district and in the new Mkambala district with patrilineal ethnic groups Nyaturu and Sukuma as neighbours only the Nyiramba have traditionally followed the matrilineal social order and have continued to do so when it has been convenient. The traditional matrilineal Nyiramba clan made the mother's brother responsible for his sister's children. The matrilineal system was officially abolished in the Tanzanian judicial system in 1964. The national adoption of the patrilineal system is causing difficulties for the two lawyers of Iramba, one of them in charge of solving the land problems, which women bring to them. The latter, himself of a matrilineal descent from Mtwara region understanding the issue indicated that the land cases he gets from women concern only the Nyiramba, not the patrilineal Nyaturu women.

By referring to this government decision men can excuse themselves from traditional responsibilities as uncles, but when it is convenient, the husband refuses to pay fees for his daughters, referring to the traditional uncle's duties. This leaves the women with all the responsibilities related to their daughters but in many cases they are not able to fulfill them. They commonly have to pay rent for the land for growing the family food crops as part of their responsibility. Household duties and growing food fill their time and energy. There are no statistics to show how common such cases of loading the woman with excessive responsibilities are in families. Women's groups frequently expressed to me in discussions the need for women to have their own fields . Discussions with some men who have taken their sisters' daughter to live in their home and pay for her fees indicate that the need for such payments are anticipated, while it might also be a way to make use of such girls' labour at the uncle's home.

An indication of the existing problem was the call of the Ministry of Labour to ILO to assist in solving the problem of the girls in danger of becoming prostitutes. The District provided a spacious quarter to an organization Kiwohede with the head office in Dar es Salaam for running the activities and a leading woman officer took over the responsibility for running the centre in Kiomboi for such young women. She had also some training organized specially for the purpose by ILO in Dar es Salaam. The project lasted three years, but has been continued with occasional funding from the CSOs and NGOs. It received special attention of President Kikwete's wife, as also the school accommodating albino youth, as we witnessed when we as representatives of Hartola were in Kiomboi.

The above problem relating to matriliny is not sufficiently interpreted and analysed as an inherited conflict between the present system and the traditional matrilineal and even at times matrilocal family system. Discussions with women's groups were carried out in Msingi village and in meetings with women in villages in different Iramba wards during ten years of local government cooperation with Hartola. The two lawyers serving the two districts are aware of the misinterpretation, and several men interviewed also admitted the problem. The situation would require counselling by the social workers and cooperation with the lawyers if the origins of such practice would be brought out into open. According to a group of women discussing their own experience, the social welfare officer had been of no help. He only sent a woman with such a problem back to her kin to sort the problem out and left it to be taken care of traditionally.

The mixing of cultural practices between the patrilineal and matrilineal systems affects not only property but also the identity of children. This coexistence of norms can be explained also by the fact that intermarriages between ethnic groups, which follow different customs, are on the increase. This has caused conflicts of interest regarding the investment in children's education. There have been instances, where a mother has secretly sent a portion of the family's accumulated wealth to her brother, who she assumes will eventually take care of his nephew or niece. Likewise, fathers have not taken the responsibility either for sending their children to school or paying for their education using the excuse that it is not their responsibility for fear that once the children get jobs they will benefit their uncles. The unsettled situation of women is reflected in the issue of land.

Regardless of the system applied, the girls are at a disadvantage. When it comes to the inheritance of property and wealth, boys are given preference, although under the matrilineal system, girls are also expected to inherit some of the family property and land. Nyaturu daughters and girls on the other hand suffer from the practice of female genital mutilation, now forbidden by national law, which had been spreading even among the Nyiramba through intermarriage. Women's organizations and female officers have made an effort to educate people on the ethically and humanly ill effects of the practice.

A great number of Nyiramba girls leave home, with the approval of the mother, who needs an additional support for her other children. The family's look for assistance to pay school fees, which they need for vocational training in Folk Development Colleges or in Vocational Institutes, which have started taking a number of standard seven leavers. Failing to get the fees, the girls take jobs as bar maids or servants often far from home. Some eventually become prostitutes and even victims of human trafficking. The acute need to pay attention to this problem was recognized by the Ministry of Labour, which enlisted the support of the International Labour Organization (ILO) in the 1990s. A branch of an organization Kiota Women's Health and Development (KIWOHEDE) in Iramba collected such girls for teaching of trades and for meetings in a hall allotted by the District Executive Director. The ILO support was provided for three years without continuation. Some NGOs such as World Vision and PRIDE and a Finnish Msingi Friendship Society have been paying fees for young girls in vocational training and have in some rare cases given them initial capital to start their own small enterprise. There is an acute need of attention to this issue, because what is being done has no permanence and is totally inadequate.

Local administration's connection with global programs

The evolution of the Tanzanian administrative and political system from centralized rule toward stronger local governments has affected the women's economy. Since 1998, the authority for local development has been transferred from regions to districts, while regions retain the responsibility for political security and oversight. Such a decision was welcomed, since bringing the Government closer to people's possibility to influence their everyday reality was seen to strengthen democracy.

At the same time, the increased grassroots participation in decision-making is contradicted by global market economy. The trend towards free markets was a far cry from the program of *Ujamaa* socialism, as formulated by President Julius Nyerere:

We would be stupid indeed if we allowed the development of our economies to destroy the human and social values, which African societies had built up over centuries. Yet if we are to save these, we cannot afford the arrogance, which our technical superiority tempts us to assume. (Nyerere 1973, 279)

Joining the market was unavoidable, as President Nyerere realized with the failing economy and rather than beginning the negotiations with IMF he withdrew, first continuing as the head of the CCM Party in 1985. Households were affected in Iramba district when the market prices of cotton were lowered. The growing of cotton continued only in three wards, while others shifted to fields of sunflower, which required further processing into oil. Women's groups, which have taken on the growing and marketing of it lack the financial resources required for further processing which required transporting the products for grinding. Women in Gumanga had been industrious in many ways and were recommended to deserve a grinding mill as a gift to save them from carrying on bicycles the loads up the escarpment to Kinampanda from grinding.

When several other women's groups were given machines for oil production and others grinding mills for maize, it became evident that all inputs requiring machinery of any kind required technically trained people in the wards and at least in the district to keep technical devises operational. Omission of technical training for requirements of villages of men as well as women is the main reason for failing in all aspects of village level development requiring maintenance and repairs.

Furthermore, also commercial training for astute observation of market opportunities has become the necessity not yet acquired by common women's groups in Iramba at the time of this writing. The only exceptions are some progressive women who are providing good leadership in the marketing of a variety of basket- and mat making products and the honey. In sunflower production, the competition by a few Asian or Arab businessmen who have remained at the local centres reduce the women's potential to further develop their trade and move up in the value chain. There are a few local women, who have initiated a variety of small income earning efforts. They are expanding them and finding marketing chains with low profit. Such local level private market chains are slowly gaining ground, providing possibilities for women even in Iramba and Singida, the administrative centre of the region. In the region, the markets centre on cattle sales, and draw other sellers to the place.

The situation for women's markets has been different on the mountain slopes in Kilimanjaro region from the dry central regions totally dependent on annual rains. The initial state control of market penetration since the villagization process affected the mountain women more radically than in regions where people had not become so cash dependent and able to handle it. The political implementation of the administrative reforms which radically affected the marketing policies, continued to be a challenge to grassroots participation. The decisions of the Central Committee, first by TANU and later after 1977 by CCM, gave the marketing power to the Regional Trading Centres controlled by the Party, which resulted in a decline in food production and in cash crop marketing. Scholars debate whether the centralization of the government system in independent Tanzania had merely continued the colonial system or whether it was strengthened after independence, when the political leadership wanted to keep control over the precarious developments in the country (Schneider 2006, 49). Be it as it may, the politicians' intention for a quick modernization of agriculture, which had led to the forced moving of people to centralized villages in 1970s, in turn had weakened people's potential of utilizing their local knowledge of land, the environment and social relations. For the people on the mountain, it meant a shortage of the goods they had become dependent on. When of indiviuals could no longer buy soap, the situation was at its worst, especially when it went together with exorbitantly low coffee prices, as I had witnessed when a woman had brought her coffee sacks for the weighing by the cooperative officer. The Kilimanjaro Coffee Marketing Cooperation (KCMC) somehow sailed through the changes and is still operational. But women did not only struggle with the low prices, they had to fight also to keep the money they earned since the handling of the coffee was no longer in the hands of men.

On the mountain, the fluctuating market prices and a sharp decline in coffee prices in the 1980s forced women to start keeping grade cows and pigs and selling milk and meat, while several coffee fields were changed to vegetable gardens (T. Pietilä 2007, M-L. Swantz 1985). Eventually many Chagga women moved down from the local markets to the growing markets in towns and cities and became full time market women as is well analysed by Tuulikki Pietilä in her study of Eastern Kilimanjaro in Mamba (T. Pietilä 1996).

After the failure of the villagization and the centralized marketing through village cooperatives and Regional Trading Centres the IMF brought in the Structural Adjustment Program (SAP), which forced Tanzania among other poorer countries into economic reforms, as another failure. In Tanzania it was fully implemented after President Nyerere's resign in 1985. The SAP measures badly affected the capacity for implementation of policies and added greatly in every way to women's workload but also women's ways of earning in towns and cities (Tripp 1987).

However, in the 1990s the participation of people in their own efforts in village development had started to gain space in official development thinking, to the extent that the World Bank under the new leadership got interested and invited experts in it to the Headquarters for consultation. They even consulted WIDER where I was as a research professor at the time. The director asked me to write a paper on it for their representative. The new direction resulted in the Global Poverty Reduction Program, as an outcome of the communication between local experts. In Tanzania, the World Bank initiated the participation of beneficiaries in project design and implementation through its Tanzania Social Action Fund, TASAF, which in Iramba District has grown to include up to 40-50 villages, depending on participatory village planning and contribution of work. Three officers have become engaged in the programmes when I interviewed them in 2012, one had been involved in the beginning years. They confirmed that the participatory planning continued to be done and repeated after every three years and villagers determined the projects for which they were ready to work as their share of payment. Women played a central roal in these initiatives.

Since the 1990s, the scholarship and analyses of the progress or the lack of it has proliferated. Critical studies see the village level projects as camouflaging global market goals and the failure of the governments to take responsibility while transferring the responsibility to the foreign financed NGOs whereby the underlying policies of the World Bank remain the same (e.g., Gould and Ojanen 2003). Kjell Havnevik has continued research in Rufiji river basin since the villagization until recent years and gives an illuminating analysis in *Tanzania, The Limits to Development from Above* (Havnevik 1993). People have not brought their dissatisfaction to political channels. They have rather taken direct action or failed to do so. As Ferguson has suggested elsewhere, the government-led project work in Tanzania that is dominated by global powers does not give much room for political influence, which is bound to lead into ground-level disagreements (Ferguson 1990, 1994). Tanzanian radio gives opportunities for dissatisfied people to raise their frustrations with the wider public.

Nevertheless, the action in Iramba witnessed in person has given evidence that the system can also be operational. The democratic basis offers both men and women a voice, if they are aware of the rights that the system offers. The participatory village planning is supposed to be repeated after every three years to give villagers potentially a voice if they know to use it. Much depends on their *awareness* of the situation and becoming conscious of opportunities, in turn requiring commercial and technical education not on offer with affordable prices. The officers and politicians are not free to misuse their power, as the local development in Tanzania leaves citizens space for action. The legally authorized village assemblies are supposed to meet four times a year. In them all, the villagers are free to gather and bring their complaints, and the Village Assembly has legal powers for implementation and making changes even in the leadership. When the District Commissioner representing the ruling party CCM in Iramba discovered that there were villages which had failed to call together the village assemblies, they were ordered to place the dates of four village assemblies in a year on the village office wall, which we could witness had been done in visited villages. I see benefits in these efforts to *create space* for village decision making, as they direct even the World Bank TASAF projects to subject their plans to the villagers' decisions. But the opportunities available need follow up, which requires astute interest, awareness and knowledge from the villagers' side, especially from the active women's groups and active nominated members in the District Council. The elected MP in the last election of Iramba District was a woman. It has also happened that people lose confidence if their efforts have not brought satisfactory response from the government, since the village plans require external funding go to the District Coucil. Fortunately the District was divided into two, each with a population of around 220,000.

6. Women groups' central role in economy

One of the academic female research assistants for Berta Koda's research originating in Iramba described women in villages as being "*wanawake wa nyumbani tu,*" "women as homemakers only," because "they do not have enough education to get them work in offices," repeating it twice in her field notes. While surely demonstrating the alienation of an educated young woman from rural reality, her remark also reflects the view that village women's productive work does not count as it is not even properly shown in statistics. This view, which is dominant and well represented, implies that urbanization is an inevitable goal to which development plans ought to prepare society, while agriculture is to be commercialized and mechanized. My experiences in Tanzania shows that women have the capacity to come forth and defy this stereotype (Swantz, Ndedya, and Masaiganah, 2001; Swantz, 2013). Persistant women do not give up even when they have repeatedly experienced resistance from men and the authorities. A couple of cases serve to illustrate this point.

A strong woman, Mwanashulu, who was engaged in the traditional netting of fish from the shore, became the frontline fighter against dynamite fishing. She boldly declared *Bahari yetu, hatutaki* (it is our sea, we do not want [you]). The unprecedented cooperation between a sole woman who dared to initiate the fight and the fishermen who soon agreed with her and came together with the facilitator Mwajuma Masaiganah, was enough to persuade the communities to ban dynamiting (Masaiganah 2001, 391-394). The fishing communities started an organization to defend their reefs which covered the whole length of the fishing villages along Mtwara and Lindi shores. They insisted they get the support from the higher administrative level, going all the way to the responsible Ministry offices in Dar es Salaam. Of interest for me, while on a visit to Mtwara to celebrate 40 years of Finnish development assistance in the two southern regions, was to read in the daily newspaper in September 2013 that dynamiting fish on the shores North from Dar es Salaam was a problem, whereas on the southern shores it was not prevalent. I had also a chance to go to Mwanashulu's home on the beach and her affectionate overwhelming reaction at our meeting was a reminder of the manifold cooperation we had with her at the time of RIPS. She was now engaged in protecting the mangroves.

A similar example of women's initiative was that of Elisabeth Ndedya in Ruangwa village in Lindi Region in 1994, where six women initially joined a group they called *Muungano* (Union). They had decided that the most profitable work was to make bricks, but they had not done it before and were ridiculed by men and discouraged in their effort to the extent that they gave up. After one season, the group disintegrated and the three remaining women together decided to cultivate maize. In that project the rodents ate the crop. Even then, the following year four of the women were more prepared to make another effort in brick making. They were bold enough to ask some young men to help them to acquire the tools they needed and they discovered that four was a good size for dividing the work. Their strengthened self-confidence as frontline fighters provided an example for other women (Ndedya et al. 2001, 388-391).

Women's limited freedom and subjection to injustice has made it necessary for women to depend on each other by forming groups. In Mtwara region, a study of women's groups showed that women of middle social level tended to form groups for cultivation and for other communal activities such as fishponds. To contrast, women from the wealthier level did not in general need group support, but joined the CCM party women's organization, *Umoja wa Wanawake*, and church groups, whereas the poorest were not in a position to come out of their homes and get involved with groups unless they were specifically encouraged (M-L. Swantz 1997).

The women's groups in Iramba villages kept the volume of production moderate to avoid overburdening members. Groups were needed to give mental and social support and were used for special projects, such as the oil-pressing machine, which the cooperation with Hartola helped to provide for many groups. Several groups presented the view that they should at least inform the men about their activities so that the women's enterprising spirit would not raise the men's suspicion and jealousy. While a saying went that an Iramba man does not live in the house his wife has built, it did happen that men did the building while the money came from the wife, who earned additionally by sewing and selling dresses. Men could also relax when women brought enough income to maintain the family.

In Gumanga Ward in 2004, interviewed women said that they had started their groups with no external funding. A group *Twende na wakati* (Let us go with the times) grew sunflower and had the seeds pressed into oil up an escarpment 20 kilometres away. Also other women's groups had meaningful names: *Vumilia* (Endure), *Mwamko* (Waking up), *Upendo* (Love), *Tupendane*, (Let us love one another), *Mapambano*, (Struggling) and *Azimio* (Declaration). The names of the groups indicated the spirit in which they were started inspired the Community Development Officer to choose the Gumanga women as the recipients of the first oil press bought with support by North -South Cooperation with Hartola. Gumanga women started also growing tomatoes and they gave them a good market along the roadside, but also brought their food items to the market in Kiomboi since the tomato business from Gumanga was a good source of income for many women. Elsewhere women were sitting along the roadsides in long rows all selling the same items, waiting for some cars to stop and buy in bulk. Especially the Sukuma households kept cattle and a youth group had built up and started a wading cattle-bath, for which the Ward offered lessons. The land was available for grazing, but the cattle keepers claimed the fee for wading was too high, so eventually the youth gave up the project.

Women's groups have been established for various purposes including cultural activities. In Kinampanda, women had started their mutual service group with 40 members in 1998, which they called *Faraja* (Comfort). The women came together the same day and time every week. They aimed to be of service such as bringing comfort to the bereaving members at funerals but also for rejoicing together at weddings and other family celebrations. Each member paid 200 shillings every month and from the collected money a sum of 5,000-10,000 shillings was customarily given to a member in whose family a death had occurred. The members shared in the celebrations and wore *sare* dress of the same cloth to emphasize their social togetherness. Even wealthy villagers, including men, wanted to enjoy the service benefits of the group membership. A well-established man paid his dues thinking that money he gave sufficed to get the service he would need but he did not participate in social gatherings for others. When his relative died, the group members did not spontaneously come to serve at the funeral, they anticipated compensation for their service. Money alone was not what the shared sociality and solidarity was about.

There were also saving groups in Iramba, which operated in the same way as the traditional groups known as *upatu* or *mchezo*, a game. Each member put an agreed sum into a cash pot on a certain day weekly or fortnightly. The amount depended on their financial capacity. Some groups could afford only a minimal sum, for others it climbed to the thousands. Everyone in turn could get an agreed sum from it for a special need. Mutuality guarantees continuity, which is difficult to maintain in individual projects. This is evident by the dying out of groups that were formed only in anticipation of loans offered by the local government. They did not have the same social glue as groups assembled for other purposes.

The savings groups were only a step away from bigger and more organized Savings and Credit Cooperative Societies (SACCOS). SACCOS serve also as the economy of care. A growing number of women's groups have organized and joined in such savings groups, some of them supporting widows as well as HIV/AIDS orphans. An elected Councillor in Ilunda Ward was active in mobilizing women in many different ways. In her village of Kinafundu, the *Tumaini* (Hope) group had 50 women basket makers. Their efficient leader, appointed as a councillor in the District Council, had found market channels in Dodoma, Dar es Salaam, and even in Nairobi. *Tumaini* group members supported widows over 70 years of age. In their opinion, SACCOS rather than a bank was the best way for getting the money to those in need. The entrance fee for the group membership was 5000 shillings. The members were carefully selected as the membership required willingness to give mutual support to those who faced death in their families. Women in *Ukombozi* (Redemption), *Amani* (Peace), and *Usharika* (Cooperation) groups in Ilunda village could rent sewing machines for a moderate fee from teachers and nurses, who did not have time to sew but could afford to buy the machines. Widows were able to use them with fair agreements.

As only people on the road to private business have the capacity to make use of bank accounts, Vigoba women's groups with metal boxes as cash containers given by the CDOs were a new system of groups started in the new millennium in Tanzania. They were introduced first in Zanzibar. The model had come from West Africa. In Vigoba, usually 25 women form the group for saving money they have earned and for providing loans when the fund has grown as a result of women's own inputs, often with some initial external input. Each of three members has the key to the box, which is opened on a given day when the fund has grown sufficiently. All are present to make financial inputs and for disbursing loans. The interest is much smaller than in official banks and the key holders, the cashier and record keeper are must work together. These groups have been gaining ground, as bank accounts would require initial capital and property or regular salaries as guarantees to be trusted to receive a sizable loan. The meetings of the group start with slogans spoken out loud. The group is not supposed to be larger than 25 after which a new group is established.

World Vision, a Christian humanist organization working in over 90 countries, has different countries supporting each a ward in the district. All the workers are Tanzanians from other parts of the country. In Iramba the organization elected local people to be responsible contacts and give them training in common gatherings of leaders. In the first years of the millennium it had given 19 women's groups training in Iramba for obtaining and managing loans in Iguguno ward. The organization had both group and individual membership, of which the latter was popular between 2004 and 2008 because of good leadership and loans faithfully paid. A savings organization of entrepreneurs called JUWAKI was started combining seven groups. JUWAKI had received from the District a 3 million shilling loan, from which it gave additional poorer members 30,000 shillings in loans to be repaid in eight months with 10 per cent interest. The groups decided when they meet for sharing experiences, giving further advice and ensuring that the agreements were kept.

Two interesting women's groups were started in the villages Sekenke and Ntwike for gold mining and salt making. Already in the early colonial times between the 1920s and the 1940s, there was extensive gold mining in that area. In the 1930s, a Canadian director living with his family in Sekenke was in charge of the mining with several hundred workers and several Europeans residing in the mining community (Danielson, 1977). In 1995, Sekenke Women Miners (SEWOMA) had begun with 16 founding members who had initially been only cooking and selling food for the male miners' community. Five women decided that they could just as well start the digging and formed their group with eleven more joining in. They bought a gold pit and started digging. At that time the District supported their venture and gave them two loans, which they returned on time, proud to have taken up the challenges of a male dominated venture. The women would have needed a water pump, a generator and a compressor for their work to succeed. The women also began to doubt the honesty of the middlemen and feared that their right to the gold pit might be revoked, as there was no guarantee of the tenure over the pits. They demanded measures from the government for supporting pro-poor gold mining, ensuring income sufficient to educate their children and meeting their health needs. When five years later there would have been further need for support for the women miners I inquired from the District CDO how the District had helped the women's mining group, he had no knowledge of its existence. According to him all the mining was put directly under the Ministry of Mining and the district authorities had no control of the operations.

Iramba women in Kitangiri were also engaged in smoking and marketing fish. They sold the fish to bigger marketeers who took the product to big cities, even as far as Mwanza and Dar es Salaam. In the same village we talked with a woman who was selling vegetables from a board in the village centre and asked her whether she belonged to any group. She did not and she said she had not heard of any groups she could belong to. In another village we asked the chairman we would want to meet women who are not within the recognized women's groups and he took us to women who brew beer and sold it to men. To our question why they did not join a recognized women's group the answer indicated a lack of recognized social level. This reminded me of the division of women also in Mtwara villages according to their social stamina.

The members of the SACCOS group in a big commercial centre Shelui had established an office in Shelui town along the main trunk road. They were initially 55 in 2005 and the group had grown to 412 in January 2008. It facilitated the marketing as all the passing trucks along the main trunk road from East to West and North stopped in Shelui. The women's organization took the name *Jipemoyo*, (Give Yourself Heart), and they had taken on some men members but so far the chairperson had continued to be a woman. The members paid once a collateral of 20,000 shillings besides a payment of 15,000 shillings, to which they added 10,000 shillings every third month. The group had 40 acres of sunflower fields and it was planning to acquire an oil press machine. Individual members had their own business of selling *dagaa* fish, which they went to buy in Mwanza. At the time of the interview in February 2007 the group had 1,289,000 shillings in the bank and they had applied for a further loan from the village. The women had retained a good relationship with their husbands by giving them money to use for the family welfare. The group leaders emphasized the importance of involving the family members in decision making such as securing loans and sharing the benefits with them. Two other Shelui groups, *Agape* (Love), and *Sayuni* (Zion), shared the thinking of the *Jipemoyo* group. One of the members specialized in making and selling soap. SACCOS had Muslim men as members, but the women chairing were Christians and without hesitation they opened the meeting in the name of Jesus. In another group in Kinyangiri, the chairwoman was Muslim and opened the meeting with both Islamic and Christian greetings.

These groups exemplify how rural women take up economic activities against the many odds they face. Far too often women are left alone to take care of the children, even to pay for their education, while the man takes the lion's share of the money the woman earns. A woman told an extreme example of how she had managed to buy a grade cow for better milk production, but the husband snatched it from her to pay for another woman. To avoid such quarrels, women place their money in groups, as it then becomes communal possession which the men cannot control through their traditional control of the family funds. I have been impressed with the firm leadership the women hold but also their sensitivity within the family. The group formation was not based solely on monetary gains but also a social and communal form of rural economy of women. Men form SACCOS with bigger initial inputs and seldom form groups for other services. They have their accounts in the Bank, where the directors have more trust in salaried customers who control their own finances.

Women's social economy in Northern Tanzania

Comparable cases can be found in the Kilimanjaro region. In the early 1970s, a woman in a village in Central Kilimanjaro began collecting banana bunches from other women, packed them on a bus top and went to sell them in Moshi city. Until then, the women were selling only in the local markets on the mountain and men took care of marketing in towns as also the income from the goods, mainly from coffee. By the time Tuulikki Pietilä started her research in 1995, the women in the eastern Kilimanjaro Mamba and Marangu had become established market women. Her study brought up the role of language and gossip in the construction of social reality. While trading, women kept up their moral reputation through their capacity to formulate language. In line with Harri Englund in his study in Malawi, relating to the argument of modernity as the cause of witchcraft by the Comaroffs (J. and J. Comaroff 1996, 260), Pietilä also claimed that women's respect of basic moral values meant that witchcraft accusations were not as likely to occur or be directed to those who "deny their relatedness by not exchanging and sharing with others." Yet, she also shows that "in Kilimanjaro few acts are unambiguous" (T. Pietilä 2007, 10-14). Chagga women had developed an intense interest in the market while they earlier only exchanged bananas from the mountain slopes with the North Pare women's clay pots at the Himo market.

In Mwanga district in South Pare, women entered the market as businesswomen in the 1980s. The research there was supported by the Academy of Finland with the project *Local Actors in Development*, also the name of the publication reporting on that research (Omari 1996, 1998; Mattila-Wiro 1998; Msuya 1993, 1998; Swantz and Tripp 1996, 1998). The involvement in Mwanga led to a two-months course for 12 members in Kauhava Entrepreneurial Institute, Finland, supported by Finnish Development Aid then called FINNIDA. The women initiated an organization of small-scale entrepreneurs of Mwanga or *Umoja wa wajasiria wa mali wa Mwanga* (UWAMWA). Some men joined in. The woman leader had an ironware and fertilizer shop in Mwanga. Another member had a hair saloon and yet another was tailoring, and some men had a wood working enterprise. The others traded food items at the local market. UWAMWA organized annual trade fairs in Mwanga in cooperation with the British supported Trade Aid operating in Mtwara, as there were also visits of women entrepreneurs between Mwanga and Mtwara regions. I was involved in both, having started working with RIPS in the southern regions. A women's seminar was held in Moshi in which a woman lawyer from Moshi was the main speaker and consultant. The women coming from different environments had surprisingly similar experiences in their relations with male partners.

As part of the Local Actors in Development research, Flower Msuya studied the Pare women's involvement in fish trade and made her Master's thesis on it for Kuopio University in Finland. The women involved in the fish trade moved with the itinerant markets on different days and had different ways of sharing their home duties, especially the care of small children by asking neighbours, older children, mothers or grandmothers to take care of them and providing food, especially fish in compensation. Some women took turns fetching the fish for food from the Nyumba ya Mungu lakeshore and sold it at the local markets on the mountain, some even owned a boat and hired men to do the actual fishing. They had the same experience as a woman employing men to cut logs in the forests in Lindi region. Men as hired workers could be trusted only for two to three months, after that they tended to take too big share of the business into their own hands.

Women on the mountain who were not engaged in trade went to the afternoon local markets to do small shopping and meet other women as a social custom. Many further research efforts and activities were initiated in the context of the research on local actors and exchange of ideas between the women groups in Kilimanjaro. Two seminars were organized with the theme of mutual learning, which remained as an idea with continuing activities strengthened by the support of the Trade Aid from Mtwara in organizing bigger market days. A seminar was arranged in which Pekka Seppälä and Bertha Koda took part. They later cooperated in organizing a research conference in Mtwara and publishing a book on women's role in the southern regions (M-L. Swantz 1998; Seppälä and Koda 1998).

The author was also involved in a study of the women in fishing villages near Bagamoyo. NORAD supported a study on the women in the surrounding villages and together with Mwajuma Masaiganah, who was at the time a teacher in the Mbegani Fishing Institute, which was financed and run by NORAD for training fishing officers. We arranged training in smoking the fish for the women engaged in small fish trade who walked there from the neighbouring Mlingotini village. Women could buy and trade less valuable fish in the neighbourhood while the Institute transported the higher priced fish for sale in Dar es Salaam. We invited Gertrude Mongella, the woman minister responsible for fisheries at that time, to speak to the women as she originated from the Ukerewe island of fishermen in Lake Victoria. In 1995 she became UN Assistant Secretary General and also the secretary general of the UN Fourth Conference on Women's in Beijing. Eventually she became the first President of the Pan African Parliament of the African Union. Her presence became a big event in Mbegani as the leaders, including men, wanted to hear her. The differentiation between the level of training of fishing officers and the ordinary fishermen leaving to the sea every night from the same shore is described and analysed in an article together with my daughter Aili Tripp (Swantz and Tripp 1996).

These experiences in Tanzania are evidence that even though small local trade had been part of women's lives in the northern areas since the colonial time, women are increasingly involved with market trade and entrepreneurship, which is unevenly developing in different parts of the country. For instance, in the 1990s markets had not been developed in Mtwara region apart from Mtwara town. Men transported goods from long distances on bicycles but women generally were not yet sellers. According to the Muslim custom, men did the shopping for the families, which meant that women were not supposed to appear at the markets. Women in Mtwara have since started growing and selling vegetables and in Lindi among other activities they are involved in growing and trading seaweed.

The research and further observations indicate that the women's way of working in groups and assisting those in need in Iramba, Mtwara and Lindi regions could be called a social economy. The women participated in the emerging modern economy on their own terms, by joining together and relying on each other for support. Mutuality means, at least conditionally, social and economic security, as such groups give women an economically secure financial base not vulnerable to male interference (Daly and Cobb 1989).

CHAPTER 6

Between the "Traditional" and the "Modern"

Traditionalists and modernizers

In our search for deeper knowledge we have asked the question what motivates people toward development and improvement of living conditions. By asking this question we assume that development is something people see worthy to strive for. It cannot be taken for granted. We have seen that people act differently from what one would anticipate from a reasonable development angle. In a consumer culture the price incentives are thought to be the main motive for improvement of life. The neo-liberal individualistic philosophy assumes that to make individualistic choices means development. If, on the other hand, an individual wants to hold on to her/his life experience and socially proven values s/he is assessed by the standards of "modern" life to be a "traditionalist." All these terms are ideologically loaded.

Development is a normative concept. Development as a "project" aims at bridging the gap between the two domains. It may appear that what a visitor to the country sees as tradition might be "modern" or it may be an invented "tradition" for the one who practices it. I make here reference to the book *The Invention of Tradition* edited and written by Eric Hobsbawm and Terence Ranger. Their use of the term "invention of tradition" shows how what has been treated as tradition was invented, such as the specific cloth models for clans in Scotland commercially introduced. The writers go through such phenomena in Scotland, Wales and the British monarchy, especially in India and by Ranger with reference to British colonial Africa (1983).

When the topic of development relates to the pastoralists the problem of tradition is more complicated. A way of looking at the relation between the "traditional" and the "modern" is to explore the ways in which the traditional can become fashionable, "modern." Much of the traditional is made use of in a "modern" context when it is marketed for tourists. This is the case with the Maasai who at one time threw their clubs at tourist cars, but today sell their tradition to tourists.

The topic of poverty and the use of the traditional as modern are treated well in the collection of chapters, *The Poor Are Not Us: Poverty and Pastoralism in East Africa,* (Anderson and Broch-Due 1999) dealing with eleven different mostly Maasai groups in Northern Tanzania and Kenya. They change the ambivalent application of the concepts of "poverty, " "tradition" and "development. " Instead of seeing "modernity" as the mark of development and traditional habitus evidencing poverty, one sees the fashionably dressed Maasai welcoming guests to posh hotels and then going home take on the traditional habitus as proud pastoralists.

The topic leads us to explore how people in Tanzania move between the traditional (*kijadi*) and modern (*kisasa*). Conceptually this distinction can be made in terms of people's everyday practice, inherited sociality, social fabric, social networks, and care systems, their ways of associating with one another compared with the new institutional forms which have taken their organizational models from the rational-legal civil and political system. I explore interaction between "the traditional" and "the modern" and how these two systems manifest themselves in people's everyday life. I assume that development does not predetermine what it as a "project"aims at in order to bridge the gap between these two domains.

I use the terms traditional and modern metaphorically, ideal concepts, to differentiate between the meanings a group of people gives to the concepts familiar to them from the socially shared context which they identify as an inherited right and obligation, and a concept the meaning of which they have to learn in a previously alien context. Even if people identify many features as African against European (*kizungu*), Indian (*kihindi*) and Arab (*kiarabu*), the difference between traditional and modern is not here understood in these terms. Many features in the traditional category were in their time new innovations, modern, many came from an alien context but have been integrated into commonly shared practice during the past decades or a century or centuries ago. They take their meaning from the institutional context in which they become fixed and their alien connection is forgotten or given a special meaning.

In Bunju, north of Dar es Salaam, I was taking part in spirit possession rituals. I talked with the *mganga* while he was resting and asked about the songs, which I had been recording. I learned of the different status of the songs and drums, depending on their origin. Some songs had heavy content and special power while others were light, entertaining, filling in to make the event a drama of long duration. In reference to the latter he said, "These are only *"kijapani,"* meaning "made in Japan," as earlier cheap merchandise was called (as later it is said "kichina," "made in China"). The songs were imported introductions, not by any means from Japan. They had been "modern," but now they had become part of the ritual itself.

In *kilinge* spirit rites on the coast, all kinds of foreign spirits were entertained and possessed people whom they chose as their seats. The German spirits were raised and made the possessed dance to the tune of a military march, the Maasai spirits made those dancing in tune of them to jump like the Maasai following the rhythm. In the Makonde dance, the *kinyago* figure appeared wearing a white mask, tight leggings, puffy pants and sleeves as the Portuguese knights were dressed when they occupied the coastlands. The white masks represented a whole variety of "foreigners" turned to spirits.

Numerous customs, songs, rites and languages have their roots in earlier foreign contacts, which later have become an integral part of "tradition" or have gone through the circle of modernity becoming tradition and again disappearing. The coastal chiefs had a full Arab apparel with black gowns, white longish shirts, turbans and a sword, as a former chief near Bagamoyo showed me in 1960s. I also witnessed how the Zaramo initiates in their coming out ceremonies *(jando)*, after staying in the circumcision camp *(kumbi)* for four weeks, *kumbi*, got red fez caps at least until the 1970s. Another use of the turbans was as a trademark for the colonial house servants and hotel waiters until the end of the colonial time. These are examples of modern becoming tradition and disappearing when rituals lose meaning.

The sword has disappeared but the turban was the sign of authority in the 1970s bestowed by an Arab spirit *(ruhani)* on a patient who was elevated to the possession state seated on a higher chair to be honoured by the spirit, the patient waiting for the spirit to rise and take its throne. This I witnessed when my adopted *mganga* father Salum Mhunzi in Bunju village invited me to come with him when he went through the first stage of raising the *ruhani* spirit. His own spirits no longer gave him the support or prestige he needed. He was laid on an elevated board and two Muslim *shehes* sat on his sides and started singing and reading verses from Koran trying to raise the spirits. Mzee Salum did not reach the trance state and failed to be raised to sit on the chair wearing a white turban, a higher degree of initiation into the secrets of the spirit world. He never went for the second trial. A patient in his own *madogoli* rites of the Zaramo for whom *kinyamkera* and *mwenembago* spirits were raised wore a turban of three colours, white, black and red, in feasting the spirits (Swantz 1986, 217).

"People" are not one homogenous group. In each community there are "modernizers" or "brokers," the term introduced by Polly Hill in her article "Landlords and brokers: A West African Trading System" (Hill 1996). Gould uses the term to describe teachers, imams, farmers and traders who have a strategizing role in communities (Gould 1997). I give examples of a few cases of modernizers.

A fisherman in Naumbu, Mtwara, decided to send his children to school and educate them. They have become economists, engineers and teachers. One daughter is a Minister in Kikwete's government. He kept one son back home to work with him as a fisherman. Yet he is the only one in his village who educated his children and distinguished himself as a leader. A grandmother in Nakala, whose daughter died, adopted her grandson and saw to it that he was educated, becoming a professor in the university. She is the only one in her community who did so. A small farmer in Kihamba decided to move out of his village because of shortage of land and moved to a village with land for cultivation. He became the wealthiest farmer in the village, developing a mill and a sawmill for others to use. Women in most villages work long extra hours to get school fees for their children with the hope that their lives would be different from theirs.

There are many theories to explain what motivates some and not others. Who become "achievers" and why? There are those who make use of opportunities, those who seek out opportunities, and others who do not. Price incentives are only partly the answer. Individualistic competition and achievement orientation as a psychological precondition partially explain social action or social differences. Cultural explanations state the obvious but do not give satisfactory answers.

One explanation sees the generational gap as the potential point of breaking tradition. In South-Eastern Tanzania young people clamour for what to them seems modern. In the 1990s, the latest fashion was Nike shoes, Chicago Bulls shirts, shiny dresses, and discos. Migrant workers have since colonial times represented such fads. They change status relations in a rural community, but city fads make only superficial changes in lifestyle and do not change production patterns, yet in some cases the returnee has more incentive of starting a shop or a small business, even cultivating different crops. Women's city ways often harden rural resistance toward girls' education. Yet women's contacts with people like themselves in or from other parts of the country influence change.

I interviewed sales people in small shops at the market place of Rwangwa town in Lindi region. Most of the clerks were young boys. I recount their stories:

Abdu has a shop and a milling machine. He finished Primary School in Rwangwa 1982. In 1979 he had started to grow sesame oil plant (*simsim ufuta*) and sold the crops. The money (31,000 Tsh) he used as a capital to start operating the village milling machine because the old one had gone out of use. He had been running it for four years. In 1993 he started a small shop with capital of 269,000 Tsh. He got supplies from Lindi twice a week, paid transport expenses of 300Tsh for a crate of bottles of soft drinks, a crate costing 3,500 sh. He made 1,300Tsh profit per crate, not counting other expenses. He also sold beer tins (500 Tsh/tin) and Konyagi (2,200 a bottle), a Tanzanian alcohol brand. In Lindi he bought wheat flour, sugar, and two types of rice (selling price 350 Tsh/kg); maize he bought locally. He was married in 1991, had four children and was doing well with his small business.

Saidi was sewing dresses with a machine, which he had obtained from his grandfather. He had finished Standard 7 in primary school in 1992 and started learning sewing by sitting and looking when his grandfather sewed. He drew his own models and people chose from them. He had another young man Mohamedi sitting next to him and learning. Two other friends also helped him without any agreed payments. A friend went to get the supplies he needed from Lindi. He paid 500 Tsh for the place on a cemented verandah in front of a shop. There was also another skilled artisan (*fundi*) on the verandah repairing watches and radios.

Wilfred was a tailor. He was from Rwangwa and had finished Standard 7 in 1981. He is one of about 300 Christians in Rwangwa, where he was confirmed. He was sent to Peramiho in Ruvuma for nine months to learn tailoring. He had also gone for refresher courses because he wants to take a grade test, but had difficulties in getting the information. No newspapers came to Rwangwa, and they heard only radio announcements. There was much sewing for Christmas and then again for school uniforms, but they had not been getting the tenders and did not have the money to buy cloth in bulk. He did not have a machine for embroidering either. He also complained that there were too many tailors, competition was stiff, and he depended on his skill and reputation.

Musa came from Lindi town where his father had a store. He started business in Rwangwa in 1989. His father sent him to start the shop and gave him capital to start with. The store building was one of the former Indian stores, which he was renting from a local man who bought it from the former Indian owner. He paid 3,000 Tsh/month.

Abdullah was selling in the shop owned by his brother. He had only started selling the month before. The shop was quite large and had dry foodstuffs, but also a good selection of shoes and cloths. The brother had gone twice to Dar es Salaam to buy things. Rice was sold for 350 - 380 Tsh/kg depending on the quality, and 600 Tsh for beans per kilo. The price of shoes was 3,000-6,000 Tsh, mainly fine sports shoes. Chicago Bulls shirts and leggings cost 4,500 Tsh each.

Omari was renting a good size empty room where he was repairing radios. He had gone to Makangilo Primary School 5 km from Rwangwa and then graduated from the Mtwara Technical Secondary School Form 4 in 1982. He took electric engineering at school and passed the Grade II and III trade tests. He went first to Dar es Salaam to look for work and got a job 1986 at Matsubishi electric factory as a worker. But he said in a factory you do not learn anything, you only work. He stayed there for three years and then decided to come back to Rwangwa 1988. (In Rwangwa there is no electricity.) He pays for the room 1,000 Tsh/month. The problem is getting the supplies. He buys old radios and takes parts from them. The room had a big pile of old radios along the wall on the ground. In the town library there is a solar panel donated by a Canadian library organization. It had gone out of operation and they had come to ask Omari to repair it. He had not learned anything about solar power but he had repaired it. The Library is now open until 10 p.m. so that students can read at night. He said he had used only common sense. Radios were run on batteries.

Rashidi came from Mnero village. He is the shopkeeper but his son Omari actually runs the shop, sells "usual" things. He started the shop 1990 and pays 500 Tsh/month for the premises. He buys things from Nachingwea, which is the nearest town.

Hamisi had a shop full of goods, sacks of flower and rice, hardware, cloth, stationary, etc. He had been a schoolboy and after finishing his school he grew tomatoes. **He** decided to try marketing them along the tarmac roadside going to Masasi. He had to transport the two cans (*debe*) with great difficulty, a distance of 70 km. He sold them, so he decided to go to Masasi to buy some goods, which he thought he could sell in Rwangwa. He added every time a bit more until he had managed to get enough money saved to hire a room and ask for his small brother to come and help him. Now he got his goods from Lindi and was doing well.

Liberu was a metalworker and ironsmith. He repaired watering cans and other aluminium articles, made keys, even repaired bridges. He had learned these skills by himself. He was an elderly man, had played flute and horn at school. He had been an employee of Mackenzie Company in Kilwa, where his brother still lives.

Chiwanga was an ironsmith. He had learned smithing from his father who had died long ago. His son, brother and grandson were working with him and learning. He sold a large hoe for 800 Tsh. He would teach young people if they came as apprentices.

It is noteworthy that none of these examples include women. In a largely Islamic area, women were not yet at the markets, either as sellers. Even doing the shopping was not a general custom since husbands did the shopping for them.

In towns, young men and even women had found ways of employing themselves in trade, small business, food processing, market stalls, cultivation, working as bar or restaurant assistants, or had taken on apprentice jobs on semi-formal or informal contracts. Young men did the marketing with bicycles or sold water from wheel carts, while others carried crops from the fields for payment. Villages had two competing football teams, which encouraged the members to do income-earning work to get the needed equipment. Groups of young men lingered along the roads in groups, often fixing bicycles and loitering.

The generational gap was surprisingly wide between young people who had gone through seven years of school and their parents who had not. The change it brought was not always toward "development." Breaking off from "tradition" is not necessary a sign of progress if it means smoking marijuana (*bhang*) and stealing.

The female youth have earlier had a harder time getting out of the bounds of home, but they too stream to towns and bigger villages where they look for opportunities. There were no women of any age as sellers at the Rwangwa market. Women sell in front of their houses and have to pay fees if the collectors come around. Youth do need challenges and the concern is what opportunities the current situation can give to a growing number of youth who either have come out of school or those who have never even entered school. This is a new phase in young people's lives, lingering with no aim. In the past they ordinarily would have been married and had children.

The lack of control by parents started when the obligatory education was implemented and the Muslim parents were not used to sending their children to school. In the elderly parents' language in Mtwara district, the children were taken from them and the responsibility was now with the school. The hours spent in school from the early morning until late afternoon freed them from the home chores. It became a custom that on the last day after seven years of school, a festive occasion was arranged for the parents who came now to receive their children who were returned to the parents as their responsibility. They had been estranged from the daily rhythm of the home chores as the long school hours had taken all their time from the early morning until late afternoon. The parents expressly felt that they no longer were responsible for their children. So now the children started going out to spend time lingering in groups on the roadsides. What differed from former times was the complaint of a father that they do not control even their daughters' going out, not even in the evenings. The communities could ill afford the idle labour force when even the young women tried to escape the agricultural work, which they would have to do when they got married.

The problem had at least as much with the male elders. They held the land and the cashew trees and kept the cash from selling cashew, or had not taken care of the trees. They did not share the income with either women or the youth. Yet in 1994 when I interviewed the young people in Rwangwa the division with its three wards had earned 1.35 billion Tsh ($2,740 000 million) from cashew nut sales.

Social scientists' solutions

Social scientists and psychologists have dealt with the topic of the generational gap extensively since the earliest anthropologists. Early individualistic economic theories led to psychological explanations and the social action theories led to socially constructed explanations. The early North American anthropologist Margaret Mead dealt extensively with the relationships between generations and the potential for change, which every new generation brings along in both Western and Non-Western societies. She distinguished between three cultural styles, postfigurative, when the future repeats the past, the configurative, in which the present is the guide to future expectations, and prefigurative, for the kind of culture in which the elders have to learn from the children about experiences which they have never had. Distinguishing these as cultural "styles" indicates static "cultures." It belonged to the configurative conceptualization of culture as the basic category of study, which was in mode in North American anthropology and of which Mead was one of the main proponents (Mead 1970).

Picturing the three ways of looking at the generational differences seem useful if they are not taken as differences in cultures, but rather as social processes going on, depending on the societies' outside contacts and their historical experiences. The future may appear to be repeating the past when a community is looked upon from outside, yet people see big differences occurring. The scale depends on the variety of experiences and the significance that a detail has in the total configuration. The process is most harmonious when the past guides the future. The process in Mtwara and Lindi or Iramba villages should be that of prefigurative change, if the school would prepare the children for work and taking initiatives, but as it has been in the school, the learning has been distant from the village life and has not prepared the youth for taking part of the work needed in homes not to speak about giving innovating ideas. In rural villages of Mtwara district, the generational break led to an impasse in the 1990s. The manner of the youth did not encourage the elders to seek their co-operation. The future gets distorted, if the youth do not learn from the past and do not contribute to the economy of their homes. The progress in the villages depended often on an individual leader as in the villages further up the Ruvuma River, where the district was slow to build the school facilities. The village went ahead and constructed a school building on their own initiative. The visiting education officer, unaware of such a voluntary effort of the villagers, condemned the effort as to his opinion the building was not constructed according to the official requirements!

With the return of neo-liberal economics and the rule of the market in the country, the psychological-based theories of achieving society were also on the way back. Before the critique of the modernization theories by the Marxist oriented development theorists McClelland with his *Achieving Society* was the recognized author for the students of development on the achievement motive in economic growth and continued to be so for the modernizing scholars (McClelland 1961). As Seligson explained:

In seeking to determine what produces this psychological characteristic (i.e. need for achievement), McClelland finds that it is not hereditary but is rather instilled in people. It is therefore possible, he claims, to teach people how to increase their need to achieve and by so doing stimulate economic growth in developing countries. McClelland has been responsible for establishing training and management programs in developing countries in hopes that a change in the psychological orientation of public officials will help speed economic growth (Seligson 1984, 53).

Having for long dealt with the social constructivist logic, whereby the social roots of any human development are firmly in place and shape the individual's and the group's way of life, it is hard to imagine purely psychological and consequently individualistic explanations. Similarly, any interpretation which separates culture from its social context and deals with it as a separate unit of study must lean on an economic theory which believes individual to be the decisive actor, apart from her social, material, cultural, political and economic ties which all play a role through the society and its institutions and orient her doings.

Tanzania rejected fully the modernization theories as did the Latin American scholars, but when the socialist economic theories failed they returned to them. As a demonstration of what one could call the "pure" modernization thesis, I refer to a study on becoming modern, which involved a survey made in the first part of the 1980s of 6,000 young men in six developing countries (one African country, Nigeria). For sociologists Alex Inkeles and David Smith who produced it, "underdevelopment is a state of mind." Their belief on youth as the agents of change was firm, with the stipulation that they were male youth: "Without modern men, modern institutions are bound to fail." Like much of the North American social study of modernization it assumed psycho-cultural factors to be primary in influencing transformation.

... transformation is the very nature of man, a transformation which is both a means to yet greater growth and at the same time one of the great ends of the development process. (Inkeles and Smith 1984, 70)

Transformation in the study is described "as the shift from traditionalism to modernity" and the objects of research were to delineate the elements of such personal change, to measure its degree, to explain its causes, and to throw some light on its observed and probable future consequences (Inkeles and Smith 1984, 70-71). They continue:

Our results provide evidence that living individuals do indeed conform to our model of the modern man, that they do so in substantial numbers, and that essentially the same basic qualities which define a man as modern in one country and culture also delineate the modern man in other places. The modern man is not just a construct in the mind of sociological theorists. He exists and can be identified with fair reliability within any population where our tests can be applied. (Inkeles and Smith 1984, 70-1)

It is hard to imagine any more arrogant way of dealing with "cultures" or being certain of the correctness of one's model. The authors seem to think that such characteristics are the precondition to national development and that they can be diffused through the population. The authors claim the characteristics of modern man fit cross-culturally. There is no indication that women also exist in this modern world.

Ethnocentric assumptions about development have fortunately lost some of their certainty during the past decades, but it is difficult to find a way in which one can present the interaction of tradition and modernity as a fruitful, creative way forward, while the powerful have the scientific means of dominating knowledge and in which one has to start from those premises and to work one's way out of them before presenting other points of view. The scientific mode is not only one of domination, it is also Eurocentric or "Northamericacentric" or even "Eastasiacentric," which leaves little room for other approaches.

The core problem in development work is to find ways of moving between the "traditional" and the "modern." "Development" as a project tries to open doors between closed rooms but the mode in which it is introduced alienates often more than it integrates. Participatory development moves between knowledge systems, seeking to bridge the conceptual chasm between people's practical knowledge and dominating knowledge, which claims its base in science, so called rational economics and ever-higher technology.

Political solutions

The demarcating line between the traditional and the modern existed also in the minds of Tanzanian planners, who started to reshape the Tanzanian society after independence. In planning what kind of social services people would need and should have, the independent Tanzanian government gave little thought to existing social organizations and traditional systems of service even if the main architect of Tanzanian socialism, President Julius Nyerere, wanted to keep the link to essentials in the old culture through the concept of *ujamaa*. What it meant in the changing society was not worked out in practice. The concept "traditional" (*kienyeji*) in Swahili, was freely translated into "as the natives do it" and was related to the *ujamaa* concept. When translated as a "sense of caring for extended family members," it was a value worth preserving, but it was poorly worked out in practical terms. The failure of the villagization experiment was an illustration of the difficulty of transferring concepts from one context to another as indicated by Goran Hyden.

When Nyerere elaborated his *ujamaa* policy, he started from three valuable points in tradition. First was "love" or "respect," which really meant "recognition of mutual involvement in one another," i.e., "each member of the family recognized the place and the rights of the other members." The second related to property: "all the basic goods were held in common." The third principle was that everyone had to work towards the common good (Nyerere 1968, 338-9). The general African *ubuntu* and Tanzanian *ujamaa* sentiment even in traditional society had its limits, which defined relationships.

The value of sociality inherent in African culture was not discussed in terms of its significance for the political process or development. Finding a sounding board in tradition, which could act as an inducement for development would have required mutual search of people's cultural roots, which would have gone beyond culture as an *ngoma*. Those who saw no relevance in tradition realized that continuity is not automatic. Nyerere himself also later realized the disconnectedness between "tradition" and "modernity." In a later interview in 1996 he acknowledged that "socialism never mixed well with the traditional ways of African villages." "You can socialize what is not traditional." "The *shamba* (field) can't be socialized"(*Herald Tribune* 2 Sept. 1996).

This is not only true about socialization it is true also about modernization in general. The external and internal domains have to find ways of being integrated as if from within. *Shamba* could not be socialized because working it was people's inalienable right of which they not only made their living but it also linked them to their forebears. The more intimate the strings, which the modern demands touch, the more acute is the question of integration from within. The issue of cost sharing is intimately related with the issue of integration.

Village women and men readily respond to the beat of a drum, and gossip goes around like a wind. In fact, the same word is used in Swahili for a blowing wind or to blow (*kuvuma*) and gossip (*uvumi*). It is harder to get a similar response when ideas from another context are introduced. There is a definite divide if something is introduced as if from outside with little connection with people's own way of leading their life. People do not identify this divide as one between tradition and modernity, they differentiate between what is an integral part of their life-world and what is as if an appendix. The tradition-modernity, development-non-development divide is of those who introduce a development project, whether it is government or some agent. The ideas need to be developed with the grassroots people themselves for the innovations to become their own.

Tradition can be dealt with as modern. By this I mean that tradition can serve society in a modern context in a way that it forms an important building block within the modern context. It is transformed to something new but at the same time anchors the present to the historical past and helps people's own self-integration within themselves and within society of which they are part. The question remains: How could it happen? How can the abyss be crossed? What is the secret of "development," which would not be linked only to the "modern"? What causes true integration to take place?

The difficulty that all well-meaning development agencies have faced in trying to build the bridge of development to developing societies confirms the necessity for integration to take place from within and to leave it for people themselves to find the ways in which it can happen. If tradition becomes transformed as if from within, it generates genuine change, which becomes creative. In my early study I referred to initiators of new features in ritual by an individual who weaves an innovation into the traditional pattern and is seen as an innovator. Also in ritual life there were individuals who were "modernizers" in their contexts (Swantz 1986, 380). In this way, a break in tradition contains at the same time creative continuity. I quote from an excellent collection of essays which touches the issue at hand here,

The unforeseeable nature of contacts with new ideas and people from other cultures and systems of knowledge, and the difficulty to predict consequences even of best external efforts, makes it that much more necessary for communication between the systems of knowledge to be of mutual learning. The development buzzword "participation" must for this reason be people's participation in development of their own making. Participation then means a process of mutual learning in which all participants discover new things and can build together on their new discoveries. This necessitates genuine self-willed, if not always self-initiated, participatory and mutual learning approaches, which open space for creative change.

My own experience in Tanzania includes the time when the country was looking for relevant organizational forms for its political movements. While the party structure as such found models elsewhere and created its own, the people in administration were looking to different directions to consolidate the women's and youth movements' adequate organizational forms.

In the first year of Tanzania's independence, some ministry officials in charge of social affairs called us as members of the YWCA committee together with the leaders of the Tanganyikan women's organization initiated by the colonial women. We met to discuss the possibilities for the new women's organization, but we soon discovered that the Party was taking the responsibility and the politically enthused women's leader from Rufiji. Bibi Titi was one of these leaders. She had been the leader of the women's branch of TANU Party started soon after the birth of TANU 1954. There was some competition should the President's wife Maria Nyerere be elected as the chair, but the strong political fervour of Bibi Titi made her more suitable as a women's leader. The women's union (*Umoja wa Wanawake wa Tanzania*) was started as a countrywide affiliate to the Tanganyika National Union (TANU), in the same manner as

TANU Youth League (Geiger 1987, Tripp et al. 2009). The interest was initially great even if the local organizations' membership and leadership were bound to be selective, as all women did not have time to spend in meetings held in village or town centres. UWT offices formed the contact point when I was working with women in different areas as a researcher.

The informal social relationships were built on the traditional institutional foundations, the women's associations were loose and they did not have leaders in the same way as initiated male age groups had theirs. A political party was different from what had existed before in society and it offered women a new opportunity to associate. As UWT did not receive financial assistance it had to start making its own ways of support in addition to the membership fees. The churches had women's organizations, which continued when UWT ran into difficulties. YWCA has run its hostel and restaurant in a central location in Dar es Salaam and has shared another hostel with the Anglican Church in Buguruni, continuing the work throughout the years until today, whereas UWT had to close its hotel in the capital.

The women who formed small income earning groups in Mtwara and Lindi regions found support from those with whom they had traditional relations. I quote from their own reporting of their ways of organizing themselves in the village of Maheha (Tandahimba) in mid 1990s:

In the villages of Maheha and Jangwani there were in 1990s traditional institutions called *likudi, kwaya (grup of singers), ngoma mkumi*. Women who belonged to one group also related to another group and they continued to help one another. They could join in an income-earning project but also at the same time belong to the traditional peer (*rika*) group or *likudi*. In the same way in *mkumi* you called your neighbours to help you to cultivate your field and then you cooked food for them. Another institution was *chikulu*. In it neighbours or friends worked together for a day on someone's field and another day they went to another person's field. They continued to do so until they had finished everyone's field. This kind of co-operation has usually from three to six members and they are people who have a good mutual understanding.

The women analysed their own groups telling that there were traditional *ngoma* dance groups in which women worked together but also played and danced if visitors or government leaders came to the village. The group members could be invited to other places and dance for a payment, dividing the money following good corporate spirit, helping each other also in cultivation. They had also a combination of women from traditional groups of different ages and income levels in special income earning groups.

During RIPS in the 1990s, women were in a similar manner encouraged by community development workers and aid organizations to organize themselves in small groups. It was evident that the women who formed the small savings and cooperative groups in Masasi and Newala had initial connections with one another. It was also found that the lowest income women and on the other hand the highest social level women did not belong to groups. The case was the same with men, who seldom formed any such groups, which is likely to have changed with the general increase of SACCOS savings cooperative organizations in the country. It has not been possible to follow up how sustainable the women's associations were which operated during RIPS, but the initial national level movement UWT was not active on local level in 1990s.

Experience has shown that traditional organizations from outside the government system cannot be converted to serve formally, but they can be called in special occasions of need to come and bring their contribution. At least two traditional groups were adopted for short periods into the formal structure when people themselves started compensating for the lack of security or came together to protect against cattle thefts. Both groups were first in collusion with the government, but when the events in the areas of their dwellings got out of hand, the *sungusungu* groups were called to help. Mwaikusa wrote about the *sungusungu* after their successful role in controlling witchcraft and misdirected traditional customs, which led to deaths of children in Sukumaland. He ends up recommending that the *sungusungu* should stay in their own traditional role and combine production with security functions, instead of becoming an alternative salaried police force (Mwaikusa 1996). For them, as also for the Maasai, the ability to stay within the bounds of law is not self-evident, since some of their activities have crossed the legal border such as revenging or recapturing stolen cattle.

One way to see which institutions villagers did or did not perceive to be an integral part of their life world was to look how they used the Venn diagram as a Participatory Rural Appraisal (PRA) tool in analysing the village institutions. They often placed such "modern" institutions as the dispensary, agricultural extension, and even school away from the centre or even totally outside the circle, which depicted the conceptual village space. Survey results also commonly showed that teachers and health personnel were left out of the samples because they were not conceived to be part of the village community. Modernity is not attractive if it does not fulfil the needs of the people. A study which counts how many times the agricultural officer visits farmers does not say much if that officer cannot relate to the ideas and ways of planting the farmer practices. I refer to the book on Indigenous Technical Knowledge published by the International Monetary Fund for details of how traditional knowledge can become the modern in an environmentally sound way. This does not mean that the potentially harmful or inefficient practices could not be changed, but that the change takes place through a rationalization process from within the configurations of the existing agricultural practice.

Having a dispensary in the village does not accomplish its task if the workers do not treat the patients with the respect they are used to getting from their traditional healers. Whether they accept their message does not tell anything about the "attitudes of mind" toward modernity. Traditional doctors take care of aspects of health, which the formally organized services do not cover. The true traditional healers go beyond the mere symptoms of health disorders and penetrate to the causes of them. They do not treat patients in fragmented parts but rather deal with people as whole human beings with social relations, which profoundly affect their health. In this they are more modern than the modern health workers. Here and there the organized health system has started learning from the traditional healers something about the significance of the social and psychological factors that influence the healing event. When the traditional healer is respected and his good ways are learned and adopted, the discussion can be carried further.

From the 1960s until the 1980s, big sums of money were still used for maturity rituals, which passed the youth to adulthood, but the same individuals claimed to have no cash to pay the Primary School fees when they still had to be paid. Now the same people pay secondary school fees for their youth. The coastal people considered the social benefit from one school year to be marginal compared to the ritual, which kept them integrated in their society. Today the money goes to medical expenses, whether traditional or organized health services.

Sharing a meal with close kin in honour of the past generations is one of the many preventive rites with which the family health is still upheld in many parts of the country. Within the "traditional" framework it is a reasonable way of sharing costs for cementing social bonds as a precondition for health. When the modern society has driven its youth into drugs and crime and alienated family members in its individualistic pursuit, it will rediscover the traditional sociality as modern. The important message, which the traditional societies have for us, is the theme of this chapter: The modernizers have no secret knowledge of what is modern. Tradition can turn into modernity and modernity can turn into traditional in this globalizing world. The way to learn is through interactive communication and mutual respect.

Sharing services

An effort was made to make the traditional as a building block in the modern context when traditional birth attendants (TBA) were given short training for acting as village midwives in the 1990s. Their services were later rejected for questionable reasons from the point of view of this chapter. The borderline between systems became problematic when people no longer compensated for the service of the traditional birth attendants (TBA), who in an effort to integrate the old and the new received short training of one or two weeks in the formal "modern" health system. Even after a short course, women attending a delivery ostracized her. In the coastal Mtwara district the TBAs told us how after they had been retrained they no longer received even a token gift in kind or cash. Yet rural people had from time immemorial had shared what they could afford for the services which they had received. TBAs retrained in a course of one week or two at most had been transferred to the sphere of the modern and were no longer part of the sharing social system in the minds of village women. The same woman could receive her share when she acted as a young girl's instructor in traditional initiation rites, because there she had not been learning anything new, but women categorized her differently at child delivery as a retrained TBA.

The retrained "traditional midwives" were referred to as *wakunga wa jadi*, but in fact, not all were traditional, some were selected by village leaders from among their relatives, some were chosen because they had a sprinkling of education and could benefit from additional learning. This meant that the position of TBA suffered from being in between the new and the old in an ambiguous way. An old truly traditional but retrained midwife in the village of Naumbu had quit her work because she no longer was called for deliveries, yet the service the TBAs gave was continually needed.

The changes were small but significant. A discussion with traditional healers attending a workshop with medical workers in Newala, Mtwara Region, revealed that the TBAs trained by the Mother-Child Health Training institute (which later was turned into a Public Health Nurses' Training Institute) were instructed to lay the mother on a bed. Mothers delivering in hospital lie on bed but no home tradition of which I am aware in Tanzania delivers on the bed. The mothers and especially the assisting older women would consider this a major change since it does away with some of the basic aspects like the carrying pad, *ng'ata* or *kata,* in the form of a ring symbolizing vagina on which the delivering mother sits, the sitting or kneeling position of delivery and the contact with ground, sometimes with bare ground, other times covered with black cloth, both with symbolic significance. The TBAs might also leave out some soaked medicine leaves for cooling, which have both healing and symbolic significance or they failed to observe taboos connected with delivery. Such small differences transformed the "traditional" into the "modern" and no longer qualified as the shared social system.

The retrained traditional midwives were accepted and compensated after the delivery in a predominantly Catholic community in Mtwara region in which the people knew their fellow Catholic traditional midwives from their earlier practice and they trusted them now after they had increased their knowledge. I interpreted this to mean that both the educational background of women and the fact that many pregnant women were also accustomed to going to a pre-natal clinic helped to bridge the gap between the old and the new. Delivery in the hands of hospital staff took the responsibility away from the "traditional" TBAs. The experiences of delivery in difficult cases have been fairly good in clinics or hospitals. The actors recognized the transfer to another symbolic system and gave up the responsibility when the clinical service was available. Lesser use of hospital deliveries still showed preference to home delivery with its familiar efficacious features (1989b).

There was a difference in the acceptance of the traditional healers, *waganga,* and TBAs. The TBAs were not members of the Tanzanian Traditional Healers' Association, *Baraza la Waganga wa Kienyeji wa Tanzania* (BAWAKITA). It did not seem that ordinary traditional healers, the *waganga,* were ostracized if they were registered even with some instruction in basics of contagious diseases or hygiene. Additional training did not remove the *waganga* from their traditional practice, but the "modern" use of the "traditional" added to the "mystery" of traditional medicine. Registering the *waganga* most likely also enhanced their professional status within the modern structure and thereby integration took place. The *Waganga* serve a wider clientele who came from outside the community and were not as familiar with the local meanings attached to the healer's practice (Swantz 1994). It is possible that the difference between the status of the TBAs and *waganga* is their different social standing as women.

The rural medical assistant (RMA) was referred to as *mganga wa kisasa*, "doctor of today," whereas a traditional healer was called *mganga wa jadi*, or *mganga wa kienyeji*, with *jadi* referring to tradition, and *kienyeji* referring to a native (Swantz 1970). As a consequence of their mediating role, more extensive cooperation and mutual learning could be developed between the traditional healers and health personnel. Healers advertise in newspapers at times as Doctors, not operating in the traditional or modern social context.

In a traditional village society services were mutually provided. How well they serve all requires historical and anthropological analyses in a great variety of societies. In a society based on reciprocity, participants keep mental records of what has been given and what return services are expected. In anthropological economics this is referred to as a gift economy.

In the gift economy, giving is an inalienable exchange, resulting in a balance between giving and receiving. The values of what is exchange are approximated. It is a topic that anthropology has dealt with since Malinowski and Marcel Mauss. The loans can be postponed even over generations, as for instance among the Chagga in the exchange of bride wealth payments: gifts and new loans are given and received based on personal trust (Hasu 1999). In the commodity economy, exchange takes place in impersonal terms, debts to be repaid are documented with interest, and commodities are alienable. Neither side needs to feel any further obligation to each other. In present day Africa, the borderline between the two is not clear, which leaves much room for manipulation and ambiguity, especially in intercultural margins. The small loan systems now promoted universally meet difficulties, when paying back exact sums or paying interest has not been the custom.

In a village community people pay either in cash, in kind or in mutual service. Payments in the form of service are seldom counted in cash value. When women help in serving at funerals, religious and ritual occasions, wedding celebrations or other family or communal events, they are at times compensated in kind or in small cash payments, collected from the participants or given by the celebrant. Poor families' celebrations are small in size and fewer neighbours and relatives attend and contribute. A family or an individual who totally lacks the means to share in celebrations can become withdrawn and social groupings based on wealth, gender, pedigree, educational level, and religion do divide local societies, but social exchange is part of life. In the southern region a man in need told us that he still could go to the wealthy neighbour for a meal when in need.

Women share in work, joining together in small groups. These groups generally have some permanency. Women know whom they can call on for help or to rally together for specific tasks. In Mtwara, the Ministry of Community Development encouraged women to join in small groups of five, but women themselves decided on the size of the groups they needed to take on fishing, farming, milling, cultivating specific cash crops, or running teahouses. In Iramba it was found that if women, who organized voluntarily, took out loans out of their own interest, they also paid back the loans while on the other hand, the returns were slower in the groups which were formed because of the promise of loans. In well working groups, if one woman is ill, others work on her behalf, also on her personal field. The care of children can also be shared. Much of women's work is of such nature that one person can do it only with great difficulty. This is the case with pounding corn, lifting heavy loads on each other's head, assisting in thrashing, going together to distant fields, carrying firewood, digging wild roots in forest, and going to a distance for water, just to mention some.

The analyses made of women's working groups in Masasi, Newala and Rwangwa districts in the southern region showed that those sharing in groups belonged mostly to the middle income category. The poorest quintile could be left without help because they could not reciprocate. The failing support indicates separation from kin and children. The breaking of traditional social systems, especially because of the alienated school youth there are a growing number of villagers who are not in any exchange circuit.

The customary work parties with which people cultivated their fields and build their houses together tend to turn to paid work assignments, although the communal work system is still known and they can be popular because they give people opportunity for sharing a drink together after work has been completed, as was observed in Masasi.

The custom of sharing in social celebrations or in each other's grief has been transferred also to urban situations. At workplaces, lists are frequently circulated for contributions in support of a colleague whose relative has died or who might be celebrating his or her wedding. The personal and social interferes with the official and gives clues about how the bridging of tradition and modernity can take place also in the "modern" context. The amounts of money spent depend on the level of the participants' income.

The estimates of remittances from relatives working outside their home areas vary, but they are substantial, and they have an impact in sustaining life in rural areas in all parts of Tanzania but the differences between areas are substantial depending on the educational level. Funeral rites and home visits because of deaths and illnesses at home and special celebrations, use a large share of migrant family members' savings. Relatives visit home areas and replenish their food stores and get socially significant services from their rural family members and neighbours. The monetary value of care given to a dependent family member, especially on account of deaths of relatives caused by AIDS necessitates contributions as well as the care of a parent, infant or other dependent. Frequently, a single mother in a city sends her child to her mother or grandmother in the countryside to be cared for. When the child grows, s/he contributes to the household by doing chores, but a school age child becomes a liability.

Often the largest contributions people give in kind and cash are for the care of infants and children under five. They also contribute to the care of the disabled and old people with no ability to contribute through work. The value of these services can be estimated from village demography documented annually with lists of the working population, children, school age children, old people and disabled the numbers of which are recorded in village books. The monetary value of time and money used for care can be estimated on the basis of opportunity cost for lost working time or reduced production capacity for those on whom the care duties fall, and these usually are women.

At no time when women were asked to describe their working schedule did they specify childcare or attending the sick or handicapped as a specific care duty. Women's workload also in carrying water often from distant places and the effort it takes to acquire is often not in fair proportion to the payments required from water users. The village women, as a category in Africa I know, should be freed from any cost for sharing in village welfare in cash. The value of the health and social care they give directly covers all that the state can expect from them until the time comes when the state or some form of insurance can cover part of their work.

In this discussion about how modernity relates to tradition for the transition from one system to another, the solution is not just to assume that a new one is better. Traditional institutional links cannot be easily shattered. Taking the traditional tasks for granted and not crediting them in monetary terms is an old fashioned tradition on the side of the self-identified modern relatives. The PRA analyses, such as have been done in the South Eastern regions of Tanzania and in other parts of the world, can potentially become fruitful institutionalized ways of mutual learning which makes interaction not only an occasional event but a continuing process.

Bureaucracies and indigenous systems

Problems under the heading "good governance" are evidence that the loss of confidence in the political system in Tanzania was largely based on the loss of leaders' personal integrity and their inability to listen to the voices from below regardless which political faction to which they belong. The issue is not only a deterioration of social trust within the modern systems of bureaucracy in Tanzania as there are signs of general social disintegration, the symptoms of which are part of the global modernization process.

African society is still a people-centred society in which personal values tend to dominate over economic ones. People-centred societies make transactions on a person-to-person basis. They nurture relationships, which have social value to them personally, but they also thereby accrue social debts. There are relationships in which trust prevails. It is common for educated family members to pay for a relative's education also outside the nuclear family, and indeed, it is common to share in the expenses of funerals, not only among relatives but also in wider circles. Among the women the sharing is more common than among the men. Both the economic and political systems are affected by the cultural features, which on the one hand preserve and protect what is best in their culture, but at the same time the consequences are counted on as corruption in the modern political and economic management systems when they penetrate into the formal system.

A case comes to mind in Maia Green's book on the African priests among the Pogoro. According to her, they lose the priestly honour by walking around wearing secular suits in place of priestly garbs and generously giving to their relatives, which no doubt comes from the church collections. This alludes to the discomfort that a priest working in his home area faces when the traditional society would accept brotherly behaviour and benefitting from one member's special situation. In common clothing, the conscience is not as likely to warn of misbehaviour (Green, 2003).

The bureaucratic system in Tanzania was transplanted from Britain under colonial rule. In Weber's categories, it would belong to the legal-rational type of domination. Under the traditional patterns of social fabric, its application has taken on personalized characteristics. Weber distinguished between patriarchal, patrimonial and feudal forms within the traditional type of domination. The African personalized type is often handled under the patrimonial and neo-patrimonial rubric. Patrimonial rule is an outgrowth of the patriarchal order according to Weber. Daniel Edevbaro refers to Jean-Francois Medard, who uses the term neo-patrimonial to refer to the African state, which is not patrimonial but rather a patrimonialised state (Edevbaro 1996, Medard 1992). Since the patrimonial model is contrary to the basic rules of rational society it is conceived from the start to be corruptive. This in itself is an indication that a system which ill fitted into the prevailing social fabric was another of the "transfers" from a foreign culture, which was bound to become corruptive. However, this is only one of the probable lines of explanation (Theobald 1990; Weber 1968).

We cannot assume that in the traditional system corresponding corruption did not exist. It simply took other forms. The analysis of the issue cannot start from an idea of "pure" traditional society in which high ethics ruled the behaviour. Anthropological evidence shows that there have always been conflicts in traditional societies. The conflicts and fraudulence took another form when there was competition for positions of power: co-wives fought for husband's favours, and witchcraft, sorcery and cursing were used as weapons. On the other hand, in close relations, people, in general, depended on each other and acted on the basis of mutual trust. There now is a break down in the social fabric of the kind, which the parties themselves find hard to explain (M-L. Swantz 1993).

Elders in the village of Kilala (Lindi Rural) complained that their male youth no longer felt the need to come home, even when they were staying in their home village. They "stole" the food items from the fields, went to the roadside to sell the products, ate at the cafes or small restaurants *(hoteli)* or cooked and shared the food between themselves. The elders saw this as the result of school. But when asked if the youth should not have gone to school the reply was that they supported the custom of going to school. On the other hand it was one of the signs that the school had alienated the youth, which I have credited to teaching and in no way do I relate this to pupils' home environment.

In Kihamba (Mtwara rural) we were told that school children had to go and earn their school fees either after school hours or during their holidays, because their parents were unable or unwilling to pay the fees. Many boys did it by fishing. (The school fees were later abolished) (MLS 07/02/1997).

In Mahuta (Tandahimba) women could not get their daughters to come and cultivate after they had been to school. They reported: "They don't listen to us." This was the case if the girls still lived and ate at home (MLS 24/01/1995).

In Nandagala (Rwangwa) fathers complained that they had no control over the girls who went out to the roads and market place in the evenings and at times did not come back before the morning (MLS, 1995).

In Matangalanga (Newala) there were no girls visible in the village centre, we were told that some had gone to town to be maids in people's homes or in bars, but they came when called out. Islamic culture prevented them from loitering in public (MLS 4/1996).

A university professor expressed worry about how to get money to his village to support his parents, when money sent even with a relative never reached the parents. These things happen frequently enough so that the person who allegedly took the money did not even feel shame afterwards. Fortunately now safer ways of sending money have become available, but the elders may not yet know how to handle the modern means.

In Samora and Magumchila (Newala) the older men who owned the cashew trees and the land refused to give part of that land to their youth. They expressed the fear that their sons would sell the land if they gave it to them. The elders would have needed their labour to improve the cashew crop and the youth could earn cash if both would hold to negotiated agreements. Because of the breakdown of communication, this did not take place without outside mediation. During the RIPS program, after the negotiations between the youth and the elders reached an agreement whereby the youth would clean, cut down and prune areas of cashew trees and be given plots of land for growing cassava as a cash crop. The cashew crop improved when the trees were thinned.

The (pseudo) self-sufficiency of the youth not needing the resources of the parents, not even returning to sleep at home requires further comment. The material is from the two southern regions in which the Muslim population is in a large majority and thus also the school as an institution had been thought to have Christian connections. In the areas where the parents had seldom been to school, the gap between generations offers one explanation. It tells something about the school as an alien institution, which had not integrated into the village, as anticipated by the Education for Self-reliance envisaged by President Nyerere in 1967. Customarily the school was conceived to be a government institution which took the students from the parents for the period of seven years. The parents gave up their responsibility since they thought the teachers (and the government) were in charge of the children. The word *kukabidhi,* to entrust, expressed this thinking well. Children were entrusted into the hands of the teachers and at the end of the seven years there was a party for which parents contributed money. This party was talked about as the occasion where the teachers entrusted the students to the parents, *wanakabidhiwa kwa wazazi,* "returning to the parents," indicating seven years alienation from home.

When the school does not relate to the needs of the home environment it indicates an outcome of "modernization" with no questioning how education could better use the resources available. When the ill effects are not questioned and the mode of development is not critiqued, the consequences outweigh the anticipated benefits.

The assumed superiority of the knowledge system since the compulsory education in 1973, was different in the Southern regions from the Northern Tanzania, where by then parents had been already for decades engaged in starting schools in addition to the government and early church schools. As also in Masasi and surrounding areas, where the Anglican and Catholic missions have for a long time influenced the schools' old tradition. This makes them different from the southerners mainly in the Muslim areas. In the coastal, predominantly Muslim areas there had been resistance to schools, which were considered to be Christian, as indeed three fourths of the schools were during the colonial time supported by the missions, Christian churches or parents. This differentiation was made also in Masasi and Newala in Mtwara region where the Anglican Church had started the first schools and the Catholic church did the same soon after, with its well-known hospital and the schools in Ndamba. They were the home areas of strong women leaders, ministers and President Mkapa.

A Muslim Secondary School was started in Kitaya, but it had a slow beginning in mid-1990s. Only few students passed the Standard 7 exams, and the only boy who passed in Kitaya could have continued, but his father did not want him to continue. Lack of trust in the youth prevented the fathers from handing over a piece of land to the sons for the fear that they would go and sell it to outsiders.

In Newala where the contacts with the outside world were of long standing, mothers complained that they could not get their daughters to come and cultivate with them, nor could they do anything about it. They would say, "I have failed" (*nimeshindwa).* The society was facing a social disintegration of a kind which had not been possible in earlier times when the elders controlled the key resources on which the rest of the family was dependent and the mature women were in charge of the upbringing of the young girls.

Mistrust was not absent in the earlier relationships, but the person thereby divorced him/herself from the family group and caused what one could call structured dissention. There were institutional ways of dealing with misbehaviour, whereas the new rules after independence made the elders feel separated from the new system, which was run with little reference to the traditional ways of dealing with relationships. If the participatory approach would have been applied it could have given the people opportunities to freely express themselves and the potential follow-ups could have been made. The participatory contacts with the Newala elders changed their relationship with their youth.

One of the villages near Mtwara pursued a constructive path. A group of seven male school leavers decided to ask for land from the village chairman and were given seven acres. They planted cassava and sold it after the price had gone up and after the first harvest they bought tools to expand the area. They progressed and eventually built a big warehouse in which they stored the harvest and made more money selling the crop when the price had gone up. They married, built homes and had families. They kept contact, inviting me on my visit to Mtwara in 2008 to come and see the encouraging progress.

Changing political environment

The restructuring of the political system through the Structural Adjustment Program (SAP) was severely criticised because it broke the social safety nets by retrenching civil servants who no longer could support their families. The average civil servant salary alone could hardly have sufficed but even before the SAP, there had been a loss of jobs. Many government servants had started income earning projects when feeding the family could no longer be managed with the salary. The low salaries also meant that people were tempted to find ways of pinching from the district funds by using parts of the ordered materials for private purposes such as building one's private house. A common effort is to make an agreement with the seller of a commodity to charge a higher price and divide the extra funds with the seller or to take part of the sheeting of a roof.

The government servants, be they administrative or functional officials, teachers or health personnel, do not necessarily share the social identity with the people among whom they are posted. While the relatives are ready to make use of the position that the bureaucratic system offers, they are angered when it happens in the government system under which they live. Antagonism between the citizens and the bureaucrats heightens when the latter make personal use of their position, be they revenue collectors, police, military, or government officials. The position against rent seeking, in which the civil servants seem to share, is a ready platform for political actors. They can lobby support from the side of those who suffer loss, be it by local or national level leaders.

While there is a general deterioration in the traditional social fabric of society, there are big differences between the areas and the ways in which external forces and influences affect the villagers. When the government confirmed that a gas pipeline would be built from Mtwara to Dar es Salaam and that a gas processing plant would be constructed in Dar es Salaam rather than Mtwara, residents reacted with violent rioting in 2013. The uprising in Mtwara was put down with arms and tanks.

The personalized system has both positive and negative connotations. A social culture which gives support to members of the same group, produces malignant growth outside its own norm system. While I recognize that similar problems are rampant also in cultures which claim to be highly non-personalized (yet individualized), it is evident that the non-personal climate of the total system provides disciplining norms without stifling the workers. Non-personalized behaviour is the norm in countries like Finland, which means that friends and relatives do not have expectations in relation to a relative or friend who makes more money.

Civil service oaths and universally accepted rules do not have the same power when personal relations take precedence in the system. Africa is in no way the only continent, in which this phenomenon appears, Asian countries offer a comparative case, but the role formal rules play in those cultures has a greater variety on account of their longer bureaucratic histories and unequal caste-based social system. Opposite to the alternative to personal rule in Singapore China has imposed strict discipline, yet large scale grabbing of funds are known to take place. Strict discipline is the weapon of dictators. Also in Tanzania prisons have the best discipline and an opportunity for learning of skills in handicrafts but also in agriculture.

In Tanzania reciprocity has been the basic principle governing social relations. One cares for people who identify themselves to be members in various composite groups, be they kin, neighbours, family or work groups. But there are limitations in this social care. The groups do not necessarily take care of all needy members around them. Group members are concerned about old people or orphans selectively depending on what kind of kin or neighbour relations they have or what social debt they have toward them. A society can emphasize social values yet have readily disposable people who today are sent to look for their luck in towns, are labourers on land or prostitutes. This is necessary to remember lest we idealize the social basis of African culture. Yet even prostitutes take care of each other, as the study of them in Dar es Salaam showed (Bamurange 1998).

I quote here a Tanzanian medical doctor who reflected on the way mutuality still operates even when it changes when resources are limited:

I am using food as an indicator of the closeness and how people feel they have to share, even if there is very little. … looking at a family today struggling in a town … the same connectedness because of the economic realities is dying. Now people have to be closer, like a third cousin isn't as important today as that cousin was ten years ago. The first cousin is still very important. I wouldn't tell very big differences between my first cousin and my actual brother . . . I would be calling them my brother or my sister, and you would not know the difference. That's still there, but now we end at the second cousin. The third cousin is still important if you go to the village, because . . . everybody knows everybody, nobody has a private life. Fortunately these traditions are still very strong in villages. We don't have personal time, we don't have personal space, and we don't have therapists. . . People are very afraid of being left alone. People are very afraid of being isolated. People tell you it is better to be poor and have all these people who are part of you, than be rich and be alone. (Interview with Dr. H. in March 1992)

There are situational reasons why a group acts in a specific way but there are also structural reasons developed over time. Shortage of resources and inability to appropriate new ones leads to limiting the contribution to a unit, which the custom would anticipate. These are some of the reasons why I have chosen "social group" as a unit of analysis because a group can be composed of people in differing relationships and situations. The same person can belong to many groups at one time or change membership over time depending on circumstances. Life can become very selective. Especially women belong to several groups as the situation demands.

Concluding thoughts on traditional and modern

A clear difference was drawn between tradition and modernity when the planners of new society started to reshape the new institutional structures after Independence. The independent Tanzanian government gave little thought to existing social organizations and traditional systems even if the main architect of Tanzanian socialism himself wanted to keep the link to essentials in the old culture. The concept of "traditional," in Swahili *kienyeji*, freely translated "as the natives do it," was readily rejected by the educated. While Nyerere elevated the well-recognized *ujamaa* familyhood concept, which could be translated into a "sense of caring for extended family members," as a value worth preserving, it was poorly worked out in practical terms.

The failure of the *ujamaa* village experiment is an illustration of the difficulty of transferring concepts from one context to another. There were many factors which contributed to the failure, and as shown above. Also Nyerere recognized this after he had resigned as president. It does not seem that the value of what in this research is called "sociality" inherent in African culture was discussed in terms of its real significance for the political process or development. Finding, a sounding board in "tradition," which could have acted as an inducement for development would have required mutual search to people's cultural roots, which would have gone beyond culture as a *ngoma*. Those who saw no relevance in referring to tradition perhaps realized that continuity was not automatic.

It is interesting to note that Nyerere himself realized the disconnectedness between tradition and modernity when he was quoted as saying that socialism never mixed well with the traditional ways of African villages, as you could not socialize what was traditional: "The shamba (field) can't be socialized" (*Herald Tribune*, 2 September 1996). The external and internal domains have to find ways of being integrated as if from within. In Tanzania in the areas where clan land was inherited through generations as in Kilimanjaro and Karagwe, *shamba* could not be socialized because working it was people's inalienable right, linking the owners to their forebears. The more intimate the old ties, which the modern demands influence, the more acute is the question of integration from within.

PART
II

CHAPTER 7

First Steps in Participatory Research

In the following chapters I go back to the fall of 1972 when I started planning the first projects in which I applied participatory approach in research as a Senior Research Fellow in the Bureau of Resource Assessment and Land Use Planning, BRALUP (later named the Institute of Resource Assessment, IRA) in the University of Dar es Salaam. The post gave me an opportunity for research oriented toward the nation's development. It gave me first an opportunity to start in coastal villages with students as assistants on their long holiday beginning in spring 1973. The close contact I had with villagers in Bunju made me believe that it was possible to develop co-operation with villagers using the participatory approach.

It seemed inevitable that research conducted in a developing community in a newly independent country could not be unrelated to the process of planned change. Building the nation on people's work demanded taking their voices into the research process. BRALUP researchers were engaged in projects in Rufiji district south from Dar es Salaam, thus the problems and needs of the communities in the district formed an obvious challenge. The program fitted well into my previous experience as I could extend the research to some villages in Bagamoyo District and one even to Bunju.

The new opportunity gave me freedom to innovate and introduce student assistants to research in an unorthodox way, studying the situation of the school leavers in the coastal area. The research was acceptable to the director of BRALUP but the approval from the Scientific Research Council caused difficulties. Implementing the project was well on its way when I was informed that the research approach was not acceptable. The Area Commissioner in Bagamoyo refused my presence but did not drive away the students. Then a letter from a higher Government officer came to the authorities not to obstruct the study, which was found to be in accordance with the national policies. The research approach in my earlier study was not new even to the President and I believe this fact removed the obstacles.

There was questioning also among the colleagues in the university. I presented the basic principles in a BRALUP seminar to gain understanding for the plans and they were recorded in a service paper *Participatory Approach to Research*, which explained the research project.

The participatory research approach combined action and training. I anticipated the following requirements of the project (M-L. Swantz 1976):

Research conducted in a community should be planned so that some part of it directly benefits that community. It should have a participatory and action oriented approach, engaging the community members' cooperation through a conscious effort in identifying their problems and in solving them. Temporary solutions are to be incorporated in the long-term solutions.

Research carried out for the benefit of, or otherwise concerning a group of people, should involve these people in different parts of the research process whenever practical. People can assess their own potentials.

When possible, research should be planned in bigger units and anticipate interdisciplinary research. Practical needs require practical solutions, which in turn necessitate the cooperation of research workers and local practitioners from different fields.

Research involving people is an educative process for all the categories engaged in the process. This needs to be taken into consideration in the planning.

The participatory research projects were planned simultaneously as training projects for all the categories of participants involved. Ruth Besha acted as a research fellow from the Institute of Education, observing the education students. The projects inevitably had political implications, which had to be taken into consideration in a country seeking to engage its people in nation building calling them farmers and workers (*wakulima na wafanyikazi*). According to the socialist system, people of all ranks were called *ndugu* or sisters and brothers, different from today's emphasis of high titles (Swantz 1976).

Paulo Freire from Brasilia had visited Dar es Salaam University in 1971 before I had returned to Tanzania. My ideas echoed his message, which was about dialogue and conscientization through education (1970, 1973). I discovered that adult educators were acquainted with Freire's thoughts, and I received support from the Canadian Budd Hall who was heading the adult education research program. He began to combine Freire's ideas with my participatory approach. In the Adult Education department they planned and implemented a participatory project on improved grain storage. Budd Hall included my basic principles in his first article on participatory research in *Convergence*, the journal of the International Council for Adult Education. He became chief editor of this journal upon his return to Canada (Hall 1975).

The director of BRALUP Adolfo Mascharenhas gave me freedom to plan the research. I benefitted from the custom of the university to employ students as research assistants to the senior staff members and received funding for my student assistants from FINNIDA, the Finnish international development agency.

The first participatory research and training project

The first project using the participatory approach was Youth in Action Research. The focus was on the school leavers and learning skills for making living. I had written the first paper on informal practical training for school leavers in 1955 while I was a teacher in a Girls' Teacher Training and Middle School in Ashira on the slopes of Kilimanjaro mountain and thus knew the need of some guidance for school leavers. I was especially thinking of the women students in the coastal areas. We found that there were no female school leavers yet in the Rufiji villages we were studying.

The first task was to introduce the students to the principles of participatory research and the research in the conditions of village life. Some of the students came from the education department and joined others after doing practice teaching. The applicants for the project took part in preparatory training sessions to acquaint them with the aims of working together with the school leavers, village leaders and officers and finding ways of initiating simple projects. Visits were made to a Small Industries workshop, vocational training institute, and the concerned ministries. Budd Hall sent a visiting Canadian visitor to attend the preparatory sessions as in his opinion we were the only ones at the time following Paulo Freire's ideas in practice. For me it was the first time I heard about Freire and his visit to the university. Many mention Freire's influence, his message on conscientization and working with people as their inspiration for engaging with people as an educational approach but initially his method was not applied directly to research (Freire 1970). Making the former informants to be participants in knowledge formation aimed at making them aware, conscious of their opportunities as responsible actors in the situation, which they faced locally and nationally.

Thirteen students volunteered and were placed in Ikwiriri, Ngorongo, and Mpima villages in Rufiji District and in Miembe Saba and Mbwawa villages in Bagamoyo district, and two students were placed in my former study village Bunju in Mzizima District. Two female students worked in Mpima and two in Mbwawa. The students had a long holiday of three months and some continued during consecutive short leaves. The education students first did practice teaching and joined the others for the rest of the leave. The preparatory training was hardly adequate orientation for working in areas totally different from the students' own home environment, but after some hesitation they found it encouraging.

A survey of school leavers was made prior to the students' presence in villages as also a sample census of the school students in the Rufiji villages, with the aim of getting a numerical account of the school youth and the attendance in the upper levels up to the seventh grade. (M-L Swantz 1974, 1975a, 1975b, 1976).

The participatory research aimed at finding out the possibilities for youth in general and school leavers, in particular, what potential these opportunities had for their own advancement, for participating in the development of their villages, and for becoming productive members of society. Another aim was to challenge the involved villages to a new awareness of the potentialities of their youth to become a transforming force within their communities. The youth often left for Dar es Salaam in search of work or to loiter around. In general, the school leavers did not see that agriculture was for them and regarded it as something left for older women. This attitude has continued until this day.

Rufiji was the first area where the villagization program had been carried through. The exceptionally high floods in mid 1960s had destroyed some of the villages along the river and a few people had drowned. It gave the government the opportunity for implementing the first villagization programme and building good standard houses in villages on higher ground. The new village sites lacked the regular floodwaters for fields, causing problems for cultivation. Water pipes had been drawn and tanks erected for drinking water, but water could not be used even for growing vegetables, as the youth discovered when they needed it for their garden project in Mpima. The girls' regular attendance in schools was only beginning.

On the way to the destined villages in Rufiji the female students wanted to show they were modern and against advice came dressed in slacks. When we stopped to have a cup of tea entering Rufiji district in Kibiti local men fired condemning remarks about the improper apparel of the female students, who quickly learned what was proper attire in the solidly Muslim district.

The students selected to go to Rufiji had initially expressed fear, as the area was known for its witchcraft, especially after reading in papers about cases leading to a death sentence in the High Court. Only one student left soon after arrival, not being able to take the sleeping arrangement offered in a half-built family house. To show the homeowners that their facility was adequate, I stayed in the room on a visit for one night. After acquainting themselves with the villagers, the male students found the boys interested in gardening, fishing or carpentry projects while the female students in Mbwawa village in Bagamoyo district started sewing and gardening with the girls. The female students in Mpima discovered that there were no female school leavers or even in the upper level in school. They worked with women and did gardening projects with the girls but also helped in care of their families. It required a change in attitude, as the reality they met was different from their thoughts upon arrival.

The practical efforts were truly co-operative as the students were as inexperienced as the local youth in the activities the latter proposed as also in the needed skills but the local students had the advantage of being more familiar with the environment. Together they sought help of experts and acquired the needed tools. The youth in Ngorongo took initiative in getting the seeds, tools and eventually even permission to obtain the water from the village tank after negotiations with the district headquarters, which the students also managed themselves. In Ikwiriri, the village with the ward head office, carpentry was initiated and fishing rights and organization negotiated, fishing was done also in Mpima.

There were many handicaps and the time was too short. In Miembe Saba, the students were criticized for the expensive way of acquiring the wood as material for the carpentry. The university students' learning process was the most important outcome, not only because they learned how to plan gardening projects, to start carpentry workshops and do fishing! They wrote one report on the research findings for their own subject and another about their experiences in being engaged in participatory research. They had encountered difficulties in adjusting to the conditions and complained about eating facilities and inadequacy of the money they had for buying food, but they also wrote very positively how much they learned during the research process and how the experience had changed their way of relating to people.

I summarized the research results about the students' work using the students' reports and the discussions with the members of the village committees in a Research Report (Swantz, 1975a, 1975b). I had kept contact with the village leadership prior and during the project and Ruth Besha had visited the villages while observing the educational students' teaching. She collected the students' reports after the project.

I quote briefly from two students' reports on their learning, which was considered significant also by the university leadership (Swantz 1975b, 1975c, 1985):

"I have come to realize (while in the village) that this was a unique programme. While the traditional research methods take the local people as objects of research, ours took them as actors, in fact the stars of the whole process. This was a revolution in itself."

Despite all the problems, the method whereby researchers stay and work with the local people is the best one, as besides bringing youth of different educational levels together, it also gives local people opportunities of learning from the researchers. During our stay in the village, people of different ages talked to us and asked important questions. At the same time we learnt a lot from the local people during our informal talks. People talk freely with people with whom they are acquainted. (Swantz 1976, 120)

From the start, PAR aimed at making research an agent of transformation in the rural community. It had to be of interest to the people in the studied community involving them in becoming aware of the problems they had which then became the study problems for finding solutions. For utilizing the educational and motivational potential of such a study it should be a common effort with villagers, elders, administrators and educators. It took time for the villagers to cooperate in such an unconventional approach, but there were those who supported the good intention, whereas it offended the authority of some of the local political and administrative leaders and could raise occasional protests and initial disapproval by other research personnel. TANU, the political party had such control over the policies and of the villagers that such research approach created the sense of interference and threat. Anyone, particularly foreigners entering the village, had to report in the village office and the confidence of the local leadership had to be gained first. My fluent Swahili and prior experience of thirteen years in the country turned out to be a threat.

The university students reported differences in the living habits of the coastal Muslims with those in their home areas. They observed difficulties that people faced but they also noted positive aspects such as the cleanliness of the areas and the clean habits in the use of the toilet. Even a child went to toilet with a dish of water. When the students as strangers in the area were responsible for the projects, they realized that the youth had knowledge they lacked. This was a decisive discovery as it revealed the basic idea of participatory research in which the researchers produce knowledge together with the researched. The students had to turn to the local government and party leaders and the parents for information, knowledge and skills. When the students became aware of the difficulties the youth faced in trying to gain suitable work, their sense of superiority as learned people faded and they understood the urge of the local youth to run away from their home areas in search of opportunities.

It fell on Ruth Besha and the author to share the supervision and participation and to provide assistance when other sources failed. Some of the funding for the resources was received from the Community Development Fund, which at that time was run by Lady Chesham, who had been an elected European Member in the first Parliament when the country was gaining its independence. Reading the student reports impresses me even today (Swantz 1975c). Staying in facilities villagers provided created trust, which occasional visitors coming with questionnaires don't gain. The university students realized the superiority they came with and the opportunity that this approach offered them for mutual learning since they came from such different backgrounds from the villagers. The students observed in the villages near Bagamoyo town that their hosts ate cassava with boiled greens and were not interested in extending their cultivation even when they praised the fertility of their land and easy access to water. The youth followed the example of their parents and did not cultivate marketable products, but rather sought casual jobs that gave quick cash. This made the introduction of gardening a fruitful educational enterprise, even with the difficulties in implementation.

An evaluation was made half a year after the first participatory research. Meetings held with the youth brought surprisingly positive results even if the activities continued with reduced numbers of school leavers. After the short time, exposure activities were sustainable only where some village leaders continued to give support. However, the quoted thoughts from the evaluation meeting arranged for the school leavers who participated in the research project in Rufiji indicated that they had learned self-critique and ideas as part of the planning:

We lack motivation and heart (*moyo*). We have not put ourselves into these projects as we should have. Money does not build up a project, the heart does. We had help in organizing ourselves. We need that help. We also need someone to come and continue to encourage us from time to time. But even more, we need expert help. We need someone to tell us why our tomatoes did not grow and why our cabbages did not take root.

We need tools.

We need to learn new things.

Some of us need to go for a few months to learn skills so that we have teachers among ourselves.

How could we get a football to gather more youth?

When we earn money we must not use it right away. We must put enough aside to develop our work. We must learn how to keep money.

These are some of the points the youth had identified and listed even more concrete ideas. In Mpima, Rufiji, where the evaluative meeting was held, the school leavers were engaged in the projects they started. The evaluative reports in Bagamoyo District gave a more discouraging picture. A quote from a university student stated:

"Negative response from the local people was mainly due for our way of life during our stay, contrary to what they would have expected from the introduction during the ten cell leaders meeting, especially from Rugaika, who was dressed in (locally worn) *kanzu,* ...we simplified ourselves too much to the extent of being feared by the village as being spies. He (officer) commented that we also did too much manual work contrary to what they expected of university students". (Notes by W. Rugaika 04.05.1973)

The statement leaves room for different interpretations. The university students were not in a position to continue more than two terms, but incorporating officials helped continue the project in Rufiji. The short time frame did not integrate the projects sufficiently into the local government program, the common weakness in all "projects." Several village leaders agreed it was a substantial learning process and the students' reports offered material for my research report on the youth development.

The students' changed attitudes toward the villagers evident in their reports impressed the Chief Academic Officer Isaria Kimambo, who circulated a letter to the university departments recommending such a research approach for using student assistants. I have met three of these students in later life, one employed in the Party Central office, another in international UNICEF service and the third as a teacher in the Cooperative University in Moshi. They credited the influence of their first research experience to their later life (Swantz 1974, 1975a; 1976, 119-126; 1982, 117-130).

Research with women in Rufiji

During the students' research period I was also personally engaged in research of women's situation in Rufiji region (Swantz 1985). I came to know the areas where the villagization had not yet been completed but the implications of it were felt in the remaining areas.

The use of a big university Land Rover for transporting the students enabled me also to make research visits on truly poor roads, leaving me walking and listening to women narrating their life histories (Swantz 1985). In the southern edges of the river people living still in houses on stilts had been informed by the government officers that it was an unacceptable way of living. People's arguments of being used to the floodwaters, moving with boats, fishing for food and cultivating when the waters receded made no impression on the decision made. A colleague from BRALUP had visited earlier the same village with his students by a boat, and joined their appeal to the decision makers that they would listen to the stilt dwellers. One of the students was Benno Ndulu, who later became a professor of economics at the University of Dar es Salaam and eventually the Governor of the Bank of Tanzania.

I passed the stilt dwellers on my way walking for many hours from Mohoro to Mbwera by the Indian Ocean. The stay in Mbwera gave me insight into the women's lives, recorded in a chapter "Woman´s Road through History and Myth" in my book on Tanzanian women, *Women in Development: Creative Role Denied?* (1985). Women told me how their throats had dried so that they no longer could sing in the girls' maturity rituals when they had lost their home sites. This left a deep impact on me.

Girls' education continued to cause problems in Rufiji. A teacher, Dawa Salum Mkono, was determined to make sure that the girls were not removed of school when they reached maturity. As the only girl in the class, she had not been able to continue her school in Rufiji. She was sent away from home because her father as a colonial government messenger was obligated to educate at least one child and her brother was too old to attend. Dawa came back to her home area as a teacher and was determined to see that girls were educated. One of her students was forcefully given in marriage to an older man who had paid the bride price (*mahari*). Dawa contacted the police, went with him to the house where the wedding was to be celebrated and forcefully took the girl out. She had the law behind her action since the independent government had decreed education to be compulsory. The parents were even threatened with imprisonment if they prevented child's education. The survey in 1973 in Ikwiriri showed as many girls as boys enrolled. The attendance was not ascertained.

When BRALUP was engaged in the study of Rufiji, staff members from different disciplines were conducting other research there. The advantage of participatory research became evident when members of the field force took one female researcher for inquiry on the suspicion of putting a bomb into the ground while she was digging for soil samples. President Nyerere was expected in the area, which kept the military forces on guard. Participatory research involving local people would have prevented such suspicions.

Malnutrition study

In 1973 and 1974 the use of PAR was extended to women's projects. A followup project called *Action Research on Causes of Malnutrition* was carried out in Kibosho and Uru wards on the slopes of Kilimanjaro in Moshi District. It was conducted by six female university students in cooperation with the local Nurses' Training School as part of their community health-training program and with the Nuru Nutritional Rehabilitation Centre, run under the Kilimanjaro Christian Medical Centre. The university students stayed in their home areas for three to four months and the nursing students two weeks each in the same villages with them to find out the socio-economic causes of increased malnutrition and its relation to the position of women. The sociologist working in the Centre Ulla-Stina Henricsson and an American graduate in sociology Mary Zalla, resident in the area, in cooperation with the Nuru staff took part in the planning and carrying out of the project.

The mothers selected for study had spent time with their children at the Nuru centre for the rehabilitation of children's nutritional status while the mothers were learning nutritional feeding habits and did gardening in a designated area for it. Each student assistant was responsible for studying the situation of a mother who had been in Nuru for rehabilitation. They also looked at five neighbouring homes of such a mother for comparison. The students regularly visited the homes of the affected mother and made visits to their neighbours who had no apparent nutritional problems. I got acquainted with the setting when visiting homes with the students. The students had a questionnaire bound into a booklet of half a page to fill after the discussions they carried with the families. The students kept impressive daily diaries in which they noted detailed observations recording discussions about the customary aspects of life and prevailing beliefs and practices related to the diagnosis, causes and cure specifically of protein calorie malnutrition (Swantz 1985).

The motivational effect of the nutritional training the women had received was assessed and by contacting the neighbours and relatives ways were found to motivate them toward common responsibility and caring for an ill-nourished child in their midst. The rotating mother-child clinics were held in the neighbourhoods but it was hard for a mother of a small child to walk to the dispensary at some distance, leaving other small children home, just to mention one problem. When mutual confidence was gained, the problems could be discussed openly. Comparison with the conditions of the healthy neighbours focused on the economic and social differentials.

Mary Zalla had participated in the earlier UNICEF Child Study in the area. According to its findings the Chagga children were found to be the property of their fathers, but the mothers were responsible for their feeding and general welfare. The economic conditions were getting poorer because of the low coffee prices and the changes in the production system. The differentiation even between closely related families was evident in the studied wards, and the show of neighbourliness could not be taken for granted. The head of the Nutrition Institute in Dar es Salaam could not believe that such cases could be found on his mountain

The analyses of the results and reading the students' diaries showed amazing possibilities in such an approach to research. The approach was made use of later in an extensive participatory health-training project (Chapter 9). The striking inequality between related neighbours indicated that the money economy had its negative consequences.

No one factor could be isolated as the main cause for malnutrition. The land shortage for growing food was one, and the sunken coffee prices affected the income, generally considered to belong to men, who drank as did the women at times. In a few cases the ignorance of the mothers contributed to malnourishment. The intention of the participatory approach was to get deeper to the actual situations than the general causes found in the surveys. In discussions with the parents the research assistants could find reasons why the malnutrition had affected one child and not others and why the child had not received attention earlier. They learned what were the relations with other family members and the neighbours, how the feeding was done, how the food was prepared, how it was divided between the family members, and how much neighbourly care or assistance was taking place.

The students found that such a research approach could raise the level of motivation and some of them continued their interest in the women's situation in their home areas afterwards, trying to start an income earning project with them, initiating a cooperative effort of a few fathers of the problem families to make educational toys. That project might not have continued but it raised the fathers' consciousness of their responsibilities toward their own children. Students gave the local officers names of the people in dire need of food distribution, which alerted them to the possibilities to plan the underprivileged in mind.

The malnutrition studies had customarily been made by measuring the food intake of children in addition to conducting household surveys. Our study drew interest among nutritionists in Norway and Finland and this new mode of nutritional research was discussed by international nutritionists in a seminar in Dar es Salaam in which the Tanzanian nutritionist, Eva Sarakikya, cooperated with nutritional specialist Wenche Barth Eide from Norway. Her co-workers then applied participatory research in their nutritional program in Sri Lanka. Also professor of nutrition Antti Ahlström in Helsinki university came along and showed an interest in broadening the scope of the teaching, which was based largely on the chemical composition of the nutritional ingredients.

Research with working women

A number of female research assistants were involved in several studies on working women's situation in the growing city of Dar es Salaam. In these studies, participatory approaches were supplemented with questionnaires (Swantz 1985).

Three students (Deborah Fahy Bryceson, Hilda Ausi and Fatuma Macha) studied the situation of women cleaners in the office of the Prime Minister, on the University premises and in the Ministry of Education. They combined the study with literacy classes for women cleaners. Deborah Fahy Bryceson on her way to becoming a well-known professor in women's studies was a student in the Department of Geography at the University of Dar es Salaam. The assistants carried out motivating talks with the women workers, who were encouraged to write about their own lives. The discussions, combined with improved reading, encouraged the women to be active in advancing their social and educational level. Deborah later reworked the chapter on the urban women into her fluent American English for my book *Women in Development: A Creative Role Denied* (1985).

A social studies student Severa Mlay did a participatory study in a cashewnut factory, which employed over thousand women workers. She experienced work-related hazards of corrosive acid on bare hands, which together with the degree of specialization prevented her from participating in the actual work process. But she spent time with the women observing their work and speaking with them on their time off work. She helped to mobilize the women as members in the labour union who took the poor working conditions to the leaders of the workers union and they in turn demanded improvements from the Italian-owned company.

Two female students from the Faculty of Law cooperated doing participatory research near their homes and in one of the cooperative *ujamaa* village in Kagera region. They deepened their understanding of the reasons why women left their homes to become prostitutes in Nairobi and Dar es Salaam or as the later research has established, eventually to become entrepreneurs (Swantz 1985; Rwebangira 1998). They returned home with sewing machines and gifts to their fathers, who according to a newspaper article, encouraged their departure. Upon their return, several established themselves as respected farmers. Both students, Magdalena (Kamugisha) Rwebangira and Regina (Mutembei) Rweyemamu became renowned lawyers. Magdalena Rwebangira became an activist and advocate for women's rights and she also continued writing about the legislation on women's rights. Regina Rweyemamu was the Commissioner for Labor and later a High Court judge.

Research on skills and education

The Department of Development Planning in the Central Government received support from ILO for making a survey of the skills and the general educational level of the rural people. The Manpower section of the Ministry of Labour asked BRALUP to make a preliminary survey in three wards before launching a full-scale survey. With a Swedish colleague Jan Rudengren we proposed that a participatory approach would be used to make the pilot skills survey (1979). Three teams were formed from different sectors of government and adult education with BRALUP in charge for the pilot project in three districts. After the preliminary project in Bagamoyo district, the full-scale participatory surveys were made in Kyela in Mbeya region and Usangi division in Kilimanjaro region.

Prior to the survey, a self-analysis was made in the village meetings called together and concluding village meetings were carried out after the survey results had been worked out. The self-analysis was a crucial aspect of the survey because the participating village members in Usangi had a chance to discuss the purpose of the survey and the participatory way in which it was carried out in preparation before implementation. Villagers of different levels of learning were instructed to carry out the survey and then with guidance they did the preliminary processing of the results before the final scrutiny. The major part of the questionnaires were accurately filled, a good share by the people themselves. The study gave the villagers an opportunity to identify their unused resources and capabilities (Swantz 1976).

The research personnel from the university followed up parts of the process. In Usangi I found the village meetings impressive in the sincerity with which people discovered their unutilized possibilities and recognized weaknesses. Whether people filled out the questionnaires by themselves or with assistance was in itself a literacy test of the household. The outcome was the villagers' assessment of their own educational level, the extent and utilization of their skills and the available natural resources in 46 villages of Bagamoyo District and Kyela and Usangi wards in eastern, southern and northern part of Tanzania. The villagers' self-assessment raised active discussions in village meetings and the results made them aware of gaps in skills, unused resources, and it created new awareness of their development potentials.

As is common in surveys, the weakness was in the follow up. It was to be done in the village meetings by the district education officer, who participated in the process and had copies of the survey results. Official survey settings seldom make allowances for the surveyors' continuing contact with local participants. The written documents went to the ministry and the district education offices for guided action and local reflection. The utility of the participatory approach is that the benefits of the approach become explicit already during the process, even if the follow-up fails.

I continued to follow the developments in the early 1980s in Usangi and on the planes below the mountain in Kwa Koa, later located in Mwanga district, in which Usangi became a ward. As part of the survey, the villagers made it obvious that they had many smiths who asked for improved working tools and methods. The area was also well known for fine pottery and the women had asked to get a shelter to dry the pots and a better oven to bake the pots. The ward was a home of a government minister who as a follow-up saw to it that the buildings for ironworks and carpentry workshop were built with fine machinery and rooms made available for individual workshops in separate buildings. The workshop was for some time scarcely utilized because the potential users of the workshop, the smiths and the women potters who had asked for the support, had not been consulted on what kind of tools and facilities they would have needed. The smiths found the machinery out of their level of skills and no effort was made for their younger apprentices to be trained in the use of the machinery. The buildings were eventually made into a vocational school. These are common failings in development projects.

The women's lot was even worse. When they asked for space in the buildings, they were told that they would get it in the phase two, but there was no plan for such a phase. The women potters rented a mud house with leaking roofing next to the workshop and they were not permitted even to use the workshop truck to transport their pots down the mountain to the market. With some interference the potters were eventually permitted to use one of the smaller rooms in the workshop. Very fortunately a Swedish NGO came to the rescue and in the 1990s they had a spacious brick house and a fine oven built for their work. They were making big flowerpots for Arusha hotels besides the traditional pots they marketed and their business was flourishing. A Danish NGO had helped to start a machine made pottery project in the neighbouring Ugweno ward and some Usangi women had received training in this more advanced workshop. The experience was one of many which made the researcher aware of the need to pay special attention to continuity.

Research was made contextual and combined with participation and action, which in today's terms would be called community-based research. The researchers and the researched interchanged places in the course of communication in exchanging knowledge and understanding people's problems. The students and the research partners learned to question the role of the researcher and to analyse how her/his presence influenced the research situation. PAR was in line with the political theory in which "peasants and workers" were to be the builders of nation. Participation of the citizens in their own development also meant participation in the political process. The legislation for the legal powers of the villagers was implemented in 1975 when the Village Assembly was granted legislative powers. It increased the possibility of the villagers for participation in the local political decision-making, as the village assembly was to meet regularly with powers to elect the village leaders and to make decisions about village affairs.

In conclusion

The planning and implementation of the early participatory research projects led to the serious effort of developing the participatory mode of research in developing contexts. After applying PAR for half a century the boards and councils granting research funds still need to be convinced that it has its merits. The participatory research has been called engaged and community based research and various other names. The development research and anthropology have gradually given space to the practice oriented research and learning. While the Sage Handbooks for Action Research had a small minority of anthropologists among the writers today there are anthropological handbooks for participatory action research relating to health. More can be read in the *Companion to Medical Anthropology* by Merrill Singer and Pamela Erickson (2011) and *Introducing Medical Anthropology: A Discipline in Action* (2007) by Merrill Singer and Hans A. Baer.

The impact of the participatory approach to research is not in its theoretical insight. The results become evident in practice while it can also be defended theoretically. Participatory research does not always end in action, rather in self-reflection, learning, and in greater understanding of the participants' own researched situation. The reason for scarce action is often circumstantial, but engaging people equips them to learn to analyse their potentials and to face the future.

The theoretical insights gained in using PAR were taken up in other chapters. The domination of theories based on historical materialism made the theoretical analysis of the infrastructure the condition for the acceptance of the participatory research in the University of Dar es Salaam.

CHAPTER 8

Jipemoyo: Development and Culture

Introduction

The study referred to as *Jipemoyo,* which means "take heart," was an extensive bilateral research project, which put participatory research approach into practice. The project was carried out in the Western Bagamoyo District, Tanzania, and got its name from the historical town Bagamoyo, which was generally understood to refer to the "beating hearts" of slaves who had been shipped to distant destinations from there during the slave trade, changing it to Jipemoyo in the spirit of the project. In this chapter, I recall the proceedings, challenges and opportunities we faced during the study.

Jipemoyo was carried out under the Ministry of National Culture and the Youth of Tanzania in cooperation with the Academy of Finland in 1975-79. The project aimed at realizing the development potential of the residents by encouraging them to participate in research as partners and to take initiative in solving their problems by using their own resources. We wanted to accommodate research in a situation demanding participation both by the traditional observer and the observed. Our ideal was to create a shared thinking process, which could contribute to the renewal of the society. While *Jipemoyo* aspired to connect scientific inquiry with people's social situation and everyday issues, what this meant in practice had to be worked out during the research.

I was the leader of the study, at the time appointed as a Lecturer in the Science of Religion at the University of Helsinki. I had prepared the way for *Jipemoyo* through earlier research projects in the same area by conducting research for two Young Child studies commissioned by UNICEF. I had also participated in a study on villagers' level of education and skills, which was financed by ILO and carried out using participatory research approach in Bagamoyo District. President Nyerere had received publications on these and earlier participatory studies and he had encouraged my husband Lloyd Swantz and me to continue research in Tanzania. Earlier in 1973, as the Chancellor of the University of Dar es Salaam, he had put the doctor's hat on Lloyd's head. We had also had him as a guest of honour in our home to congratulate our friend, Member of Parliament Barbro Johansson, for receiving an honorary doctorate from the University of Gothenburg, Sweden.

Through my earlier research I was familiar with the people forming the majority in the area, the Kwere in majority around Lugoba, Msata and Chalinze, the Zigua around Miono and the Doe along the road to Bagamoyo. The Parakuyo Maasai pastoralists were latecomers in the area, but their role in *Jipemoyo* was to become central. Their neighbours of other ethnic backgrounds and the government people called the pastoralists Kwavi, but they identified themselves as Parakuyo, and considered the Kwavi to be a derogatory name originally belonging to another group further north (Beidelman 1971, Brain 1962, Cory 1956). However, from the beginning we decided that our concentration was not on ethnic groups but rather base the study on the villages the population of which could be of more mixed composition.

The tentative proposal for the Tanzanian-Finnish participatory research project was presented in the spring 1975 with the theme "The Role of Culture in the Restructuring Process of Rural Tanzania," shortened to "Development and Culture" in project publications. Its objectives were:

- To analyse the role of culture in the process of change a) as a motivational and creative element, b) as a deterring element
- To participate in the process of development and to experiment with research methods which incorporate people from all social levels and create in them awareness of their development potential.
- To collect, document, study and organise a system of archiving for cultural material, such as oral tradition and music, which is likely to disappear in the midst of change.
- To assist in the training of Tanzanian and Finnish scholars to carry out participatory research.
- To create models of field training for cultural officers, party and government leaders, and students working in villages.

Political and social background

Julius Kambarare Nyerere adopted the concept *ujamaa,* communality, while he was the Prime Minister. It was published in the pamphlet *The Ujamaa – The Basis of African Socialism,* five months after the country gained independence in 1961. Six years later, a policy for the consecutive political decisions was formulated in the *Arusha Declaration* (Freyhold 1974). The Declaration was widely broadcasted. I heard it while sitting in our village house during my research in Bunju, when it was declared for the first time.

Arusha Declaration is not the work of someone or some people schooled in classic socialist formulations. Rather it is a product of experience in the field of nation building in Tanzania. It sprang from the hard and real struggle, for the realization of people's interests (Arusha Declaration 1977, 11-12). The principle of communality and national cultural continuity were central in the Arusha Declaration. It encouraged research and practical measures realising *ujamaa* on the village level. In Nyerere's words,

The Tanganyika we have inherited is a very different Tanganyika from the one we are setting out to build and to bequeath our children...I believe its culture is the essence and spirit of any nation. A country, which lacks its own culture, is no more than a collection of people without the spirit, which makes them a nation (Julius Nyerere's inaugural address 9th December 1982)

In 1967, the government implemented *ujamaa* by moving people from the Rufiji river valley to higher grounds, as unusually high floods had destroyed some people's houses near the river. New houses were built with new schools and government buildings and the operation was considered to have succeeded well. Similar operations were carried out in the Mtwara and Lindi Regions, where the involvement of Tanzania in the independence war in Mozambique in the early 1970s necessitated the evacuation of the villages north of the Ruvu River. These operations served as a model when villagisation was declared as a national program.

Instead of living in remote and isolated settlements, the rural population was to live in planned villages. The emphasis was on raising the level of living conditions so that people would have access to clean sources of water, educational and health facilities. Expanses of cultivated land were to be owned and cultivated cooperatively. While the ultimate aim was to change the mode of production to cooperative, the rural transformation was first implemented without a definite schedule.

Already in 1968, some people in the Bagamoyo District had heeded the call to move voluntarily into co-operative *ujamaa* villages, "People are to be encouraged to live in Ujamaa villages," *Watu washawishiwe kuishi katika vijiji vya Ujamaa.* To exemplify, first, most people of Matimbwa village were not willing to leave their houses, cashew trees and coconut palms to start anew in virgin land, but by the end of 1971 around 120 families had started their own "*ujamaa*" communal farm. They moved four miles to a neighbouring uninhabited area and established what they called an *ujamaa* village by the name Ilongo. They cleared 20 acres of forested area near their village, made charcoal and grew simsim (sesame) for their living. However, local government officers did not at first recognize their efforts, since the official plan to build *ujamaa* villages had not yet been announced.

After the villages were created, the local government had to be organized accordingly. According to Michael Jennings (2007), Ward Development Committees Act legislated in 1969 made it possible "to make an order requiring all resident citizens of the United Republic resident within the ward for which the Committee is established to participate in the implementation of any scheme." Anyone not participating could be charged with a fine of cash or goods.

The presumed success of the first population transfers induced the nationwide implementation of villagization. In 1973, the TANU Executive Committee ordered, "People must live in villages," *Lazima watu waishi katika vijiji.* The rural people were to live in villages by the end of 1976. When they did not move fast enough, special operations, such as "Operation Coast," i.e. "*Operesheni Pwani*," in the Bagamoyo District were launched. Most of the moving had been carried out in the area of research when *Jipemoyo* fully had begun in 1976.

In reality, deficient planning of villagisation set development back in many ways. The Ministry of Land in Dar es Salaam had been given the task to draw the general layouts for villages, which were then given to respective Regional Commissioners. There was Finnish architect serving in the Ministry of Land who had the task of drawing the plans, wondering how it could be done not knowing the locations for them.

The officers followed the orders regardless of whether they had comprehended the intention behind villagisation or not. Matimbwa people, who had started their own *ujamaa* village, were not the only ones who declared that nothing less than physical force will make them shift to a new area where they would have to start anew from the scratch. Misconceptions were inevitable, when the villagisation program was carried out using force. If people did not move voluntarily, field forces were brought along, even burning people's houses, including our former house in Bunju.

Before the Jipemoyo project started, I had visited destroyed villages in Kisarawe district. I recorded voices of people sitting under trees in miserable conditions, their old houses broken down and the new ones haphazardly built of grass and mud. The destructive implementation of villagisation gave no consideration to the property value in Maneromango: a brick house with windows and water tanks was half broken for family to move a few yards into a temporary mud house. Opposite, on the other side of the road another well-built house with a shop had been totally destroyed to make room for straight streets drawn on surveyors' boards, but never implemented. I took the reports and recordings to Vice President Kawawa in charge of the program and to the media officer of the Party and presented a list of recommendations. Kawawa referred to the successes in Rufiji and in the southern regions, which in his mind had offered a good model to continue. While the TANU Executive Committee in Musoma made changes in the strategy in line with my recommendations, it was too late to repair damage caused all over the country. Also our house in Bunju, built with a local family, who had to move to the next village, had been taken down!

In the Western Bagamoyo, the area of research, people were expected to join in large-scale communal cultivation in concentrated new villages near the roads, each family providing labour at least three days a week. With some exceptions, the required labour inputs were not provided as anticipated. It turned out that president Nyerere's theory of the communal *ujamaa* spirit did not apply in the case of cooperative fields on the village level. When the communal cultivation failed, the villagers were told to cultivate *bega kwa bega,* "shoulder to shoulder," joining individually cultivated plots into unified fields for efficient ploughing by tractors, which the District would provide until the village would be in the position to buy a tractor. The village would then act as a productive unit, selling the crops co-operatively to the Regional Trading Offices. Even merging the fields for easy ploughing did not bring results, as vermin appeared in some of the fields, which were left unattended. People also blamed government officers for using the tractors for their own fields.

Jipemoyo took place right after and partly during the main moving of the people when the villagization program had not yet been fully completed. Tensions increased further as the Parakuyo herders were supposed to move to the western side of the main road while the farmers' fields were to be on the eastern side in the Lugoba division. Neither the farmers wanted to leave their fields nor were the cattle keepers satisfied with being next to the forest because they were infested with tsetse flies causing sleeping sickness. Because of the ostracizing that the pastoralists suffered, researchers tended to sympathise with them, causing the farmers to call the *Jipemoyo* researchers, including anthropologist Peter Rigby, as friends of the "Kwavi." However, Rigby, doing research with the Parakuyo Maasai, indicated that in the opinion of the Kwere, the main ethnic group in the Lugoba area, the pastoralists had been favoured when settling the people in the new villages (Rigby 1992, 67).

Shaping the Jipemoyo research team

Jipemoyo was a multidisciplinary project, in which sociology, ethnology, ethnomusicology, social anthropology, geography, theology and science of religion were represented. While the team was bound together by the participatory approach, individual researchers followed methodologies based on their own disciplinary groundings and personal capabilities.

The Director of the Department of Research and Planning at the Ministry of Culture and Youth Dr. Isaria K. Katoke was appointed as the Tanzanian Director for *Jipemoyo*. The Tanzanian Ministry of Culture and Youth also nominated two researchers with newly earned master's degrees, Kemal Mustafa and Bernard Kiyenze, to join the team. Kemal was from an upper class Indian family, whose father was a High Court judge and his journalist mother was one of the elected Indian members of the first Legislative Council in preparation for independence, when one African, one Asian and one Tanzanian member were to be elected from each constituency. Kemal had done his grammar school and BA studies in England and MA studies at the University of Dar es Salaam, writing his Master's thesis on President Nyerere's home village Butiama. In *Jipemoyo*, he did research with the Parakuyo pastoralists. Kiyenze from a Sukuma farmer's family in Shinyanga engaged with groups of aspiring smiths, carpenters, and women skilled in various handicrafts, encouraging them to take advantage of the government's intent to promote cooperative groups and small-scale industries.

Ethnomusicologist Philip Donner, with earlier research experience in Senegal and Mali, and his artist wife Ariadne, or Ari, settled in their Miono village home with two small children, the third to be born during the research period. As an artist, Ari did artwork for the project. The family made themselves quickly at home in the yard of a Zigua house-owner's family.

The contribution of Donner was a great professional addition in the field of ethnomusicology. He had outlined a dialogical research plan for getting into the music of the Zigua people working closely with a *selo ngoma* specialist

Juma Nassoro. The Zigua extensive girls' maturity rituals and instruction offered opportunities to a variety of music. Donner went through all the stages of building the drums and together with Juma Nassoro they started a drum-making workshop in their resident Miono village. He took pictures of all the phases of drum building and the dances performed, which formed a big part of the collection of thousands of Jipemoyo pictures. Together, they developed a teaching program for secondary schools utilizing the expertise gained from the *selo ngoma,* developing the notation for the music. Later Nassoro came to Finland and contributed to the Finnish musicians' *selo* dance groups. Interestingly, I met an elderly woman during the writing of this chapter who told she had been part of such a *selo* dance group started in my present hometown Lahti. Donner's interest in music included the songs sung during the Islamic Ramadhani months of fasting when the Muslim youth went around singing through the nights. Later on, he studied and recorded *taarab* music with specialists in Zanzibar as part of the MEDIAFRICA project.

Philip's wife Ariadne contributed with drawings to the pamphlets distributed to people and to the covers of the Jipemoyo publications and together they included a project on water with the school students and villagers in their programme. Living with the family of small children without a source of clean water even for themselves enticed to cooperate with the school students in an inquiry how people traditionally managed their water problems. When the Donners' third child was born during the research period, the family stayed for a period in Dar es Salaam in Member of Parliament Barbro Johansson's beach house, which had been my family home for six years. Philip Donner shared his time between the two places before the family eventually returned to their village home.

The second Finnish recruit came with his wife and a small child, but returned home after finding the conditions unsuitable for the little one. As the Director, I had to look for another scholar who could also take care of and archive the research materials, since the Tanzanian Ministry wished that the archiving system would be developed during the research. Ulla Vuorela was the choice. She had her Master's degree in ethnology and had attended my lectures on Tanzanian ritual symbolism when I was teaching general ethnology in 1971-72. Her family lived in the house of the Finnish Literature Society, which in Finland serves as a home for folklore collections. Thus, in my mind her family tradition made her fitting to become responsible for the archiving and for relating to the Finnish Embassy. Ulla Vuorela's first task was to build the base for Tradition Archives and Documentation Unit in the Ministry of Culture and Youth but she also settled in Msoga village. Being fluent in many languages, she was quick to learn Swahili and was interested in listening to the stories people told as they gathered around the fireplaces. She was an accomplished pianist and acquired a piano for her home in Dar es Salaam. Also for *Jipemoyo,* she took along her accordion and enlivened the women's evening seminars with music. She did concentrated research on Msoga women and worked out a theoretical frame for her doctorate after the Finnish support to Jipemoyo was finished. She went there with other scholars to develop drama performances with the villagers who played out key problems they faced. For years, Vuorela continued to correspond with the village women, who turned to her with their sorrows or reported joyful events. They in turn expressed their sadness when during the visit to Msoga in 2013 I told them about Ulla Vuorela's early death.

Helena Jerman had her Master's degree in anthropology from the University of Helsinki and had served as an assistant to Professor Arne Runeberg of Social Anthropology. She had written on the concept of ethnicity attending to courses in the Scandinavian Institute of Africa Studies in Uppsala. Prior to joining us in the Bagamoyo District for five months, she handled the administrative work based in Helsinki. Her duties included material acquisitions, transport and travel arrangements, financial responsibilities and literary work. During the relatively short time Jerman made intense use of the time in the study area, continuing research on ethnicity and the colonial influence in its creation. She made intensive interviews with elders, men and women mainly in Miono area, where she lived by her sister Ariadne Donner's family. She listened to people's views of their lives and histories, which followed family inheritance and social relations based on kinship. Jerman got the name for her doctoral work *Between Five Lines* (1997) from an elder who drew five lines on the ground to explain his family history. Jerman made an analysis of the clan based social systems emphasizing different dimensions of belonging, which had more significance to the interviewed people than the ethnic identity. She finalized her doctoral work with the history and critique of the ethnicity concept, which in many documents had divided the population according to tribes in Bagamoyo district.

Two Finnish missionaries working in Tanzania fluent in Swahili joined the team as research associates. Arvi Hurskainen had been a pastor in the Southern Highlands and later a teacher at the Makumira Theological Institute later turned to University near Arusha. He came to do research based on his sociological studies with the Parakuyo pastoralists, but disassociated himself from the team as disputes became tenser assumedly based on ideological and professional differences between some research partners working with the same ethnic group. Hurskainen related to different Parakuyo clan groups apart from other pastoralist scholars and thus was able to continue his research with two assistants, and to make an excellent collection of pictures and recordings as well as research notes included in the Jipemoyo archives. He did his doctoral thesis *Cattle and Culture* (Hurskainen 1984). The photos found their way to the University collections in Pennsylvania where Rigby became settled before his rather early death.

Taimi Sitari, a geographer, was a teacher in the International School in Moshi. As an affiliate, she divided her time between her teaching duties and substantial periods of research staying in Lugoba and Msata villages. She came into close contact with the people and cooperated with the officers who dealt with people's moving from their former homes to the new village sites. She visited systematically the houses and noted down the movements of the households, in the villages, which she selected for thorough scrutiny. Her surveys and drawings of maps of the villages were useful for the officers and other team members alike. She was the first one to get her doctoral thesis *Settlement Changes in the Bagamoyo District of Tanzania as a Consequence of Villagization* (1983) accepted and published. It has subsequently provided background information for many studies. In 2008-2010, Sitari led a research project in the same Bagamoyo divisions with an international group of researchers who followed up the changes that had taken place during thirty years. The combined research report was published in Swahili (Sokoni 2010).

A number of research assistants joined the research. Daudi Kitolero carried through the whole project. After *Jipemoyo* and writing a thesis on his own people, the Ngindo, for the Institute of Social work, he acted as the leader of the research section of the Ministry. In 1978, an indigenous Parakuyo student Melchior Matwi returned from his studies in the United States and joined the research team. Later on, he continued for a period as a research officer in the Institute of Adult Education.

Jonas Ruben Wanga, originally a Maasai from Arusha, was an assistant for the pastoralist research with the background of seven years of primary school and two years in the Lutheran Bible School in Mwika. Other assistants were Eva Liwale and Mariamu Marijani, who both had academic education, and a local musician Juma Nasoro, whom Philip Donner had found and discovered as an expert in all aspects of Zigua music in his home area in Miono. Later on, Nasoro visited Finland and initiated some *selo ngoma* dance groups.

Dr. Katoke retired in 1977 and Odhiambo Anacleti, with a Master's degree in history from the University of Dar es Salaam, became the Tanzanian Director of *Jipemoyo* while appointed as the Director of Research in the Ministry. He took the task seriously and was at times needed in soothing some of the arguments that developed within the research team.

Odhiambo Anacleti represented the Ministry of Culture in the *Jipemoyo* advisory group, as also anthropologist Peter Rigby, Professor in the University of Dar es Salaam, who was doing research with the Parakuyo in the same area. Also another teacher, a well-known scholar and political activist Marjorie Mbilinyi, initially with American background, attended the meetings of the advisory group. Both University teachers contributed to the publications of Jipemoyo, as did also Deborah Fahy Bryceson, who had served as my assistant when I was Senior Research Fellow in the Bureau of Research Assessment and Land Use Planning (BRALUP). Today a well-known scholar, Deborah Bryceson was doing her doctoral research related fairly closely with *Jipemoyo* and as an advisor took part in creating the historical materialist theoretical framework for the study.

Starting Jipemoyo research

After the initial contacts with the people were made, we organised a seminar to introduce the research team and our ways of working. The seminar was a chance for around a hundred villagers we had so far worked with to bring out problems they faced in their efforts to develop their community. The event also gave the staff representing the wards and elected village leadership an opportunity to discuss their views and goals. In the welcoming session, the Tanzanian research director Israel Katoke represented the Ministry of Culture and Youth. Eeva Ahtisaari was there on her own right, but also on behalf of her husband the Ambassador Martti Ahtisaari. Among the higher government officers were the Regional Director of Development and the District TANU party leader. School youth entertained the participants through songs and dance. A local historian Timoteo Kambi related a personal experience with the French and German Catholic missions. After the Germans had defeated they trusted him with the keys of the *boma*, their colonial fortress, to be handed over to the British.

After the school students' traditional dances and welcome speeches, we welcomed the participants to meet in four groups. Pastoralists formed a group, women potters and mat makers another, and miscellaneous traditional craftsmen, carpenters and woodworkers gathered in two more groups. The leaders met in their own group and ended up also eating separately in a class-room, while others were sitting on the ground in groups. This separation was part of the local practice, which we had not anticipated. The groups were then asked to share their thoughts with other seminar participants. The Parakuyo selected a spokesman to give their problems and views about government plans. The other groups had to be probed by asking them questions. While such seminars became a way of gathering thoughts together with the selected participants, it turned out later on that informal discussion in daily encounters with individuals and groups prepared the ground for more purposeful meetings.

Throughout *Jipemoyo* the researchers and assistants recorded their observations and discussions with people in notebooks copied in three prints simultaneously. The notes, referred to as UTAf, were to be available in the Ministry archives and in the Institute of Development Studies in Helsinki. Also each writer kept a copy. As some members of research staff did not follow this informally agreed rule, not everyone's research notes are in the archives. The discussions were informal even when specific questions were in mind. The hope was that the officers would also learn a more informal way of communication with the people, which would help the decision-makers to draw a truer picture of how the policies were affecting ordinary people's lives.

Participatory research in action: Mediation

As the legislation passed in 1975 made the Village Assembly a legal body, the potential involved with villagisation became apparent. Village leaders could make bylaws for commonly agreed responsibilities, and villages divided into cells of ten houses with an elected chairperson enabled the government to reach the people. Villagers aware of their rights could thus influence decision-making for their own benefit. *Jipemoyo* increased villagers' awareness as participants, who could bring out their thoughts and concerns about the implemented policies. At times, the researchers' contacts with the community were utilised in mediating local problems to bureaucrats, politicians and even the top leadership of the Central Government.

Rajabu Roweza, the chairman of the Lunga village in Lugoba ward, had lost his trust in the political leaders and did not believe that we as outsiders could have any significant role in the local situation. He had inherited his leadership as a member of the former rulers' lineage, his grandfather's grave was still honoured and the political leaders had trusted him as he had complied with the policies of the Party. In the early 1970s, he had attended a conference of the ward chairmen of the Coast Region in Rufiji. After the conference, Roweza had gone around the villages in his ward, Lunga, Mboga and Diozile, telling people about the coming plans on villagisation (M-L. Swantz 1979):

We were told, 'Go and do things together'. I told them 'We are asked to cultivate together and to live together'. We cultivated fields everywhere. The second year there was a meeting, *baraza*, short for *Operesheni Pwani*, which is Bagamoyo for 'Operation Coast', where we were told that the representatives from the whole region come to Lugoba for a *baraza*. It was a nine-day seminar. We were told: Villages are these: Lunga, Mboga, Mazizi, Msata, Chalinze, Makombe, Diozile One and Diozile Two. Two people from each village will be taken to a seminar. I finished five years and I was re-elected, we cultivated and went through the *kufa au kupona*, "to die or to survive" (as people were told to do in difficult years, especially in 1973) and we built the hospital by self-help, with my politics (which became the Health Centre in Lugoba).

Roweza invited me to a meal and I slept one night in his and his wife's house, with no doors in the rooms. He told of an incident. The Regional Commissioner was to come with the Area Commissioner to Lugoba, and people had gathered and waited for the whole day. It was the season for *kulalia nguruwe*, to go to the ripening fields to protect the harvest from wild pigs and birds. Roweza had given in to the waiting people and allowed them to leave at 6 pm so that they could reach the fields before dark. The visiting dignitaries came at 6.30 pm finding no crowds welcoming them. The chairman was told: "You are no good, you have let them go." In the following elections the people elected him again but the officials returned the papers. The reason given was: "You are like a small child, you do not know how to read." His reason for not reading was his poor eyesight. Roweza considered his treatment abuse as he guessed the real reason.

Another similar case was that of Aloisi Muhode, the village chairman of Diozile One. While bold in words and uncouth in appearance, as a Christian he had gone to school and knew how to read and write. Muhode, as many other village leaders, had his complaints about the bureaucrats. As he explained:

They all come on their own time, they have no schedule in village visits we do not know their agenda. The cooperative officer comes 3 p.m. without giving notice every person has his schedule, first comes this one, then another all the things get stuck with no leadership. "Do this, do that." We have no teacher, no guidance is given.

The division had three officers resident in Lugoba area, who were related to the Ministry of Agriculture. When asked why they did not coordinate their work, they answered, "We have not been told to work that way." Lack of coordination turned out to be a negative consequence of the new bureaucratic mode. The officers represented different branches, such as cultivation, animal husbandry, training donkeys and oxen for ploughing, and bee keeping. They did not see the need for cooperation, which in turn would have made people's lives easier.

The Chairman of the neighboring Msoga village, which was initially ordered to move to Mboga, put the complaint against the bureaucrats in the following words: "*Sisi tunalalamikia vingine, serikali inatuletea vingine*, We complain of other things, government brings to us different things." In 1959, he harvested 40 sacks of sesame from a field he had cultivated, but now the yield was decreasing. He explained that the decline in production was caused by the leaders' detachment from agriculture. According to him, the officers had multiplied in number and drew fat salaries for holding meetings and writing minutes, but without doing productive work. Only the President and the Vice President were exempted from criticism of leaders "who only sat in expensive cars visiting villages." We were also spared from the critique, as we lived with the people and listened to them.

In case of Msoga the mediation succeeded particularly well, although some villagers doubted whether our research would be of actual use to them. Initially, the Msoga villagers had been ordered to move, but they had not wanted to move.

When Taimi Sitari and I visited Msoga village after the general moving process, we discovered that most of the villagers had not moved. We found them as a big group preparing a vegetable garden near the village. Upon seeing that we were carrying a sizable tape-recorder, they immediately got an idea to send a message to the President. They got together and in half an hour they were ready to sing their story. They wanted the President to know that there was no need for them to move, because they had done everything the Government and the Party had ordered them. They had cultivated a big maize field together and ordered a tractor to plough it. However, the school in their village had already been moved elsewhere. A school-leaver wrote down the story of the village and the rehearsed songs told about the accomplishments. As the recorded message reached President Nyerere, he sent his assistant to come and see the village. As a result, the Msoga village was recognized and allowed to continue, and the school was rebuilt.

Interestingly, the villagers told Ulla Vuorela a different story ten years later (Vuorela 1987, 133). Her informer believed that a collection of money had been made and given to a Ward Party Officer, who had then influenced the decision. Not even the highest local government officers, Regional Commissioners would deviate from the orders from the highest level. Sending a message to President Nyerere through a song sounded to them like a fairy tale. Msoga village turned out to be a special case, in which villagers' obstinacy produced results. No one knew that the future president Jakaya Kikwete was growing up in Msoga, his birth village, and was at the time attending the Kibaha Secondary School, where he even had Finnish teachers.

Inevitably, our participatory approach caused apprehension among the district party leaders and bureaucrats. Continuing the research required at one point a letter from the Prime Minister's office sent to the district officials. Some politicians and officers feared that the researchers would act against the Party rules or reveal their private fields. Informal discussions, meetings and seminars with the researchers opened to the villagers new ways of thinking about their own situation, even when solutions to their problems were not in agreement with the decision makers.

Participatory Research in operation: Education

One of the goals for concentrating population in bigger villages was to improve people's opportunities to send their children to school. In 1973, attending school had become compulsory and the officers tried to implement the order diligently. The problems that educational officers of Bagamoyo District faced were a starting point for the researchers' participation in village life.

An officer had gone to a Parakuyo village in Chamakweza to get the "Kwavi" boys to school, but had been chased out by a throw of a hammer. The cause for such a reception had been another officer's earlier beating of a reluctant Parakuyo boy who was already a junior warrior. I witnessed another such a throw of a hammer after a European when a car stopped to observe the opening of the TANU office for the Maasai in Chamakweza, an event, which I was attending. Nevertheless, the officer was afraid of further contact with the "Kwavi" and, having heard of our contacts with the pastoralists, asked us for assistance. Hence, poor relations between the officers and pastoralists formed one departure point for the participatory research (UTAf 1977/27-30).

It turned out that one reason for dissatisfaction was the teaching program followed in local schools. Mtumia Samsindo, the elected chairman of the Parakuyo in the Western Bagamoyo district area and an inventive pastoralist himself, held the program in low esteem. He had paid toward the building of the school in Mindu Tulieni from the cattlekeepers' income in cattle sales and had sent his boys there to learn. Pastoralists like him wanted improved cattle keeping as a subject in the school program. They were even willing to contribute to teaching by giving two cows and a person to look after them. The teaching program became a topic of successive meetings with educational authorities, including with the Ministry of Education, to little actual effect.

Another reason for dissatisfaction related to the new location of the Parakuyo village, which was forcing the farmers in Makambo village to move out of their village area. The farmers rather sacrificed the children's school attendance than left the fields they were cultivating (UTAf, 1977/27-30). The new location appointed to the pastoralists was at the edge of a forest infested by tsetse flies, which needed clearing so that the cattle could be kept away from the farmers' fields. Instead of clearing the forest a unit for treating the forest against tsetse was prepared to come from Morogoro. Ultimately, the farmers had burnt down the trees, as coal was the villagers' main source of income. Mtumia Samsindo, the former chairman of the Parakuyo, told this to me when I some years after Jipemoyo asked him what happened to the forest. This became also evident in the research thirty years after (Sokoni, 2010)

Our intimacy with the villagers gave us a good position to have a close cooperation with them. Some *Jipemoyo* team members lived with the villagers throughout the study with some necessary breaks, while others took times off for other duties. In Msata, we rented a village house. In Lugoba, individual poorly insulated rooms were rented in villagers' houses, which meant that the researchers learned to share the life of the families. The researchers cooked their meals on small coal burners or ate in small restaurants and teahouses, "*hoteli*," one of them owned by the Parakuyo chairman Mtumia.

We helped in mediation not because facilitating the officers' work was on our agenda, but because we also felt a need for a deeper understanding of the situation. There was confusion about why the cattle keepers refused to send their children to school and completely forbade girls to participate in classes.

The local government officers and party leaders were not accustomed to close participation of the researchers in village life. The researchers tended to be sympathetic to the people's critical views of the government dealings and consequently often critical of the employed local staff's way of ignoring the pastoralists' problems. The officers hardly communicated with them, and as we discovered, the pastoralists' chairman had not before our time been invited to the meetings when higher officers visited Lugoba. Local staff usually held views following the party line as they interpreted it in fear of otherwise losing their jobs. Thus, participatory research unfolded as a search for *nafasi*, space or opportunity, which people had in the situation. At the same time, we cooperated closely with officers in charge of people's movements, who benefited from Taimi Sitari's drawings of the maps and the movements of the villagers.

The leaders had tried to gain the interest of the youth in different ways. They started a group for young boys for making sandals of tyres, which the Maasai wore, some youth prepared hides for drums for ngoma drumming and formed dance groups which drew interest. The names were recorded and the numbers of those who attended grew. But the older warriors wanted the youth for herding, even girls took part in herding but the freedom that it gave to boys attracted them more than schools (Notes by Jonas Ruben Wanga UTAF 1977/27-56).

The education officer invited Jonas Ruben to attend in several meetings with the local people. The observations he wrote about the meetings and events give evidence that the first Jipemoyo seminar had activated both the leaders and village representatives to follow the Party educational programs. The following are Jonas Ruben's observations on the progress of pastoralists' education and of their Kwere neighbours' unwillingness to move.

Samsindo Mtumia, the ward chairman of the Parakuyo, enticed the families to send their children to school and a Chagga local education officer formed a school committee in Mindu Tulieni. On 20th May 1976, it was recorded that the school, which had been built with a substantial contribution from the cattle auctions with the Parakuyo income had 188 students so far only up to 6th standard and they were mainly Kwere from neighbouring Makombe village, which was supposed to have moved to Lugoba but refused to do so.

In November the same year the number of Parakuyo students was 15, of whom two were girls, the daughters of Paulo Moreto and of Laban Moreto, the traditional leader of the pastoralists in the area. Another school built for the Parakuyo had at the same time 12 pastoral students in Chamakweza east from Chalinze, where a TAPA, Tanzanian Parents' Association had built a school.

The education officer invited Jonas Ruben to attend in several meetings with the local people. The observations he wrote about the meetings and events give evidence that the first Jipemoyo seminar had activated both the leaders and village representatives to follow the Party educational programs. The Jonas Ruben's observations tell of the progress of pastoralists' education and of their Kwere neighbours' unwillingness to move.

The leaders had tried to gain the interest of the youth in different ways. They started a group for young boys for making sandals of tyres, which the Maasai wore, some youth prepared hides for drums for ngoma drumming and formed dance groups which drew interest. The names were recorded and the numbers of those who attended grew. But the older warriors wanted the youth for herding, even girls took part in herding but the freedom that it gave to boys attracted them more than schools (UTAF 1977/27-56).

The education officer and the chairman Mtumia Samsindo of the Parakuyo together with his nephew Ikoyo Mtumia tried their best to get the male students to stay in school. Ikoyo told with a firm voice that boys go to read but the girls never. When the author visited the place ten years later Ikoyo had become the chairman of the Maasai proudly declaring that his girls were at school.

According to Kemal Mustafa's notes, mothers had resisted sending their daughters to school, other information tells that the resistance came from fathers who were afraid that they would end up as girls in bars where men were drinking. When I in June 2013 met Mtumia Samsindo's daughter in a church service in the President Kikwete's home village Msoga, she told me that her father had not sent her to school, so she had not learned reading.

Adding from my own notes, to encourage boys' school attendance Mtumia Samsindo made the recommendation that a pre school would be started for children in his compound. The Tanzanian YWCA assisted by the Finnish sister organization established a branch in Lugoba. The chairman asked them to build a house for the pre-school children in his compound and two young women were taking turns teaching there. Some connection continued over the years, as when the Tanzanian branch celebrated the World YWCA Centennial with a big event in the Diamond Hall in 1986, two young women from the Parakuyo YWCA branch attended and offered their Maasai beads for sale.

Participatory research in operation: Women

President Nyerere had expressed that the weak side of the traditional society had been the position of women. Interrupted by a century of mercantilism and slave trade, followed by colonialism, the traditional societies had not followed the ideal course. However, Nyerere and his supporters were hopeful that the new society would rediscover its communal roots. Not only *maendeleo,* development, but also *mapinduzi,* revolution, was turning things around.

During the years of *Jipemoyo,* the research team cooperated with women from all ethnic groups. Bringing up women's issues in seminars and personal contacts began to influence attitudes between men and women, the men did not consider their customs to be discriminatory. They insisted men and women to have different tasks in life.

A major event during the study was a two-week seminar, to which we invited women leaders from the headquarters in Dar es Salaam and women community officers of the district and ward level to discuss the issues that village women would bring up. After responding positively to the invitation, many of the leaders from the city inquired about the *per diem* payments. This was the first time I experienced such a request, as I had thought that such visits were the participants' professional duty. Several failed to come since we only covered expenses and fed the participants but did not pay per diems. Fortunately, Kati Kamba, the chairperson of the women's organization of the TANU *Umoja wa Wanawake wa Tanzania* (Womern's Union of Tanzania) and Ms. Kaisi, a representative from the Ministry of Education came from Dar es Salaam to take part in the seminar and to meet with the female community officers from the district and ward levels and with women from the visited villages.

The seminar started local discussions on women's situation. The seminar participants stayed in ordinary houses with walls made of mud plastered and whitewashed, and found it better to eat in local *hotelis* instead of having a male cook to make food for them. We visited selected villages for informal visits, meeting women and invited some of them to share meetings with the leaders. Following our research approach, we wanted to keep the interaction informal, as it was obvious that people's problems were not delivered through formal channels. Thus, seminar participants from the district were encouraged to arrange local meetings using the same approach.

Some evenings were devoted to discussions and women's *ngoma* dancing while Ulla Vuorela provided music with her accordion. These sessions opened up opportunities for free exchange of views also on women officers' personal lives and problems. They indicated that their husbands' customary behaviour and superior attitudes toward women had not changed toward the way the leaders taught about women's rights. Sound recordings of a standard then available were made of the sessions.[1]

The conflict between social policies and cultural traditions relating to women placed the female researchers in a sensitive situation. For instance, although the Parakuyo women had not been invited to the seminar, their different treatment came up when they gladly welcomed adult reading lessons organized for them. The local teachers told us they had not had any contact with them, as the Parakuyo lived in some distance from Lugoba. However, once the lessons started we learned that the Parakuyo women were insulted, because the teachers appeared to think that they could not read just like the others. Further, the teachers wanted to teach the women how to cook chicken for a meal, since they knew that the Maasai do not customarily eat chicken. The teacher's sense of superiority over the adult students, which is far from an exception in development work, reminded us that sensitivity is required when trying to change things.

Another sensitive issue that came up during *Jipemoyo* was women's circumcision. I did not initiate the discussion myself, but after witnessing a ceremony in which a Parakuyo girl's clitoris was cut, the first wife of the Parakuyo chairman consulted me about it in great secrecy. She wanted to stay with me when I was invited to spend the night in their kraal. In the secrecy of the room, she asked worriedly whether the cutting of her sex organs could have caused her barrenness, which several of the pastoralist women had suffered. She expressed her concern in these words.

"If a man suspects his wife to have had relations with another man he can beat her without mercy, but he himself is free to have any relations he wants. Men want women to be circumcised so that they would not have sexual desire toward other men. Many girls have died or become infected after their organs have been cut."

She had not given birth to any children and was already past the age of pregnancy. While she had kept her position as the first wife, her husband had married another woman, who bore three children to him. Since I had seen the mutilation ritual, I could talk about it with some knowledge, but listened to her thoughts before giving my views. I told her that it was indeed possible for the organs to be affected. We also discussed how women could be freed from that operation. Rather then staying with me for the night she went out and gathered other women around her. I could hear them having a serious discussion about the matter sitting until late into night in the moonlight. I did not understand the words, as I did not speak the Maasai language.

A third instance on women's issues came up during a seminar, which the Parakuyo men had organized with the government officers. "Where men eat meat they have butchered women cannot attend," was the rule of men.

---

1 Recorded discussions are available in Jipemoyo files.

During a two-day seminar, the men ate meat of two cows they had butchered. Their refusal to allow women participate came to the women researchers as a surprise. Women advisors could not risk the success of the seminar by insisting on women's participation. The women themselves avoided arguing against the men: they had their own seminar, where they could bring up their complaints and demands with women researchers.

The custom of men and women eating separately has continued until today. When I visited the Parakuyo in Mindu Tulieni in 2010, I was taken to a new Lutheran church, which the Parakuyo had helped to build after an increasing number of them had become Christians. When the food was served after the worship service, I found myself eating together with the men, only realizing the situation after one of them made the remark, "The women went over there." Visiting another Parakuyo area in 2013, we six European visitors, women and men were invited to eat with the Parakuyo men while the women did the cooking. I used the opportunity and invited some women to join us to eat the meal with some Parakuyo men and with us. Three of the women came to eat with fingers from the first dish but left when the soup came to the table set out in the open. Only later I realized that there was meat in the soup. No one said a word, but I was left with a question in my mind whether I had made a mistake inviting the women thus thinking that eating separately meant discriminating women. I realized that it was a general custom in the societies I had shared life with in Tanzania and questioned whether we westerners too readily interfere with people's customs in the name of women's rights!

A similar occasion took place with the Zaramo men in Bunju, when I was invited to the home yard of a Muslim teacher *shehe,* the holder of the flag of the specific Muslim brotherhood, *kadiria tarika (qadirriyya tariqa),* for a *maulidi,* the celebration of the birth of the Prophet Mohammed, the name referring to the name Mawlid, the author of the story of the Prophet's birth. I was seated in a front row with men on chairs while the women were behind a bushy fence. I ate meat with men from the cow they had butchered, while the women were drinking tea in their area and could take their share from the meat afterwards on their side (M-L. Swantz 1985, 129-130). I interpreted the breaking of the custom and inviting a woman where only men were supposed to be to mean that the European woman did not belong to the internal social gender categories, as I had discovered also in other similar occasions.

Peter Rigby in his writings about the rights of women in Parakuyo society emphasized the fact that the women had cows in their possession, had rights and did the selling of milk and had to be consulted about sales of these cows or keeping them, at least nominally. Marjorie Mbilinyi and Deborah Bryceson challenged Rigby but were more informed about the women's position historically in Usambaras and in reference to the situation in Uru in Kilimanjaro region according to their challenging article in Jipemoyo 2, 1980. The chapters written by Rigby in *Jipemoyo* 1 and especially in *Jipemoyo* 2, p. 32-84 show his close penetration to the life of the Parakuyo and the significance of his deep knowledge of the pastoralists' everyday life is impressive, sharing life with them in their huts, as also his interpretation of the social structure and the rules embedded within the society giving meaning to their social life, yet facing harsh critique with the voice of equalizing policies. Rigby based his theoretical knowledge on the *Grundrisse* and *Capital Vol.1* of Marx and the *Ethnological Notebooks,* but his last book *African Images* end with the impermeable solutions. He quotes Johannes Fabian (1978, 170) and Marcus and Fischer (1986, 11-12) and ends with pessimistic thoughts, in his mind seeing the solution with Marx, but not foreseeable in practice.

Participatory research in operation: Culture documentation

The central aim of *Jipemoyo* was to involve participants in the culture research but also to encourage documentation of cultural material. As a response to the request of the Ministry of Culture and Youth, Donner with Juma Nasoro created a problem-oriented documentation of cultural materials, which could be used in the development process while making the material available to future generations (Donner 1977, 22-32; 1981: 53-59). One of the projects was to study, code and prepare notation on *ngoma*-form of music as a course for secondary schools. Further, Kiyenze documented forms of old crafts and local histories and many aspects of pastoralist studies by Mustafa and Rigby became included in university courses on development. Thus, *Jipemoyo* aimed at integrating aspects of specific cultures to the national cultural heritage, but the theoretical interests of the researchers occupied the researchers minds. These discussions are available in articles concerning women and pastoralists' studies for reading available in the doctoral theses (See Bibliography)

Ulla Vuorela had the task to organize the documenting of research notes, pictures, films and recordings in three copies. The personal notes were written in three stenciled copies in notebooks. The original copies were collected in the research archives of the Ministry of Culture, the second copies in the Institute of Development Studies, University of Helsinki, and the third copy remained with the scholar (Vuorela 1980).

The Ministry of Culture and Youth of Tanzania were involved in organizing a training course for the cultural officers. Professor Lauri Honko was invited for a three-week course in collecting histories of cultural heritage. He was professor of Folklore and Science of Religion in the University of Turku, at the time research professor in the Academy of Finland and the chairman of the *Jipemoyo* steering committee.[2] The first week consisted of lectures, discussions and demonstrations held in Miono. During the second week, the officers did practical work, staying in selected villages, interviewing elders, visiting graves honoured by people and other places of local historical significance. It gave the villagers opportunities to recall their family and clan histories, which were recorded in two impressive archived volumes (Jipemoyo 1976). During the third week, a seminar was held in Dar es Salaam in which the Ministry staff and other researchers attended to discuss the work of collecting histories and poetry.

---

2 Academy of Finland appointed a steering committee for the projects it financed.

Such aspects of *Jipemoyo* helped filling a gap in cultural studies in Tanzania. The work devoted to lifting up the ancient cultural heritage suffered in Tanzania during the rapid Africanizing of the government staff in the 1960s, when the British archaeologists had to leave the country. While Africanization helped to raise national self-identity, the fine restoration work that had gone on in the Kilwa mosque, the Sultan's palace and several other sites along the coast, were left to lie idle until Tanzanians were trained for the field. Also, anthropology was considered damaging to the self-consciousness of the citizens. Hence, it was not introduced as a subject at the University of Dar es Salaam and instead replaced with the Department of Theatre Arts with foreign staff. This led to analysing young girls' maturity rites as a form of drama, as was the case in a study of the Kaguru by Penina Mlama. There was a further pragmatic interest in promoting role-plays and drama in villages. People were obviously gifted in role-plays, as the experience showed in women's seminars and later in health seminars. The drama and role-plays have shown to be an excellent medium for informing people about HIV/AIDS, but it had delayed the study of local cultures. Anthropology was reintroduced as a part of rural sociology no earlier than in the 1990s. Individual researchers had scholarships in USA and could do their research in anthropology there, such as Simon Mesiakini and Joel Lugalla, the latter did not return to Tanzania.

While culture histories are valuable in themselves, they were not the central theme in *Jipemoyo*. We did not line up with the Finnish tradition of folklore collection, Claude Lévi-Strauss or Adam Kuper, for whom the most important task of the anthropologists was to save the culture for posterity. Instead, our research team believed in the creative powers of cultural renewal based on peoples' "living culture": the neglected discoveries of the retreating cultural forms and values were brought into the attention of those charged with the task of developing the country.

An example of such cultural forms is the traditional legal practice. Traditionally, the Kwere and Zaramo quarrelling parties performed the legal debates by singing and the middleman judged whose presentation won the case. The whole procedure performed with singing indicates great creative capacity of the people. Such procedure was the *kitala cha kutagusa* of the Zaramo, also described by Father Cornelius Vermunt to have been the practice with the Luguru and the traditional practice by the studied Kwere (Described in Swantz 1970, 399-400; 1985, 421- 422). I asked Tanzanian President Jakaya Kikwete at the time the Minister of Foreign Affairs, on the way to become the next President, whether he still knew the same Kwere tradition, as he was born in Msoga and had gone to school in Lugoba. His answer was positive. I suggested that it could be introduced in schools in some form acknowledging the origin of the tradition. Such debates of two sides taking an opposite view were practiced in schools following the British system, not debating while singing as did the Kwere and Zaramo. A good example of such debates is in the autobiography of Edwin Mtei, the first Governor of the Bank of Tanzania, who describes how he beat the British Headmaster of the Old Moshi Secondary School in such a debate in the colonial time (Mtei 2009).

Jipemoyo researchers wrote extensively on cultural descriptions and analyses. Helena Jerman analysed the colonial influence of "tribe" or an ethnic group as a concept. Bernard Kiyenze's work dealt with the history and practices of the artisans and the neglected effort of the Government to encourage village based small-scale industries. Kemal Mustafa wrote extensively on the debates and the readiness of the pastoralists for change, and Arvi Hurskainen on the traditions of the Parakuyo. I wrote an extensive study paper about the Parakuyo after working two years with them, parts of which are included in this book. According to my interpretation, the Parakuyo met the *ujamaa* transformation as a communal group of pastoralists, whose life-style was about to change. Unlike for the farmers, this meant a new kind of perception and total change of their culture. As I wrote, "… Their dilemma provides an excellent illustration of what happens in general, when people are pushed to accept alien ways with no regard to their own culture - but also, how the same situation can be turned to look entirely different, if people's self esteem is given constructive channels of expression" (M-L. Swantz 1980, 105).

Theoretical disputes

In the 1970s, the University of Dar es Salaam had gradually become a hub of radical scholars, who found the policies of Nyerere too idealistic. President Nyerere as a Catholic Christian spelled out in his speech in Cairo that his socialism was not based on any one book such as the Koran, the Bible, or Marx's Capital. He was socialist of his own making. In general, the academic community at the University of Dar es Salaam rejected his political formulas as ideological and supported their own variation of socialist policies based on historical materialist theories. They refrained from making suggestions on how to implement villagisation better. Against this background, our Tanzanian-Finnish group of researchers had to find its own line between the theories governing the discussions "on the hill," or at the university, and the practice of the implemented *ujamaa* policies.

I had my own theoretical grounding in hermeneutics. Guides for my approach were those who felt the same need to cooperate with people and relate the created knowledge to the ground. For my doctorate study, I had acquainted myself with the anthropologists, such as Victor Turner and Mary Douglas, who had done research on ritual symbolism, and others who had been engaged in research other areas of Tanzania, such as Monica Wilson, T. O. Beidelman and Hans Cory's *African Figurines* (1956). Professors Terence Ranger, Marcia Wright and Swedish professors Claes-Fredrick Claesson, and Ulf Himmelstrand had been supportive of my approach. I enlarged my theoretical understanding by reading history of philosophy, phenomenology and hermeneutics and looked for anthropologists who would have been near to my striving to get nearer to the people with whom I did my participatory research. I was encouraged by Bengt Sundkler, who found in my approach similarities with his own human-centred approach. My primary concern was not how theoretically sound the starting point was, rather how to accommodate research in a situation, which demanded the common participation and contribution of the traditional subject and object (M-L. Swantz 1980).

For theoretically oriented research partners, it was impossible to start the study without a worked out historical materialist theory. Building the theoretical framing based on historical materialism was led by Kemal Mustafa, who hardly found points in common in that respect when he spent nights with the warriors and worked closely with families of the Parakuyo Maasai. Deborah Bryceson and Marjorie Mbilinyi elaborated the framework further, with Ulla Vuorela placing an emphasis on the women's weak position in her writings. The ensuing publications found both support and criticism in Participatory Action Researchers' conferences (Mustafa 1977, 33-51; Bryceson 1980, 10-25; Bryceson and Mbilinyi 1980, 85-116; Mustafa and Bryceson 1982; Mustafa 1981). The associate members Peter Rigby and Marjorie Mbilinyi contributed to the theoretical thinking as did Deborah Fahey Bryceson. All three shared in writing for Jipemoyo publications, but Bryceson did not take part in a participatory research project itself.. Nor did Rigby mention the *Jipemoyo* publications, when his chapter was reprinted in another context nor are Bryceson's Jipemoyo articles mentioned in the bibliographies of her well-recognized later works.

As a research associate, Professor Rigby guided Mustafa to line up with materialist phenomenology by referring to Karl Marx, Alfred Schütz and later to Maurice Merleau-Ponty (Rigby 1985). Rigby's phenomenological views offered a common departure point in which he took a more sympathetic view to my line than the other fellow researchers in the discussions. Similarly with me Rigby criticized the traditional anthropological method based on "field research" and "participant observation" by accusing the vocabulary to be deriving from natural sciences (Ferguson 1990). According to Rigby, the "participant observation" implied false ontological objectivity; the observer wrote down or recorded what s/he gleaned from participation in specific social situations. What Rigby insisted was that the observer did not merely objectively scrutinize her or his surroundings rather became involved as a "whole person" with the interpretive equipment of scientific discipline. Those studying the scientific results were thus "interpreting an interpretation."

Mustafa was influenced by Rigby's theoretical line, but during *Jipemoyo*, Rigby did not see the Parakuyo as divided into classes. Mustafa presented a logical explanation on how the classes conditioned consciousness, but only briefly summarized its meaning in his dissertation focusing "on the level behind appearances in social interactions in order to explain and then work towards transforming what was experienced at the level of appearances." Mustafa's critique was mainly against the government's treatment of the pastoralists, but he differed from Rigby by analysing their problem as a growing class differentiation caused by the government policies. Thus individuals pursued their own interests within a particular social class and created certain historical materialist ideology (Rigby 1984; Mustafa 1989).

Mustafa evidenced a growing class distinction within the formerly less materially differentiated Maasai by pointing out at the growing differences between the numbers of cattle, which the herders owned. Some herders who Mustafa knew well agreed to count the heads of their cattle with the researchers' assistance. The account evidenced the decreasing numbers of cattle; many herds were too small even to support the owners' households. In his research, Mustafa recorded the differentiation among the pastoralists by dividing them into three income groups, of which only the richest had enough cattle for reproducing themselves. Ultimately, the research helped to put halt to the Government order that ten per cent of the herds were to be annually sold at the cattle market near Lugoba. The Government had assumed that the cattle herds were growing in size (Mustafa et al. 1980, 64-87; Mustafa 1989, 111). Rigby considered that the Parakuyo still maintained social commonness even when the numbers of cattle differentiated the households. In his last book he came to different conclusion and expressed his frustration (Rigby, 1996)

Yet, there were basic differences in the founding principles, as materialism as the dominating basis of analysis did not leave room for humanistic interpretations, which the social and cultural life of the societies we studied would have required. I could not see that the sole determining forces were the modes of production, especially in case of an emerging society, such as Tanzania, with its own social context. While I was not denying the basic significance of the productive forces and their influence in creation of differentiation, this society was not easily analysed through defined classes. As anthropologists, many of us found it hard to apply the historical materialist theories to our research.

Theoretical disputes affected the actual study. The rejection of my non-theoretical approach was looked down about, making my position as the director difficult. It affected me to the point that I never worked my final report into a publication. Arvi Hurskainen dissociated from his position as research affiliate and did his study independently with different pastoralist groups, taking fine photos of their ritual events and daily activities and providing copies of his dated research observations to Jipemoyo archives. With Yonas and Paulo as assistants, Hurskainen stayed away from the debates and developed his own theoretical frame apart from the others. In his doctoral thesis, he made an extensive analysis of the structure of the Parakuyo Society, which, alongside several other studies, gave him the post of a Professor in African Studies at the University of Helsinki (Hurskainen 1986).

Ultimately, both the theoretical and practical lines were pursued. As we entered the research from several disciplines, I claimed that we needed time to work out the theoretical and philosophical basis for a participatory approach. The prior practical experience of three years engaged in participatory action research, while struggling to interpret it to the Marxist scholars, had prepared me for the challenge. For me, it was important that the theoretical problems were not perceived separate either from the social situation, which the researcher shared with the people, or from their concrete problems. At the same time, we all agreed that although the social scientist shared the life with the people she or he was researching, the researcher's task was also to make the situation scientific.

Further, we all agreed that while the participatory approach used in *Jipemoyo* was bound to lengthen the study period of the Tanzanian and Finnish scholars who were aspiring to do their doctorates, the process of knowledge production had to be shared with the social groups we worked with. Surprisingly, both the Ministry of Culture and Youth and the Academy of Finland as employers and funders were patient and supportive for the entire period of four years.

Mustafa had a chance to present and face criticism of his framework in the meeting held in Mzumbe in Tanzania in 1977, where African and international scholars met. Later on, Mustafa recognized in his doctoral thesis that the researchers as well as the government employees were "members of the petty bourgeois class in control of state power" while the fight was of "the oppressed and exploited class" (Mustafa 1989, 166). However, he had to be more lenient to the thought that the terminology of the different versions of the Marxist theories was not fitting in the situation of the rural petty farmers or even less of the pastoralists in Tanzania.

Follow-up after Jipemoyo

The leadership of the Academy of Finland followed closely the implementation of its first development study project in Africa. Professor Juha Pentikäinen, who as the chair of the council of the Academy for Humanities had initially advised me to prepare the research, and Elisabeth Helander, the Director of Research in the Academy of Finland, visited the research sites in Tanzania. After their visit the funding was released with greater confidence for the last three years.

The closing evaluation was held in Helsinki in autumn 1979. The conference was opened by the Director of the Academy of Finland and chaired by the Director of Research of the Academy, which evidenced the attention that the project had received as a pioneering development research in humanities and social studies. *Jipemoyo* brought attention to the Finnish academic research conducted in Africa, apart from the earlier research written by missionaries, some doing their doctoral work as also the author of this. Among the participants were all the Finnish and Tanzanian researchers in Jipemoyo, the Director of Research Anacleti Odhiambo and evaluators coming from West Germany/Switzerland (Action Research theory), Ireland (Ethnomusicology), Norway (Women's Studies), Denmark (Handicraft and Small Scale Industries) and Finland (Pastoralist Development).

The evaluator of my work and of the research methodology of Jipemoyo was Heinz Moser, a Swiss expert of PAR theory and history working in Germany, who had acquainted himself on the earliest user of Action Research in USA after WWII, the German scholar Kurt Lewin, and had continued to take interest writing several books of the history and application of Action Research in German language (Moser 1975, 1978). The evaluation conference was followed by a meeting of the European Association of Development Research (EADI), Basic Needs Working Group, which I was chairing and which added to its name participation, Basic Needs and Participation. 25 foreign delegates from 15 different countries attended. Jeremy Gould reported the research he had done with the funding granted to him in relation to the work of the group by the chairman of EADI professor Lois Emmerij, who also attended and was supportive of the participation concept (Gould 1981).

Following *Jipemoyo*, five doctoral theses were presented at the universities of Dar es Salaam, Helsinki, and Turku, one licentiate thesis in Helsinki, and some lower degrees in Dar es Salaam. Kiyenze had a scholarship to Finland and did his licentiate in sociology in the University of Helsinki and Mustafa's doctorate was done in the University of Dar es Salaam.

Two researchers became professors: Arvi Hurskainen in African studies in Helsinki and Ulla Vuorela in Anthropology in Tampere. Taimi Sitari held a senior university position at the University of Turku and Helena Jerman has been a long time Senior Researcher and teacher in the Institute of Development Studies in University of Helsinki.

When the funds from the Academy of Finland ended the Ministry of Culture and Youth was willing to continue the project. It had recognition in the Parliament as a Tanzanian conducted participatory research and the University employed Mustafa as a lecture in social science, when he finalized his thesis. Anacleti worked later under the Oxfam headquarters but had to return to his home in Tarime because of illness and relatively early death. Kiyenze started first as researcher in the Institute of Adult Education and then had a position in the leadership of the Tanzanian Red Cross. Mustafa was later in charge of the Canadian Aid civil society in Tanzania, married and moved to Canada.

The immediate results of *Jipemoyo* were in bringing the Participatory Action Research into the academic discussion and international research conferences. The basic principles of participatory research I had recorded in the initial Jipemoyo plan became stated and further analysed in Budd Hall's edited issue of the journal *Convergence* already in 1975. He referred to the guiding principles presented in my initial Service Paper of BRALUP (M-L. Swantz 1975, 1976). Hall became the General Secretary of the International Council of Adult Education (ICAE) with headquarters in Toronto and was also the main organiser of the First World Assembly of Adult Education in Dar es Salaam in 1976, during which some Latin American researchers made contact with the *Jipemoyo* team and visited the research site. As the centre for PAR networks, ICAE co-ordinated participatory research projects all over the world. Methodologies, theory and practice of PAR were debated in regional and international conferences held under or related to ICAE. In Europe, a European Adult Education Participatory Research Committee was established, which held its meetings in different European cities. In Tanzania, participation became a dominating concept in village development after it had been applied in the mode of Participatory Rural Appraisal in the Finnish supported development programme, RIPS, in the southern regions. Participatory approach in the form of Participatory Rural Appraisal was adopted as part of the countrywide programme for village planning, of which more in other chapters.

Three decades after *Jipemoyo*, Taimi Sitari conducted an international research project with four other scholars in the same Western Bagamoyo area (Sokoni 2010, Ylhäissi 2010). The study showed that 35 years after villagisation the villages in Western Bagamoyo have remained where they were created. A village-based local government system has been in operation, primary schools have been provided in villages, and dispensaries or health centres are available in bigger centres. In the beginning of the new millennium, secondary schools were built in all the wards with villagers' enticed efforts. The population has greatly increased and the numbers of cattle have grown, but so have also differences in wealth among the pastoralists (Sokoni 2010, 17). The area has received additional attention as the home district of the President Jakaya Kikwete, whose home village is Msoga, where he had a country house built for his free time use.

I have made frequent visits to the area after the Jipemoyo project. In June 2013, I met some of Ulla Vuorela's friends in Msoga who were sad to hear about her death. Ulla's doctoral thesis *The Women's Question and the Modes of Human Reproduction* (Vuorela, 1987) was based on sharing her life with the women and then systematically reviewing the kinship and power relations. The study has detailed descriptions of the cultural features of the matrilineal Kwere, including comparisons with related ethnic groups. Reading the work today as the theoretical divisions of the 1970s have toned down, one is reminded of the fervour with which the discussion was carried out between my effort not to accelerate class conflicts but rather to follow the idealistic effort through people's participation to increase their understanding and awareness of their development potentials in their situation. In other chapters I return to the theoretical backing for this thinking. The country was very different where I had been teaching on the slopes of Kilimanjaro before independence and where the educational opportunities had been made use of and the differentiation was beginning to be based on wealth acquired with other means. The rural people in the Western Bagamoyo lived in a traditional clan based rural society and the classes were not yet in formation. The Tanzanian adoption of *ujamaa* policies consciously aimed at preventing the class formation. Well-known anthropologist Maurice Godelier, who with other scholars had adopted Marxist theoretical grounding, yet had to recognize that the societies based on kinship were not class societies. The societies he was studying did not think that the differences within the kin groups would be based on externally influencing capital. Marx did not have a ready-made theory for such societies. The battle in the UDSM on the hill had to go through the same difficulties, but people's struggles in Western Bagamoyo were on a different level.

Perhaps more than with studies in general, the results of Jipemoyo have become part of the on-going social processes. The research was part of the everyday lives of people, who were the actors. The research was successful if it was not a memory of alien people among the villagers or pastoralists, who tried their best. When I some years after Jipemoyo met Mtumia Samsindo I asked him whether in his opinion *Jipemoyo* had brought some positive result in their lives, he did not in a customary fashion answer positively. He was not satisfied, he had anticipated more with what had been tried to accomplish. The educational system did not even yet offer Pastrolists education, which would have facilitated a pastoral way of life. He had also reason to be disappointed, as he had not received any public recognition of his many efforts to improve pastoralists' lives. Nevertheless, participatory research had political connotations. The individual and group discussions which were carried with the Parakuyo, the seminars in which the decision makers and the pastoralists met and the latter had chances to speak for themselves did influence people's courage to speak for themselves, a result which they would not recognize as a result of Jipemoyo. Jipemoyo at the time encouraged decision-makers to hear the discriminated people when solving their problems, but it is not a result, which would be visible with the changes in leadership. It increased people's awareness and made those in power conscious of people's right to speak. Ikoyo who followed Mtumiahad gained courage to face changes and send his daughters to school among other changes. The Parakuyo pastoralists are still herding and in much bigger numbers than before. Their rights, for which they have fought, have so far been recognized in the Western Bagamoyo and even around Morogoro where as members they have contributed to building of churches.

In conclusion

Jipemoyo was a significant milepost in developing participatory action research. It drew much high-level interest already during the research and has been documented in international publications. Participatory research has found recognition in three volumes of Sage Handbook of Action Research in which I have been on their Editorial Committee, as well as in the Advisory Board of the journal Action Research. Googling Jipemoyo gives results, but sadly the archiving system in the academic context in Finland has not yet provided the needed funds to get the rich Jipemoyo material with original texts, sounds, rich photography and data safely archived.

Jipemoyo research had a component of culture as one of the key ideas. It assisted the nation at the right moment to get the cultural aspects included in the development of the country and in strengthening of the national language. Finland assisted the erecting of the building for the Swahili institute, in which also the Development Studies Institute has been located. The contacts made between the Swahili institute at the University of Dar es Salaam and the Finnish academic and national cultural institutes have had an impact in the belated interest in research of ethnic languages in Tanzania. The establishing of Swahili as the national language first prevented the research on the over hundred ethnic languages and cultural traditions, which have been revived since the 1990s.

In conclusion, *Jipemoyo* initiated lasting interest in participatory research. *Jipemoyo* served to establish the role of participatory research both in national policies and even at times in development research, which has continued over the years. Participatory action research has also had its place in the academic and national development.

CHAPTER 9

Participatory Research in Support of Public Health Training

The Ministry of Health in Tanzania had initiated an extensive Primary Health Care programme and was starting to build it up towards the end of 1960s. The new programme was branded "Health For All" and was seen as a communal responsibility. Prevention was a priority rather than building the health programme on the basis of an expensive curative system. People's concepts of the causes of diseases needed clarification and the healing traditions had to be reconciled with the new health services.

The Ministry of Health had put forth *An Outline of Medical Development 1964-1969,* which set goals for health institutions by the end of the decade. The document was addressed to The Honourable Minister S.M. Maswanya and the Medical Development Committee was headed by the Principal Medical Officer Dr. Akim. The committee included one female Senior Medical Officer, an American administrator and seven British doctors. The document listed the health institutions and the anticipated extensions during the five-year period under review, "in accordance with the general principles recommended by the Committee for adoption in planning future development." There was no mention of any indigenous health system. The hospital facilities in the cities were government run and some facilities were run by Asian communities. In the rural areas they were run mainly by Catholic, Lutheran and Anglican Churches and Missions. The majority of the planned new facilities were anticipated to be government-run as the government eventually took over the majority of the former mission hospitals.

The big change came in the 1970s, when the Health For All (HFA) was implemented with the adoption of Primary Health Care (PHC) at its core in the ten-year Health Sector Plan 1971/72 – 1980/81. It was to serve the community-based health care system with an emphasis on prevention, even if the hospitals, clinics and dispensaries continued still to play an important role. It aimed at reaching the maximum number of people in the rural areas with basic health services. The number of dispensaries grew fast. According to the survey 1978/79 supported by SIDA, the International Development Agency of Sweden, in ten years 72 per cent were to live within five miles of a health facility, including the facilities in the process of being built (SIDA 1982 and URT 1991).

The plan to provide services for all was given much weight by the Ministry. The number of health centres grew from 161 in 1976 to 260 in 1986; the dispensaries increased from 1,847 in 1976 to 2,831 in 1986 and 65 per cent of the health expenditure was spent on rural areas, where 90 per cent of people lived. On the other hand, while in 1973/4 nine per cent of the GDP was spent on health, in 1981only 2.8 per cent was directed to recurrent health services.

Observationd in the late 1980s indicated that the health students' work practice in villages required funds not made available.

The village based community health system was well under way before the United Nations conference in Alma Ata in 1982 declared its *Health for All by 2000* programme based on Public Health. The Ministry of Health began remodelling its system according to the new directives, even when its own system had already followed the same principles even if details differed. The same pattern of changes, made according to external wishes and payments, has been repeated over and again in the field of health, in education and in development programs in general. Conditions tied to donor support are repeatedly taken up, resulting in the loss of initiative, energy and resources while peoples' own accomplishments fade away time and again. I listened to ideas of foreigners during the RIPS program in Lindi region in mid 1990s when a leading Education Officer had gathered District Education Officers from the southern regions for new instructions, as according to him "Tanzania had decided to adopt the Irish education system." He had heard an Irish educator giving such instructions in the Bagamoyo educational training centre and found an appreciative education officer to declare its acceptance in Tanzania. I experienced another such surprise when the District Executive Director of Iramba told me in 2007 that the country was following the participatory approach in district planning, which the Japanese had introduced.

The assessment of the primary health care was made throughout the country in the end of 1978/79 and it was thoroughly documented in numerous volumes. Finland had financed the building of 11 training centres for Rural Medical Aid. It brought the Minister of Health of Tanzania for a visit to Finland together with his Permanent Secretary. He reported the tentative results of the health sector evaluation, but the reports did not give sufficient information about the capacity of the Primary Health Care to reach and serve the women in the specific maternal and child health problems. The Minister inquired whether the author could take on research of the capacity of the health care system to serve the women's health needs. FINNIDA was prepared to finance such a program as it was in its interest to assess its own support to the training centres for the Rural Medical Aid in different parts of the country in 1973-1976. One of them was in the process of being turned into the Centre for Educational Development for Health (CEDHA) in Arusha and it was given the task of educational development and retraining of health educators from the 97 health workers training institutes throughout the country. FINNIDA saw an opportunity at the same time to launch the evaluative study *Effects of Finnish Development Cooperation on the Lives of Women* with an additional component of training. It became an extensive research and training project titled *Village Participation in the Health-Workers Training Program With Special Reference to Women*.

The preparatory work for the research project was started in 1979 and the first research round was made in 1980. Some of the training events were continued after the evaluative phase with the participation of a number of

Finnish doctors representing their organization, Social Responsibility of Doctors (SRD). The support of SRD's participation in health workers' training events continued until 1993. Combining the evaluations with the training program of the Ministry of Health gave the possibility to get deeper into the issues rather than visiting a number of places and studying some documents. The participatory approach to assess the health training practice opened up the opportunity to influence potential changes.

The Primary Health Care initiative was built on communal care and it aimed at giving more responsibilities to the citizens. The plan was extended to elect two village health assistants, preferably a male and female, for observing the health related needs in the village, recording people's special needs and happenings and so assisting the paid health workers. The assistants were to be given some training in first aid measures in district hospitals. If there were special campaigns, the village health assistants were involved in them, but as their services were dependent on the villagers' support, some left the work and disappeared to cities to look for paid work. Short training of traditional village midwives in basic hygiene was also implemented, giving them simple equipment for hygiene.[3] In some cases the problem arose, as experienced later in coastal Mtwara, that after the traditional midwife had received a little training she lost her traditional identity and with it the neighbourly compensation in kind at the delivery of a child.

UNICEF implemented village-based training in selected regions organizing seminars to which groups of villagers were gathered for learning events. The participants were given refreshments during the seminar and small payments as compensation for their missed workday at home. This continued practice created a pattern of dependency, which has been perpetuated in donor-supported projects. The villagers have anticipated payments for attending seminars also after the donor money was no longer there. The government officers' expectation of per diem payments for their visits within the district became even greater hindrance for attendance in training programs.

Participatory research combined with health workers' training

My experience with a participatory approach combined with training in the earlier malnutrition study served as a precedent for its application in the health assessment project in relation to women. In place of assessing women's health care in some part of the country the decision was made to broaden the research to include in it the health-workers' training preparing the students for village health work with special reference to women. The research was to be implemented in cooperation with the health workers training institutes as a combined research and training program.[4] The implementation was worked

---

3 Village health workers are no longer found in villages and the use of traditional retrained midwives is forbidden because of some errors made. The health system has no longer the same emphasis on community-based health care.

4 The officer responsible for development cooperation in East Africa Ritva Jolkkonen, who later became the Ambassador in Tanzania, cooperated with the initial plan. Dr. Elina Visuri followed and gave the same keen support to the project.

out with the Ministry of Health whereby two Tanzanian officers responsible for health education Dr. Mnzawa and Ms. Mnaulau did not only agree to the approach but cooperated in the project.[5] They came along to the preparatory round of visits to health training centres of various levels, and they continued to follow the work subsequently. They came also to Finland to take part in a workshop organized around the theme in Finland. Dr. Rumishaeli Shoo represented the Ministry and his participation was particularly significant and his lectures in the workshops gave authority to findings. Decades later he became the responsible director of the UNICEF programs in East Africa and benefitted from the earlier experience, as he told me at a casual meeting of him and his family in Meru in 2004.

From the Finnish side Margareta von Troil from the Institute of Development Studies at the University of Helsinki acted as a research/training co-worker in this as also in several other projects and did thorough recording in English for the training and research documentation. Architect Outi Berghäll, with experience in an infrastructure program in Manzese, Dar es Salaam, joined the first round of visits and meetings with staff and students in 1980. The health-workers' training program continued in cooperation with the SRD, three members of which participated from the first phase and some doctors continued later with the Tanzanian staff in seminars during Finnish summers until representatives from all the health-training institutes in all the zones had attended such a training seminar. Dr. Kati Juva followed the programme starting in 1981 until the final positive evaluation of the Finnish participation in 1994. The representatives of the Ministry had expressed their opinion that the training would continue with or without the Finnish support.[6]

The research on the impact of health services on women and children, however, pertained only for two years and six training workshops with village visits and the recorded village contacts related to them. The first workshops were held after the study tour in 1981. Päivi Kokkonen specialized on the effects on women of the FINNIDA supported projects in the RMA training institutes (Kokkonen 1985) of which the training institute CEDHA was one. It became a central place for the research-training project.

The participation of the students in training for health work in villagers' everyday life and getting acquainted with their problems was a central part of the formulation of the training approach combined with participatory research. People's participation in the upkeep of their own health meant their *becoming conscious* of their health needs but also of the potentialities they had for preventing disease and precautions they could take. The teachers would visit the villages in preparation for the students' work in them and meet the villagers during the

---

5 The doctors participating through the research period were R. S. Shoo, Dr. Mnzawa, Dr. Hingora and E.M. Teri, the head of CEDHA and on the part of the nurses Mrs. Mnaulau and Miss E.E. Zebulon. The Permanent Secretary A.S. Dhalla was most helpful all the time. Director of Manpower was Dr. Mkumbwa and Senior Medical Officer in the Ministry Dr. M. Amri.

6 Doctors Kati Juva, Åsa Westerlund, Matti Mäkelä and Ulla-Maija Rautakorpi participated in the programme as distinguished scholars and holders of positions at home. See Bibliography.

students' learning periods. Together with the students they would learn to know people's views and problems in informal discussions with villagers. The health workers had to get closer to the patients' world, and to know the problems and potentialities of the women in their everyday life, not only during their visits and stay in the hospitals, health centres or dispensaries, which women often made at the last stages of their pregnancies when they were getting ready to deliver. The health workers had to acquaint themselves with the general conditions of the villages in which the mothers went through home deliveries, took care of their babies after delivery, and they would learn the reasons why the women would not come for treatment or delivery to the health centres.

A significant principle in planning the training program was to mix the levels of health workers, doctors going together with mother-child health workers and rural medical aids with nurses and environmental health workers and taking part in the training seminars together. They would learn to know the living conditions, the beliefs about causes of illness, the traditional medicines, practices people used for cure and prevention, and the fears they had towards school or hospital medicine, which the workers represented. They needed to observe how the dispensary or hospital served the needs of the people, the experiences people faced with the official medical system, and the need to have staff available for home visitation. The learning process aimed at giving the medical staff greater understanding of the need to be inventive in the variety of situations to which the staff had to adjust and to know the traditional practitioners from who they sought help. The workshops were to serve as an introduction to the way of training, as even samples of information served as significant signposts toward an improved approach to work with the villagers.

During the years 1982-1983, four participatory workshops for preventive Public Health Program were organized in cooperation with the Ministry of Health staff, with the researchers from the IDS in the University of Helsinki and the members of the Social Responsibility of Doctors. Gaining understanding of the people's use of traditional medicine, the workers' and people's conceptualization of health and medicine as well as the inquiry about the concepts, which the media perpetuated about traditional and modern medicinal practices, were included in the project.

The participants in a seminar in Kibaha Health Centre gathered an amazing amount of information, which the people in surrounding villages shared with the teams who spent a day visiting them. The villagers did not hesitate to present sharp criticism of the existing service they had experienced, not least experienced by the delivering women. The information about the traditional medicine and the curing methods of the local practitioners, who the villagers customarily preferred to consult with their problems in the coastal belt, were openly shared when the clinical medicine was experienced to be of little use or not available when needed. The coastal rural population was obviously well acquainted with the traditional practices, even when they had some experience of the new services on offer at some distance.

The first version of a health handbook was prepared in a question form with 25 subject areas of health. It was intended as a guide for discussions with the villagers as active participants, whom the health-workers traditionally encountered only as patients. The book changed its form as the years went by, and a totally new version with informative instructions in Swahili with some of the drawn pictures retained was published in 1993 on behalf of the Ministry of Health by the Centre for Educational Development in Health (CEDHA) and supported by SRD. It was entitled *Ways of engaging people in improvement of their health. Guide for health workers. (Mbinu za Ushirikishwaji wa Jamii katika Kuboresha Afya, Mwongozo kwa Wafanyi Kazi wa Afya).* There was an evident need for better communication between the health personnel and the patients. The consequence of the initial project was the inclusion of participatory learning in the training programme of the Ministry as part of the syllabus for the different levels of health workers and as an examination requirement even for the doctoral candidates (Swantz 1979b, 1983, 1989c, 1992, 1994b).

Getting acquainted with the health training curricula

The experiences in participatory projects, in which research was combined with training, gave me the urge to develop the approach further. During the Jipemoyo project in Bagamoyo District in the latter part of the 1970s I had begun to work with a couple of women teachers and student nurses in Lugoba toward a self-generating training program. The teachers became involved in adult learning lessons with the Parakuyo women in what to them sounded like a dangerous adventure going to the Maasai *boma*, teaching the women to read and trying even to teach them some cooking.

The aim with the nurses was to learn women's health problems from their point of view. The nurses indicated a desire to spend time with village women, but having no initial training for such an approach they found it hard to carry out. As professionals, the teachers and nurses were taught to act as teachers dispersing knowledge. It was evident that the training prepared workers to teach and to give health directives but not to listen to the people or to address their taboos and customs. Learning from the people was not a familiar concept, nor was mutual learning the custom (Swantz 1979c).

The initially intended evaluative study was turned into a participatory learning program for the health workers training institutes' staff members and students. The participatory training combined with evaluative study aimed at giving the trainees more understanding of the people' ways of living. Together with an investigative tour and participatory training seminars the curricula for the training of the different health professions were studied to find out what the expectations were in regard to the needs of the communities.

In all, the curricula of the health workers' training programmes included a period spent in villages and in them the communal aspect was expressed in varying ways. The first task was to acquaint the researchers with the curricula for the different categories of health workers. It was found that the stated community and preventive objectives involved the health workers in initiating, organizing, supervising and directing community activities. The village period was to induce in the trainee a conviction of the "environmental womb from which disease takes birth" and to teach him/her how to cooperate with the villagers in improving the environment and instigating self-help projects. The period practised in villages aimed at exposing the students to the village reality, giving them experience in discussing with mothers the care of their children, in terms meaningful to them. The students' work was to relate to the health priorities of the villagers, which needed to be analysed. Maximum community participation presupposed also knowledge of and cooperation with the traditional healers. Thus it was found that the curricula included the aims of the research-training programme and the task was to find the ways to implement them during the training period and to research the existing practices and potential obstacles to why the community participation was not implemented as guided.

The curricula inclusive of village periods also strengthened prejudices by reference to "the effects of ignorance, custom and prejudice." The health-workers were not taught about the positive healing customs, beliefs, and practices, nor the taboos or fears of the people who would come under their care. The Medical Assistants (MA), who later on were promoted to the position of Assistant Doctors, were to be in charge of the health centres or the outpatient wards of the district hospitals and the managerial functions were included in their clinical training. They received practical training in such workplaces and two or three weeks were reserved for the village environment. While the understanding of "the causes, conditions and processes of diseases within the body" was basic to clinical medicine, there was no acknowledgement that the patients they treated might seek the causes from a totally different angle. Not recognizing the potential difference in the perceptions of the cause and nature of illness was bound to create a wall between the healer and the patients who would bring their own medicines to the hospital for treating causes not perceived to have physiological causes. The curriculum indicated, "The main purpose is to help the student interpret the symptoms and signs of clinical diseases and to appreciate the rationale of the treatment." Not knowing the patient's rationale, the transfer of knowledge to the patient might not be understood. Such was the case with a woman from Bunju whose stomach had been operated on at Muhimbili hospital. She told me that her suspected neighbour had caused a *jinni* to enter her stomach, which now was removed, showing the ways the threats were mixed up in her mind.

Environmental health training, included in the MA program, was closest to the villagers in stating: " The aim of this course is to induce in the medical assistant student a conviction of the environmental womb from which disease takes birth. It is hoped that this conviction may be strong enough to result in overt action in improving the environment of Tanzanian villages. In other words, the purpose of studying environmental health is to improve the environment."

The MAs were expected to encourage self-help projects and to assist, reinforce, direct and supervise the work of health officers and health auxiliaries in these efforts. This proposed course was village centred and recognized "the living in the village" for three weeks to be "an essential part of the MA curriculum" as "he learns at the first hand the actual problems of the rural areas and this makes the subsequent learning realistic and practical." They were not only supposed to discuss the health problems with the villagers but to assist in harvesting crops or construction. They were even warned against displaying "a superior attitude toward nursing and a resistance to learning its techniques". There was also a political section referring to the Tanzanian socialism and the structure of the health service. MAs were advised to discuss with mothers, "in terms meaningful to them", the care of the patient. In discussing the spacing of children, "the various social and religious beliefs and customs" within the Tanzanian society were referred to. The Health Education section stated that the MAs "should involve maximum community participation and be related to community health priorities." The MA should plan the health education project for the Health Centre and be able to conduct interviews, identify community leaders and use principles of good communication in leading discussions. The MA should even be able to cooperate with traditional healers in treating mild mental illness and neurotic reactions. In conclusion, s/he should assist patients with sympathetic counselling. In general, the curricula included many of the aspects which the participatory training covered.

The categories of workers that needed the most village-centred training were the Environmental Health Officers (EHO) and the Rural Medical Aids (RMA). In the manual of the EHOs it was clearly stated that their place was firmly among the people, and the purpose was to produce a practical and technical "man," who could actually make and build things. The syllabus did not indicate what they should do in the two weeks in villages during the first year of training. They would spend eight weeks with the District Health Officer during the first year and four weeks in the Dispensary or Health Centre in the second year. The practical work included an attempt to identify a community problem and solve it with the community as a participatory effort. The aim was "to enable the student to relate accurately to any environment in which he happens to be working, both physical and human" (underlining in the original text). It was important to convince mothers of immunization. The EHOs had less emphasis on the significance of the environmental factors than in the MAs' syllabus but they needed "a number of skills in perception, analysis and communication" with the emphasis on the visible, demonstrable and practical.

The Rural Medical Aides worked closest to the rural life. For them it was important to give assistance in the care of mothers and children and to manage a dispensary. They were supposed to "talk with mothers of malnourished children in the hospital wards and try to find out the social causes of malnutrition." They did a village project of three weeks, but no details were supplied about the activities. A part of the syllabus dealt with the traditional beliefs and attitudes toward them, pointing out that there were also good customs, beliefs and taboos. RMAs learned about the dispensary management and public relations with village leaders and attending village meetings. RMAs were to make educational visits to rural houses and to discern the features of healthy human environment, clean water and improved housing, food hygiene and storage, important tasks if the RMAs could provide such assistance.

Thus the curricula were well planned and full of good goals, which showed that the health system aimed to be communally implemented if the good aims were carried out as intended. The review showed that combining training with participatory research fitted well into the programme of the Ministry of Health as spelled out in curricula. At the same time the aims were too extensive for the capacity of the workers within the conditions in which they would be working and the preparatory phases were not equipped to demonstrate the ways of implementation.

Participatory study-training visits to training institutes

Acquaintance with the curricula gave background to the visits into the health-workers' training institutes for finding how the policies worked in practice and what the teachers and students considered important in their training. I had done another part of the preparatory phase, collecting materials from the newspapers and journals over a period of several years to indicate what the general public knew on the basis of press, including the Swahili press, about the diseases, exceptional birth events, children and mothers, perceptions of the causes of diseases and accidents, traditional medicine practitioners and interpretations reported in papers. Such collections of materials were combined in an extensive file distributed to the doctors and representatives from the Ministry of Health gathered to discuss the future on the basis of the results of the previous extensive health survey reports.

During the visiting tour to the health training institutes the curricula could be further discussed, worked on, put into practice, and compiled in cooperation with the teachers, trainees and the communities. Special emphasis was to be given to the treatment and teaching relating to women and children and their specific issues, to which the curricula had not paid special attention. These things served as the background for conducting meetings with the staff and the students in the training institutes and for introducing community participation as the key topic for discussion with special emphasis on women and children as well as observing the students' contacts with villagers during the training.

Six training institutes were selected for the initial study-training phase with the aim of finding out the existing approach, organization and implementation of the training for the students' work in the villages. The institutes included two nurses' training schools, one in Tanga and another one connected with the Kilimanjaro Christian Medical Centre (KCMC) in Moshi, two Environmental Health Officers training institutes in Tanga and Arusha, one Mother-Child Health-workers' school in Same, and the Assistant Medical

Officers training in KCMC in Moshi, upgraded from the Medical Assistant courses. The simultaneous evaluation of the RMA training institutes covered that sector, but the difficulty of travel at that time because of the shortage of fuel permitted a visit only to two training centres. The concluding workshop was held in cooperation with one of the RMA training institutes in Arusha, which was being developed into an institute for health trainers as the Centre for Development of Health Education (CEDHA).

During the visits to the health training institutes, I visited two villages with the students who were doing their practice in them, one near Tanga and another in Suji village in South Pare. Discussions were carried out with the staff and students where the practical phase was not in process. Attention was paid particularly to the students' contacts with the village leaders, different categories of villagers, especially women and small children and the potential length and nature of the stay in the village. In general the institutes evidenced an attempt to implement the contacts with the villages as part of the training for varied lengths of time with the resources available following the accustomed modes of implementation. The approaches and lengths of time devoted for village work differed according to the funds available but also depending on the interest of the teachers, the nature of the students' future work and the need to pay attention to the opportunities for deliveries of children and child care. For the environmental health workers the periods in villages were longest and for nurses and MCH students longer than Assistant Doctors / Medical Assistants. My visit to the training facilities and meeting health workers in Mtwara in 2009 indicated basic changes in the system. Mother Child Healthcare workers have since received more training and been upgraded to Rural Health Assistants and Medical Assistants have become Assistant Doctors. The change of titles changed their work descriptions.

During the study, the student nurses were at the time in the village. We visited households and spoke with people while the students also met patients coming to the local dispensary. It was a common approach for the students to settle in a dispensary or health centre and use it as the base for visits to homes mainly to fill household questionnaires. In Kilimanjaro the MAs had assisted in making latrines and slabs for wells, but often the poor housing arrangements made the village periods short or transport was arranged for going back and forth daily.

The reports from the village visits revealed that the villagers treated the students as *waganga*, the title used for all healers, while workers assumed to be of higher level were called *madaktari*. Some teachers reported that the students had earlier considered the time in a village a holiday.

After the visits to the training institutes three workshops were held with participation from the visited training institutes. The workshops were conducted making use of a participatory approach, thereby involving representatives of all the groups in the training program. The principals and other representatives of the staff of the training institutes, senior students with some experience in village training, a few village leaders or ordinary villagers and health auxiliary staff in village dispensaries were involved in the week long workshops, which included a day or two spent in visits to villages. By bringing together health-workers and students of different levels and sectors it was hoped that in encounters with each other the different groups would be in a position to listen, to express views and to work together on recommendations. The participants were involved in the process of rethinking the more engaged approach of the health workers in their village work. The exercise was also part of developing further the participatory research process. There was general interest in such an approach at the time and the cooperation with the Ministry was genuine.

Training in Community Participation in Village Health

After getting acquainted with the requirements and the working methods, the participation in the exercises gave grounding for changing attitudes, while the weaknesses in village based health work and the difficulties encountered were also recognized. The active participation of interested leading doctors directly representing the Ministry of Health and giving well prepared informative lectures built an excellent base, from which to develop further the training program. The research findings during the participatory training, the potential for the implementation of the changes in the training mode and crucial findings in discussions with the villagers became part of the further development of the community based health education. The effort to make the training more community centred and communicative demanded additions in the curricula, but it required also funds allocated for the purpose, realizing that participatory training was part of the health care itself in practice. The section of participatory village health work was added in the curricula for the teaching programs as part of the community health program even in the medical doctors' requirements in the Faculty of Medicine.

The significant part of the concept of the basic health service in the 1980s was that the health workers as well as the village communities learned the concept of sharing the responsibility of caring for their own and the village health. The village experiences helped to clarify which preventive measures were possible for people to implement. Had the participatory inquiry results been implemented much would have been accomplished. Protecting water sources from interference, boiling drinking water, drying pools or covering water sources, which bred mosquitoes, making slabs for latrines and digging latrines were included in the programmes, recognizing that different circumstances required a variety of considerations. It became clear through the inquiring participation, not by the teaching mode of the learned health student. Preventive health service required finding reasons for malnutrition, traditional taboos and eating habits keeping children from eating the most nourishing food or the segregating eating habits causing at times unintended gender and age based malnutrition, as had been discovered already in the earlier malnutrition study in Kilimanjaro (Swantz 1979b, 1985, 1994b).

It became obvious that when the people once had a chance to talk with the health personnel they were interested in bringing out the weaknesses they experienced in the care they received within the health system rather than being ready to discuss their own responsibility and role in the communal health. The coastal villagers conceived that their only trusted support system was the traditional medicine and healing practices. The main difficulty with pregnant women was the distance and transport to dispensaries or health centres and the patients complained about the expense of the medicines, if they were at all available. It had been especially inconsiderate to send patients back from the dispensary or health centre without any attention, if the queues were long or the health workers had other interests to care for. Such experiences led to the use of local midwives who did not have the training they could have had. At later phase in the new millennium the practice of weakly trained local midwives were officially forbidden, as they were not considered competent.

I include here briefly some results from the findings during the participatory training period. The recorded material is from two of the training workshops, one in Kilimanjaro Singa Chini, the other from the coast relating to the health centre, hospital and nurses training centre in Kibaha (Tumbi), which reflect the differences but also similarities in people's experiences. Only samples are quoted here of the plentiful material preserved

Samples of health-workers study notes during village visits

After the first training workshop in Singa Chini, Moshi extensive health-workers training workshops were organized in Arusha, CEDHA and in Kibaha Nurses' Training Centre, which had dormitories for housing participants. The Singa Chini participants were housed in school dormitories as it took place during the Christmas holidays.

In Kibaha after the common sessions eight groups were formed for the participants to visit villages off the main road where none of the participants had been before. Each group was given a couple of subject areas as starters for talks with the people they met, but the discussion spread to other topics according to the interest of the people encountered. One group was guided by the village chairman, who influenced the discussion with readiness to answer the questions, another group visited all the houses in one ten house cell while another group found that people were on their fields and the discussions were limited to a few older people remaining near their homes. One or two village representatives from the visited villages were invited to the centre the following day for discussions on the findings. In the teams participants from different professional levels went together in order to get a broader view to the health situation.

The health issues relating to women and children, problems at childbirth, the use of prevention, planned timing of birth, use of medicines, nutrition, availability of food, the care of the families, the ways of earnings often relating to agriculture were discussed, but villagers' thoughts turned readily to the weaknesses in the system relating to health care as they had experienced it. The role of the traditional healers and midwives came up in most groups. Villagers' responsibility in their own health care, boiling water and washing hands were discussed. One group indicated that the drinking water was boiled when there was the threat of cholera, but when the danger was over it no longer was done. The role of the trained villagers for first aid and the failure to get the assistance from them were the topics brought up. In one case the village had contributed to getting the village health aide trained in Lushoto, but when she had started to work and she was not paid for the work she left the village for Dar es Salaam. This had been the case also in another village where the health centre had paid the training.

In the experience of the villagers the service of the health workers in the Kibaha hospital and health centre had not been good, and the health workers' negative attitudes in addressing the people became the heated topics. Such opinions could be interpreted as a defence for not making use of the service offered, but it caused also the Finnish participants to question why the Nordic influence had not had any longer enduring impact as since the building of the centre and its occupation by Nordic personnel had taken place less than two decades earlier.

Expenses related to health care was a topic brought up in all the groups as were concerns about the difficulty in transporting the patients to the health centre or dispensary, particularly of the delivering women. They were also concerned with the high cost of the medicines when they were available. Not only was the treatment at the Kibaha hospital, referred to as Tumbi with the traditional name of the area, not satisfactory but the medicines were not available when they were prescribed. The residents' negative experiences had led to general mistrust in modern medicine.

The participation of residents made it clear that more mobile health care and children's check-up cards with recorded weight of children were to be given to all mothers and stations for nurses' visits to homes or at least close to people's home areas were obviously needed. People had turned to traditional practitioners, as they were the most trusted. People continued to placee amulets around children's stomachs, wrists and neck to protect them from bewitching or spirit power. It is possible that in defence of the general use of the traditional medicine the negative aspects of offered health care became overemphasized, but the complaints had to be taken seriously. The preference of the traditional beliefs and practices and the use of traditional practitioners were topics given specifically in one group, in which the visiting group gathered detailed knowledge relating to the illnesses and problems that the traditional healers solely could treat, but most groups reported using traditional practitioners and medicines.

Here are some of the findings from the study:

<u>Childbirth:</u> Difficulty in transporting a delivering mother to the health facility led to home births assisted by the local midwives who had no additional

training. The placenta and umbilical cord had to be buried together in a hidden place, which had later both negative and positive significance, negative if misused by an enemy. Bathing of the mother every night or twice a day after delivery was a general important coastal custom, "*kumkanyaga mzazi maji*," for cleansing and returning the functions of the sexual organs. In the discussion when going through the experiences it was found to be a good custom and was recommended for all. Part of the population in the area had been moved there during the villagization, partly mixing different ethnic backgrounds, thus also the customs of the coastal people's were different from the upcountry groups, in relation to the extent of engagement in cultivation and in eating habits, and the grains and roots grown.

Birth-control: After giving birth mothers abstained from intercourse until they stopped breastfeeding. They knew of the need to time the births but had not received enough information about the birth control. Above all they did not like the methods offered for prevention and they did not get sufficient teaching about them. The information given at the health centre was not followed, because those who had tried using modern preventives had run into problems. The most usual way, about which the visited villagers knew was to wait until the mother ended nursing, which might also work the other way around so that they ceased the breastfeeding when it was the time to restart sexual intercourse.

Childbirths and deliveries: Home delivery was the trusted norm with some difference between villages. There had been a noticeable dependence on the services of the village health worker who had left the village and gone to Dar es Salaam. The traditional midwives were trusted and called to assist. No mention was made of the trained midwives.

Causes and Care of Diseases: Diseases were caused by God, by circumstances or appeared in children as *dege dege*, an attack they commonly get, which if not treated in a traditional manner would cause paralysis. Fainting, hernia and sexual disease were treated with Islamic means called earthly knowledge, *elimu ya dunia* (in opposition to divine knowledge, *elimu ya ahera*); or attacks were treated with *falaki*, rinsing written words of Koran with water into a clay pot and drunk, or the cause of the illness was gained by going to a *mganga* for divining with rattles, *manyanga*. The traditional healers were preferred to modern medicine since they treated people in a friendly manner, gave medicine right away and above all had the right understanding of the situation of the patients.

The above is only a small sample of the recorded information from the groups. It was filed and reports were left with the Ministry to disseminate, as the results of research have significance only if they are integrated into the teaching program. It would require a training system in which the participatory approach is continued. In any case, the health workers' teachers and the students taking part in the exercise learned substantive information and above all became aware of the significance of the attitudes toward the health workers and the need to adjust the care according to the situation of the people. Interestingly I met one doctor practicing in Mtwara whose visits to local health units where women gathered drew my interest. He had been one of the candidates who took part in the participatory training.

Participation in community based training of health workers

Thirty years ago the community participation in village health work was an accepted policy in the Ministry of Health and the doctors participating in developing the approach were committed with real interest. The significant role of the volunteer doctors from Finland in the seminars continued for over 20 years until the 1990s. The last effort the Finnish doctors' organization supported was in 1993, when the Ministry of Health published a completely new handbook for participatory training. The abbreviated history of the involvement of the Finnish doctors, and their participation in all the seminars in different parts of the country was instructive both ways as the different versions of the guidebook indicate.

In numerous cases, the mothers with complications were transported to distant health centres with the means available. In one case two men tried to transport a delivering woman on top of a bicycle. When the nurse arrived at the dispensary, she discovered the woman was curled up and convulsing. My Land Rover could take her twenty plus miles to the health centre where the child was born safely, but lack of transport prevents many from having safe deliveries, even when people are willing to carry their patients over distances in makeshift stretches.

The dependence on self-help and communal support has not had the same emphasis since the time of *ujamaa*, which was embedded in the planned health system. The community responsibility was at the core of the plan while the health service was being implemented through the system intended to be near the people. The self-help has since that time taken different forms.

The "economy of affection," the concept Goran Hyden (1983) recognized being at the core of the local mutual care when he pointed out that economy based on affection breeds mutual obligation and trust. Consequently the communities were inclined to prioritize informal arrangements rather than a formal kind. Hyden considered it to be detrimental to the further development of the country, because it did not promote economic development in the country. The socialist program considered the joining of the world market harmful rather than a necessity, yet it put the country behind and could not in the long run be beneficial (Hyden 1983, 11-12, 207-211).

At the same time the communal assistance by relatives has increased the family economy based on mutual aid. It has saved people facing health problems and the increasing deaths in families caused by the spread of HIV/AIDS. Grandparents commonly look after small children and families frequently adopt children of relatives when necessary. In Iramba district, World Vision has helped children to have their own house if one of them is big enough to build a simple house for his/her sisters and brothers. Mutual care has become important also in education. When the first seven years require funds only for the uniforms and special collections, any additional formal or informal education and training require fees, which people put together through extended family, when not succeeding to get external funding.

Later developments in health care and concluding thoughts

In 1990s the Community Health Fund was initiated on the village level or the Ward has taken it on later. Thereby with a payment of 5,000 Tsh (at that time) villagers were entitled to health services, but the services to women for deliveries and children's vaccinations were supposed to be given free.

In the new millennium the change in the health-workers' training programs with increased professional quality meant also changes in the titles, which no longer indicate the community based focus of prevention and service delivered in villages. The training of village health workers, who could be trained to give first aid, as also of briefly trained traditional midwives was discontinued. When the professional quality of work was emphasized, trust in the utility of the traditional services weakened. It appears that the initial emphasis on prevention, hygiene, sanitation and clean water, which went together with the Primary Health Care based in villages, lost its urgency. UNICEF has had for many years emphasis on improvement of the water systems.

The growing prevalence of HIV/AIDS since the beginning of 1990s has brought external support on preventive measures, which have been generally financed from international funds as special programs, which made it an effort to reach village people. The HIV checks financed externally are voluntary and thus do not reach all the affected, even if the offer for tests is within reach. With the change of the personnel in the Ministry of Health and with new streams of external influence together with the changing political program the communal participation in villages has changed direction.

My visit to the Ministry of Health in 2011 looking for the Health Education office was not successful. Two research staff members directed the visitor to a health research office where two reseachers had no knowledge about the past research and training efforts. The first edition of the booklet used in the participatory program was delivered to them (Swantz 1981).

The direction of the health workers training has in the new millennium made a turn to institution-based health services, but the needs of the first three decades of the independent nation were also different in many ways from what they are today. The *Ujamaa* politics and the cultivation of common fields did not succeed at the level of whole villages, but the examples of village groups having their common fields were common. The communal spirit was alive in several ways but villagers who agreed to work together also secured their family food by cultivating their own fields for food.

Today there is a quest for necessary upgrading of the professional level of health workers but it goes together with gaining degrees and fine sounding titles, but not always in ways which serve the practical needs of the village communities. Not having any longer workers in the Mother Child Healthcare or Rural Medical Aid categories is a great loss, especially when it has meant elimination of village midwives and trained village health workers and has turned the Mother Child Health workers to Public Health Nurses of whom some take diploma in midwifery. People now turn to the traditional village midwives probably even more than before, but the traditional midwives are not getting any training in hygiene and this can be a hazard to mothers who cannot make use of distant health centres or dispensaries. The number of early deaths is an indication of that. The schools for former RMAs were turned to schools for Clinical Officers, *Shule ya Watibabu*, "School of Healers".

The discussion in 2009 with the teachers in the school for Assistant Medical Officers, the former MAs, and the officer in charge of upgrading the staff in the Regional Health Workers' Training Centre in Mtwara indicated the eagerness of the lower level workers to get a better life and rank. The pattern is the same as in Finland where doctors do not want to seek posts in rural communities. On the other hand, *Maafisa tabibu*, the former Rural Medical Aids, are destined to serve in the rural Health Centres, and the improvement of their skills is prioritized in the policy of the Ministry of Health. The clinical officers and nurses will be in charge of helping the ward and village health committees oversee the availability and hygiene of water and latrines as well as the general hygiene.[7]

In closing, my experience with the inclusion of traditional healers has been more positive rather than with the middle level modernized self taught "doctors," whose medicines and ways of treatment are doubtful. The experience of women can be trusted when discussions are held with them. People living long distances from health centres need to be given more thought than is the case today and the standard of local services need close oversight. Drawing people from all the levels of the health care system into participatory efforts for improvement of the local health services encourages all concerned to greater efforts.

---

7 Information about the health system and policy was obtained in the Regional hospital and training center in Mtwara 08.12.2009.

PART

III

CHAPTER 10

Knowledge Production for Development

This book has moved on the border between theoretical and practical knowledge, which I have called "living knowledge" because it connects theoretical knowledge with people's every day life and common sense world. It is essentially also about broadening knowledge creation. It does not deal only with ways of sustaining life, but rather how the kind of knowledge is broadened, which sustains life beyond its daily subsistence. I assumed that in dealing with studied people's existential problems related to their sustainable livelihood different knowledge systems have to interact. On what level and for whose benefit the knowledge interacts needed to be defined.

In this book and during my whole career I have struggled to find what support I get as an anthropologist and a student of development studies from these disciplines in participating in the lives with rural people in Tanzania, so that they not only would sustain their lives but enrich them by deepening and widening the ways in which they conceive their life situations beyond mere daily subsistence, beyond making their basic living, in brief, how people could broaden their conception with questions, which deal with knowledge creation. The central question has been how the knowledge system we use serves the purpose for which we need it, in this case not only creating sustainable livelihood for the people we relate to but seeing them as active participants whose problems, knowledge and lines of thought and culture could enrich their lives and contribute to universal wisdom.

Research has enriched my life, yet every time I have tackled the task I was left with the thought that there would be much more to know and much deeper to go. I have had 70 years to improve my understanding since I first began academic life right after the War in autumn 1944, yet I feel I am only a beginner.

During 62 years I have been working as a Northener in intercultural situations in Africa trying to understand the ways of the people I have shared life with. I face the question of what I have learned during those long years and what wisdom I can bring forth from the treasure chamber of experience. I have moved between two forms of knowledge, practical everyday experiential knowledge of the people I have shared life with and theoretical knowledge, which equipped me initially for my work and which has during the years accumulated in thousands of volumes on my shelves and in my aging head. I do not want to privilege one form of knowledge over the other, but what I have sought is "living knowledge."

When I leaf through the books and articles I have written and speeches delivered I ask whether this work has been of some significance in the field of science and development or has it only fulfilled my own inner need to understand and analyse life. I let others decide, but in this book I have sorted out ideas and factors which have influenced my scholarly work.

I have found it difficult to stick to my professional role as a scientist and distance myself from the personalized approach to research. I see people as humans and as neighbours, not as informants or objects of research. Yet I convert the knowledge gained with them into a scholarly analysis. It means that unexpected events in life turn to occasions of new learning and overtures to new vistas.

My early history and basic academic training in Finland influenced and gave meaning to my later work. I transformed the term "folklore" into "people's knowledge." Throughout my research career I have wanted to bring out the people's common knowledge, which I have encountered in different contexts and environments. I have returned to these influences frequently and have brought out, what these contacts have meant to my scholarship and to me as a person.

All scientists build their own world of science with its academic and applied science structures. With the development of high-technology based on refined theoretical science, the separation of science from the common people's practical reality widens. In the human and social sciences they are brought together in terms of basic and applied science, but in this book I have tried to show that human sciences need to integrate scientific knowledge with people's knowledge more explicitly.

Scientific knowledge is not produced apart from people's practical knowledge. A scientist appropriates everyday knowledge unconsciously even if s/he is not aware of the sources of her/his knowledge. Common sense thinking is always at the base of scientific thinking and common sense thinking is based on practice and knowledge created in practical situations. Any cultural contact situation requires a greater cognisance of the contribution that each collective contributes in an encounter. As ethnography bases its knowledge on differences in cultures and in ways of interpretation rather than generalisations, I have endeavoured to understand the phenomena I have studied from the point of view of my research companions, who in traditional anthropology were named informants.

At the meeting point of cultures as the science-based actor I have recognised the role of practical everyday knowledge in the theoretical thought. I have maintained that if the development agents fail to recognise this, the development projects fail. The practical knowledge of people is born and draws from common sense knowledge of a collective, a group or community, and is applied in action. Participating in people's action accommodates bringing theory to the level of action (Swantz 1989, 59 122).

The conditions in Tanzania are changing quickly and educated and trained women are engaged in bigger business. The descriptions here are from the time when women were rapidly getting into bigger business but differences between various regions were evident.

Studies in Iramba District and in the southern Mtwara and Lindi regions over the last two decades have dealt with women's ways of sustaining the lives of their families in village communities, which in the World Bank "objective measures" belong to the category of the poorest. Women sustain the lives of their families in the midst of hardships by forming groups, which they develop into savings groups through the introduction of new ways of saving such as Vigoba groups and take leadership in further developed SACCOS groups. Even then, women face precarious conditions, which prevent them from getting larger sums from the local Banks for enlarging their business efforts. Men have formed SACCOS in order to get significant loans for business purposes, but do not otherwise form mutual assistance groups. Women's savings organizations cultivate a very different culture, aimed at achieving both social security and financial income. More than men, they construct a social economy for supporting their families.

Highlighting the social aspects of women's economic pursuits does not imply ideal communities: quarrels occur, groups break up and new ones are formed, and women with poorer initial starting points seek ways to manage their demanding life situations. Yet experiences so far have been encouraging. Women make use of opportunities for individual progress when they occur, but at the same time build social foundation for family and motherhood.

The western scientifically empowered world has given heavy weight to theoretical knowledge and only secondary significance to practice-based knowledge. It has led the developing countries unfortunately down the same road and has influenced the learning in schools. Yet, the history of science has plenty of evidence that great discoveries and leaps of creativity have resulted from the practical mode of knowing, which forms part of all true scientific work, whether it is recognised or not.

In development work it happens that engineers cannot handle technical jobs as a consequence of their theoretical and non-practical training. This became evident in the process of transferring technology in the Finnish water project in Mtwara and Lindi regions (M-L. Swantz 1989a, 1989b). The same was evident in Iramba in the skills of technicians whose training in practical skills has not given them the versatility, which was required in practical working situations. The local self-trained handymen come to rescue where repairs can be made in makeshift manner on the spot. The interaction of practical knowledge and theory are required for technical change. What is true in the technical world is equally so in the human and social world (M-L. Swantz 1989).

Scientific knowledge is not produced apart from people's practical knowledge. A scientist appropriates everyday knowledge unconsciously, even if s/he is not aware of the sources of her/his knowledge. Common sense thinking based on practice and knowledge created in practical situations is at the base of scientific thinking. The scholars around ethno-methodology research, initiated by Harold Garfinkel (1974), demonstrated the basis of common sense knowledge by scholars in science. Henri Elliot brought into scientists' attention the fact that scientific reports and accounts were tied to the everyday practices of the working scientist. The language was acquired against the backdrop of ordinary language, and the syntax of practices and methods accredited as correct to the task at hand, were conducted in same ways as any concerted activities warranted by a collective (Elliot 1974). Recognising this becomes especially important at the crossroads of cultures. The cultural contact situation requires greater cognisance of the contribution of each collective in an encounter between them. Ethno-centricity arises from the lack of this realisation. An ethnocentric (social) scientist fails to recognise that the common knowledge from which s/he draws from is not every collective's common knowledge. Ethnography is a discipline, which bases its knowledge on different points of view and ways of interpretation rather than generalisations. It endeavours to understand the phenomena from the point of view of those it researches.

I have referred to Stephen Marglin's book *The Dismal Science: How Thinking Like and Economist Undermines Community* (2008), in which he uses the Greek terms *techne* and *episteme* to signify two basic systems of knowledge: *algorithmic* versus *techne* knowledge (1990, 217-282). For Marglin, the fundamental difference between the two was whether the conception and execution of work were separate processes or a single process (1990, 173). The ways of knowing are distinguished on the basis of how knowledge is arrived at, how it is made use of, how it is modified and what political relations prevail between those who make use of the same system. *Techne* knowing is part of practice both in the learning process and as an outcome. Particularly important for me is that *techne* organises experience in a way in which, according to Marglin, *episteme* is inadequate (1990, 234, 239).

Feeling and sensing are central to *techne* as knowledge is gained through touch and emotions. Knowledge is learned through practice and learning is a process of absorbing. The learner learns from one who has the knowledge and skill in body, mind, and hands. Through a heightened sense of touch and feel, and through intuition, *techne* creates and transmits. This is akin to Lévi-Strauss's "*bricolage*," in which people develop new solutions to problems using existing resources embedded in their collective social consciousness. This "science of the concrete," which as also a mythical reflection according to him, "can reach brilliant unforeseen results on the intellectual plane" (Lévi-Strauss 1969, 16-7).

If the *techne* and *episteme* concepts are used as ideal types, they can be useful in our attempt to better understand the economics and social conduct of common people. *In fact, what lies behind these concepts is at the heart of this study.* During the 60 plus years I have witnessed development in Africa, I have again and again seen how development projects grind to halt or end in failure because of little regard or understanding of people's *techne* knowledge to the point that the whole dominating concept "development" is questioned as a "lost illusion" (Escobar 1988). Cases from different areas of life illustrate lopsided development in concrete contexts and give evidence how a dominating system creates its power relations when practical knowledge, ways of learning and executing skills are given secondary attention, and when ways of person to person interaction are not familiar to owners of epistemic knowledge.

Knowledge as a continuum from practical to theoretical knowledge

My basic assumption is that there needs to be a search for a wider base for scientific knowledge that places different forms of knowledge on a continuum: Common people, who are experts in their own life situation, can consciously contribute to scientific knowledge in a process of mutual inquiry and learning. Scientists can develop questions and find answers through communication with the non-specialists. They can also consciously expand common people's knowledge base with new information and new ways of analysing their life situation. A natural consequence of such a process in a developmental situation is that the people who thus get involved participate in the subsequent analysis, planning, and action. Action becomes part of knowledge formation while it contributes to the solution of the commonly identified problem.

When knowledge formation is seen as an interactive process between practical knowledge and theoretical knowledge, *action generates knowledge.* This is at the base of Participatory Action Research. The new paradigm researchers who grouped themselves around a "quality inquiry" theme under the leadership of Peter Reason of Bath University questioned the conventional goal of scientific knowledge. The extended numbers of scholars following similar lines have then contributed to the two volumes of *The SAGE Handbook of Action Research I and II* and the third volume finalized in 2015. According to John Heron, one of the initiating members of the action research and participatory group, the traditional form of research produces findings for *knowing that,* while *practical* outcomes have to do with *knowing how.* This way of looking at the rationale of research has obvious consequences for the participatory research setting (Heron 1996).

In participatory action research, *knowledge is formed in and for action.* This was the case also in the co-operative research in which Reason and Heron had specialised. The main outcome in scientific work is writing books and articles for the scientific community, not for the researched community, although "often the knowledge that is really important for them is the practical knowledge of new skills and abilities" (Reason 1988, 13). Heron takes this idea further. He points out that there is a hierarchy of knowledge, which proceeds from experiential knowledge through presentational and propositional knowledge to practical knowledge or the realm of skills. "The deeper way to do participative research is to make skills in a domain, not statements about a domain, the primary intended outcome" (underlining mine; Heron 1996, 45). According to Heron, practical knowing how, the active execution of skills, is the true consummation of an inquiry, not a paper or a book, even if these are also necessary as a secondary outcome:

After trying it both ways — I now believe we get deeper information about the nature of our realities when our prime concern is to develop practical skills that change these realities than we do when our prime concern is to get information about them through the exercise of certain skills. (Heron 1996, 45)

It is especially pertinent to differentiate between the outcomes of the types of knowledge when we deal with people's knowledge and the outcome they want from common inquiry. To consider the action, or learning a practical skill, as the consummation, does away with the power of theoretical knowledge over the practical. According to Heron, this does not rule out the validity of direct information gathering, which is the method of choice, but it is complementary:

Because our realities are subjective-objective, the point about true excellence of action is that it is reality transformative for the person who acquires that excellence. And the transformation brings into conscious relief both what that reality was and what it has become. . . . The essence of knowing how to do something is having the knack. It cannot be reduced to 'knowing that' or 'knowing what. (Heron 1996, 47)

Heinz Moser, who worked with the theoretical problems that an action research faced, showed that the usual criteria for the validity of research results are not relevant in action and participatory research. According to him, the central concept is transparency. The different ways the research results have been gathered need to be written out. Second, the researcher's way of working must accord with the research aims. Third, the researcher should not influence the course of action in the research process so that the result in fact is her doing not of the actors (Moser 1975, 120-125).

Scientists have built a hierarchical world of science with its academic and applied science structures in science-based technology. Only after the end product is in the hands of the consumer the user is informed how to use the product. This kind of problem becomes particularly evident in the transfer of technology process from one culture to another. The introduction of a simple water pump in developing the shallow well water supply systems in Southern Tanzania is an example of how one-way communication led to failure. The World Bank tendered a 10 million dollar study to find a pump that would work, while the best usable pump had already been put to use in co-operation with the users' pump model. The best way would have been to involve the users in all the stages of the project process (M-L. Swantz 1989, 147-154).

For solving the basic problems leading to poverty it is necessary to bring into interaction different levels of theory, practical life and technology in people's everyday situation. Interaction between different knowledge systems occurs only if the researcher leaves her realm of science and enters the everyday world of the people for whose development she is working.

The social scientist needs to recognise that the researcher is not there only to learn what the informants have to give, by then turning it into epistemic knowledge for transmission of her expert knowledge. That is necessary, but the context and the ways in which health education, for example, is put to practice makes all the difference. Indigenous medicine has lessons to teach the modern practitioner, especially in treatment of the patient and its psychological effect on health. The closer the theory adheres to practice, the more fruitful the scientific enterprise is for the world in which it is created.

In participatory research we move on the border between theoretical knowledge, practical knowledge and practical action. The assumption is that in dealing with people's existential problems different knowledge systems have to interact. On what level and how they interact is the crucial question. One problem is that of communication: How do the different knowledge systems communicate? It is a question of language, personal contact, and preceding knowledge of "the Other," a concept which in anthropology and in practical life has gained much momentum. Participatory Action Research (PAR) is not only a tool, but a mode of interaction and an end result in an encounter between knowledge systems. PAR consists of search, interaction, action, reflection, intercommunication, and action. The failure of PAR is that it has rarely been institutionalized. Only if it becomes *a modus operandi* in the hands of motivated citizens can it begin to have political influence with structural consequences.

When new paradigms such as PAR, with its high regard to *techne* knowledge, try to interact and break through to the epistemic system, they are tolerated for a while but their welcome is generally short-lived. Transmission with any permanency and continuity fails, because the epistemic system's corpus of scholars is consistent with the orientation of the system itself. This coherence also develops exclusive knowledge communities, which prevent links with other systems of knowledge, not only between disciplines but also schools of thought. I experienced great difficulty in trying to defend the need of case studies, not to speak of participatory case studies, equally among the Marxists, neo-classical economists and economists for whom the status of economics as a science depends on abstract mathematical models.

Heinz Moser noted that when he was starting to work on action research (AR) in the late 1960s, he found that the interest in it had waned although it had been intense after Kurt Lewin had brought the concept up, written on it and worked with it with minorities right after World War II. The social science handbooks barely mentioned it and all the quotes put it into a negative light. Moser quotes at length the few paragraphs he found in handbooks of several languages. He also gives the basics of Knut Lewin's *Action Research Theory (Aktion Forschung Theorie)*. Since Lewin was German-American and died rather soon after writing on the theory in English (1947), it was easy to bypass his work and what was written showed how false the understanding of the action research was. Among other things it assumed that the researcher becomes the practitioner and then works it into his analysis. The same process is probably happening at present to different kinds of participatory research when they are under massive criticism. Moser, who was the critic of my share as the director of Jipemoyo, did not think that the new action research and participatory research were the same as Lewin's, but it was important to build on what had been done before. The quoted book of Moser gives a thorough grounding to action research also in its new form (Moser 1975).

McCloskey, a Chicago economist who referred to himself as a realist, wanted to free economists from the rule of methodology and epistemology. He wrote about '(t)he violence with which economists outside the main stream (are) excluded from the conversation'. McClosky had organised an economists' manifesto, which states:

We the undersigned are concerned with the threat to economic science posed by intellectual monopoly. Economists today enforce a monopoly of method or core assumptions, often defended on no better ground (than) that it constitutes the 'mainstream'. Economists will advocate free competition, but will not practice it in the marketplace of ideas. (McCloskey 1994) Julie Nelson describes well the fears that the "hard scientists" have lest they be called "softies" or "sissies" (Nelson 1996, 6-7). The lack of respect toward social sciences is evident even by the fact that the use of the English term "science" is generally restricted to natural, technical and mathematical sciences. Calling the strict border politics into question is in these terms already a sign of slipping. For me, the scientists can keep their criteria if it fits their cosmic vision, but it does not mean that the continuum of knowledge should be chopped into fragments. Scientists are humans who need to question their knowledge base in the same way as others. According to Baert, economists are "renowned for the technical nature of their activities" and "*mutatis mutandis* less prone to meta-theoretical reflection than other social scientists." Criticising realists, Baert goes on almost rebuking them to say that even those who earlier had applied mathematical models to game theory are now "happily committed" to repudiate most of what has been established in their discipline (Baert 1996, 513).

The phenomenal growth in sheer quantity of writings devoted to understanding and explaining science is indicative of the experienced need to reconcile science and the lived world with "its pervasive effects on everyday life" (Baber 1992, 103). For an essentialist view of science, "social" means mere circumstances and effects that lie external to the intellectual activity of the scientist, disregarding the fact that interpreting, proving, giving evidence and making observations are also "social" (Woolgar quoted by Barber 1992). The privileged position of science endows it with the dominating role that it has assumed in shaping today's world. In the words of Marglin, "It is not matter of the good will or bad will of the expert. It is rather a systemic problem, a problem of the knowledge system" (Marglin 1990). The power of science lies in the cultural authority of science as an institution (Chandra Mukerji, *Fragile Power* quoted in Baber 1992, 116). Science can exercise power to disregard other forms of knowledge as being authentic. Yet the scientist has to concede that her/his knowledge is only temporal knowledge.

A self-evident reason why PAR has little space in the academy is that if it tries to combine the theoretical knowledge with practical knowledge, it would require a practical base also for the way it is transmitted and written up. There is no practical base for anthropology and social sciences in general in the academy as there are laboratories for natural sciences. The science villages that I am acquainted with marry business and "hard sciences." PAR would require research spaces in which interaction with researched communities is based on community initiative and in which people's knowledge has the same space as scientific knowledge. I would like to think that such places exist in different forms at least for technical and natural sciences, but whether they have been able to break the division between scientific knowledge and *techne* knowledge needs questioning, whatever brand the research takes in different contexts. The developments in Community Based Research and Action Research referred to in previous chapters indicate a new direction combining higher education with *techne* knowledge.

To the question whether PAR has made progress in the "scientific sense," one probably has to answer that its success has been in a different kind of practice. Practice does not become known because the people who are part of it do not write books. The scientific results are more in explaining how PAR works and what kind of knowledge it produces rather than showing numerous "scientific results" as such. I refer to Heron's view of the supremacy of action over an end result in the form of a book, *knowing how* as the prime aim rather than *knowing that*. This is one way of looking at the matter. Today's world with its high unemployment and incapacity of people to solve their problems of living and sustaining life, one solution is to learn to think in terms of interchange and interaction of knowledge and learning to respect the consummation of the search of knowledge *in* domain of action instead of *about* the domain of action.

Knowledge base in rural Tanzania

By suggesting that people's knowledge in rural Africa belongs largely to the category of *techne,* the intention is not to divide knowledge in dualistic realms of life. There are no "pure" categories. Even less should we think that *techne* and *episteme* cover the whole field of "knowing" and can be placed in an evolutionary scheme. I do not suggest that "tradition," which is mostly based on *techne* system of knowledge, is to be distinguished from the "modern," a hallmark of *episteme* system of knowledge. Tradition has no permanency. Tradition continues to change constantly. In the place of a dualistic view of social life, *techne* and *episteme* rather intertwine, in some context one predominates, in another the other. They feed one another and both are dependent on one another, but, what is significant here, they are in an important way complemented with the third kind of knowledge formation within symbolic ritual and art forms.

The African university as an academic institution clings to the universal scientific epistemic system, which distinguishes itself from the local. There is very little engagement with *techne* knowledge, which is at the base of African society. Universities transmit knowledge in the academic mode inherited from scientific communities in industrial countries, hardly daring to innovate, so as not to divert from the rules of the universally approved system. In the research conference on Action Research in Australia I experienced that universities there were further along in approving different forms of AR. The PAR, which began to flourish in the University of Dar es Salaam in the 1970s, had little continuity at that time but participation has been applied in village planning with a method derived from Participatory Rural Appraisal (PRA) tools. The academic system shares the power structure, which the epistemic system creates, regardless of its locus. Part of the reason might be the political connotations that PAR had in the 1970s when many of its adherents insisted on Marxist ideology to be the necessary precondition for the application of participatory research. e.g. (Kassam and Mustafa 1982, Mustafa, 1989). Today we learn of the new line of Indigenous influence in thinking from Frederique Apffel-Marglin and Arturo Escobar. It is also possible that the methodology, which was created for development planning in action, has been used as a research method, not only a way of gathering data, as Maia Green's critique would indicate (Green 2000).

African social life is under global influence in such a way that its changing traditions are also part of the "modern." Yet in Africa, there are distinct cultural mores, modes and norms created and transmitted under a knowledge system which is local or regional, and does not claim universality nor any literary or scientific, epistemic, and not always even a *techne* origin. The book *Postcolonial Identities in Africa,* edited by Richard Werbner and Terence Ranger (1996), included an interesting discussion about the modern, postmodern and postcolonial concepts. Frequent reference is made to Achille Mbembe as a scholar who has freed himself from the rationalist western model and from the bondage of established lines of thought (Mbembe 1992a, 1992b).

The need to be free from the power of established knowledge systems is reminiscent of the struggle of Latin America scholars, who first developed the theory of underdevelopment and under influence of Paulo Freire (1970) as a pioneering educator and moved on to Action Research in the fight against the cruel treatment of the indigenous Indian population. Orlando Fals Borda, in turn, was a leading social scientist in Columbia engaged in liberation scholarship and action and later after contact with Tanzanian scholars adopted Participatory Action Research as the approach to knowledge formation (Fals Borda1979).

The *episteme* and *techne* categories leave us in a void when we try to delve into Africa. My assumption that the wide recognition of Africa's flourishing cultures is the prerequisite for the continent's road to healthy economy and "development." This presupposes a broader concept of knowledge than what the *techne-episteme* dualism would permit. I refer to symbolisation beyond words as symbols, language as a symbolic system or mathematical symbols, which belong to the category of discursive symbolism (Langer 1956, 14, 70-80). The wealth of presentational symbolism in all forms of performing and expressive arts reveal more than anything else the heart and soul of Africa. It cannot be fitted into a knowledge system if knowledge as a concept is limited to the realm of discursive symbolism (M-L. Swantz 1970, 51-3; Lévi-Strauss 1967, 197-200). Whether fetched from the past of a specific group through collective tradition: myth, ritual, song, any symbolic act or performance, given expression in individual art forms, or created through discursive logic, all these forms of "knowledge" are an integral part of the human experience. Within any collective they are subject to numerous external influences. It would be restrictive to analyse this kind of "knowledge base" only through dualistic categories or in fact limit it only to a specifically African experience. "Practical knowledge" or *techne* as concepts are too utilitarian to cover the artistic symbolic expressions of experience.

I present snapshots and narrate events in a variety of social contexts. Exposure to practical knowledge requires a practical base also for the way it is transmitted in writing. The concreteness of cases rather than theoretical categorisation serves the purposes of this book, but is not easy to achieve. Any effort to identify people's knowledge based on *techne* and presentational symbolism are bound to be defective. By elaborating the areas of presentational symbolism I wish to remind the reader that the pervasiveness of aspects of life which people do not experience in terms of utility (even if an analyst would force them into such a category) have an effect on the interpretation of the concept of poverty as also on the external well-meaning efforts to alleviate poverty. A theoretically interesting issue is what place different aspects of culture should be given in the analysis of poverty. An even more debatable question is whether poverty has its own culture.

I would need visual illustrations to do justice to a presentation of people's knowledge base for sustained livelihood. I identify the following traditional categories briefly:

Women's reproductive knowledge.

Ethno-sciences: -methodology; -geography, -meteorology, -geography, -biology, -medicine, etc.

Indigenous Technical Knowledge (ITK): agriculture, health, fishing, woodwork.

Oral tradition: narratives, proverbs, poetry, myths, folktales.

Symbolic knowledge: rituals, symbols, metaphors.

Performing arts, artforms, artefacts.

Communication: language, codes, gestures, mores, norms.

Music and dance: different uses of music, songs, dance, rituals.

The categorisation is an epistemic way of identifying knowledge. The categories overlap and are used here mainly to illustrate the broad spectrum of people's knowledge base, not in any way to exhaust the content of each field or the scope of them in the cultural context which they illustrate.

Women's reproductive knowledge related with practical knowledge

Rural women's knowledge and skills, with which they manage their households and their often very complicated life situations have some regularity of patterns. The development politics and practice have paid scarce attention to the traditional cultural features. In them symbolic ritual and art forms are integrated into the productive and reproductive elements. The reproductive symbols were taken from the shapes and substances of the everyday household utensils, containers, tools, daily activities, prepared foods, and from the animal and bird life around them. Women's rationale, knowledge, skills, wealth, and social relations are derived from their reproductive and productive roles and the social and symbolic presentation of them. They have been the material which has shaped rural women's lives and economics. Yet I have no recollection in any development context that these creative aspects would have drawn interest in how they enter into the lives of the people who are deemed poor (M-L. Swantz 1992).

Traditionally a young Zaramo girl learned where her place was when she saw her mother and grandmother doing daily chores. She listened to the stories older people told her and she felt the changes in her body until she "broke the limb" (*alivunja ungo*), whereupon she was secluded, often for many years until a suitable husband was found. Then a feast was arranged when she emerged from seclusion, and many gifts were given for her future home. She was carried on someone's back to the future husband's home. She was taught that it was the original woman who discovered the edible plants, which she cooked one after another and gave them to her husband who ate them. She found that if she gave birth to a girl, women ululated with joy twice as long as for a boy child. Women was regarded as more precious because they gave birth and continued the lifeline, but a woman was not to be proud about it. She was taught to be obedient to her husband and to serve him. The penis symbol of the wooden spoon (*mwiko*), which a man had carved, was given to her when the marriage started, as a sign that the husband stirs the *ugali*-porridge in the female clay pot. If she was not satisfied with the behaviour of the husband, she left the spoon unwashed against the wall and no harsh words were required. The husband went to the wife's advisor (*kungwi*) to sort out the problem. Small symbolic elements were ways of communication (M-L. Swantz 1970).

Women learned through lifelong apprenticeship within marriage and family life that at best, a woman was a hidden treasure, of which the man was in charge of safekeeping as he was in charge and set the rules. Men established themselves as caretakers of women who were instructed by the *kungwi* and *somo*, a woman from both mother's and father's side, how to respect and serve the man. But in a matrilineal society she had a refuge in her brother's estate (M-L. Swantz 1992).

People's experiences in the changing society made the old ways gradually less meaningful when the girls even after going through the maturing girl's *mwali* rites found that neglect of details did not have the harmful consequences as the teaching indicated. Young women could have a beautiful healthy child without the ritual during the seventh month of pregnancy, which was intended to secure a safe birth (M-L. Swantz 1986, 208). During my research in Bunju, issues relating to women's private life could be discussed only in secrecy with related mature women. Nowadays, women learn through the increased use of the media, attending meetings, through their own travels, and school has to different degrees become the source of literary learning. Such aspects from other knowledge systems enter into women's consciousness and affect men's thinking of their roles. Even then, the basic skills women use for managing their households and families are still learned through practice. The role of the school in domestic skills is negligible, even non-existent today in Tanzania, and practical subjects are not part of the basic level educational program.

There are differences between areas, as in Kilimanjaro where the Lutheran church started schools since the beginning of the 20th century. The girls filled the existing classes on the mountain so that in the survey made during early British rule in 1924 there were more girls in the primary school classes than boys. This led to having further educational opportunities. Tuulikki Pietilä's book gives an interesting picture of how the women who remained on the mountain managed their situation. Women's issues cannot be taken up without recognising the differences in localities and the changes that occur in urban and rural areas (T. Pietilä 1999; Swantz 1970, 1985; Larsson 1991; Seppälä and Koda 1998).

The modernizing life brings new demands, the way the chores are done, the way new materials have to be cared for, the new demands of hygiene for health, new types of houses, which change the way of life of women as well as of men, and as culture determines the manner of change. The life story of Edwin Mtei from a herder sleeping on a hide on mud floor with his brothers to the Governor of the Bank of Tanzania and Minister of Finance in Nyerere's Government is an instructive, warm story of human capacity and flexibility. It shows the influence of mother in the beginning stages of life but also how such a boy had to adjust to fit the traditional into the modern (Mtei 2007).

The problems of the transfer and exposure to new cultural scene are not included in the education at this time. The models, wares and fashions coming from India and the Arab countries have shaped the changes alongside with the western influences. The capacity of people to adjust is remarkable, but in the process people lose their cultural identity and self-esteem.

Feminist scholars have overstressed the point that women are not only homemakers and men have to learn the same things as women do. The early newspapers in the independent Tanzania headlined time and again that women have to come out of the kitchens, but women have continued until today as the homemakers even if the wealthier women transfer many of their duties to servants. The feminists have criticized the schooling from the colonial times for concentrating on home-craft in women's education. Aili Tripp has shown the efforts British women educators made in Uganda to secure for the girls the entrance to the University College in Makerere from the start, but in addition the female students in Uganda as well as in Tanganyika teachers' training classes got a thorough practical introduction to all aspects of home care in the subject called Domestic Science. The girls had the same teachers training program as the male students, except in the teaching of crafts and domestic science, which differentiated the skills. The female students in Ashira, my learning ground to life in Africa, learned even childcare with an adopted baby rescued from the local hospital after her mother had died at delivery. The child was returned to the family, when there was capacity to rear the child. There was a tendency to channel the female students to secondary schools with less scientific subjects, because their domestic role was considered unavoidable.

The disparaging arguments relating to gender on points on female education, have lead to abolishing not only domestic science but also other practical subjects from Primary Schools in Tanzania, where at least 90 per cent of households depend on women's cooking and home care. 18 kinds of life skills as additional subjects in Primary Schools were on paper for choice, but teachers' training for such subjects was non-existent and the subjects were taken out of the scheduled teaching program.

Without going here into further details I conclude by pointing out the misguided global message, indiscriminately propagated, which has discredited women's domestic and caretaking service. It has had disastrous effects in people's lives. It has had its effects in the field of education in Tanzania, as elsewhere, as thereby the practical subjects were eliminated in the Primary School programmes. It has been detrimental to the total process of development but specifically for homes and the housework, which is still left for women but without the needed facilities or guidance. Tradition is stamped as harmful and oppressive customs, which deny the indigenous development path for women and men.

Anthropology in the service of indigenous culture

I have indicated that anthropology was not seen in a positive light in Tanzania, when it was not included in the university programme until the 1990s and even then only marginally. Anthropologists were blamed for wanting continuity and not seeing the necessity of rapid change. The anthropologists do have the task of demonstrating that people's culture can offer inspiration in the national development process, as the studies of cultural background have done in Finland, which has fitted itself into the modern life under hard conditions of war, cold climate, and fields dug out of stony ground with thick forests. Anthropologists can bring out the values in the passing culture and help to lift it to a greater visibility, consciously build it into the new life skills and become the source of inspiration for musicians and artists of many descriptions. They need to counteract the negative concept that has been spread in Africa of culture. I have criticised the excessive interest of anthropologists in witchcraft and the negative aspects of traditional culture.

Different everyday aspects of women's practical learning are still perpetuated in much of the village life in most parts of the country, although the changes take place unevenly depending on the exposure to the outside world. Through the media people do not see the best features of foreign cultures and the news and TV shows from overseas tend to depict the negative aspects of life. The wealth that Tanzania has in the communal environment could be grouped in 1) practical life skills, 2) relational skills needed in social communication, conduct, and mutual service; and 3) knowledge related to life-world, "*cosmovision,*" involving symbolic communication and the sense of community. In many parts of Tanzania the symbols which elevated physical sexuality into another level of meaning, integrating it with social relations and skills, have little relevance today. The epistemic emphasis in the world religions, Christianity and Islam, has partly compensated for the practical learning which the African inheritance gave the youth in matters of everyday life. Professor S.J. Mamuya in the community health department of UDSM wrote a book on the *unyago* and *jando* initiation rites, hoping that some of the key features of sexual education could be consciously introduced into the training of the youth. As an anthropologist one would have hoped that what the name indicates, the book would have related more to the traditional teachings in *jando* and *unyago*. This is not the case. I am not aware whether the book has been used in formal education.

Jando as a ritual for boys is losing value because the circumcision as the central part of the ritual is done more often than before in hospitals (M-L. Swantz 1973). Girls' maturity rituals have been preserved on the coast until today. Women's knowledge accumulates as they continue to learn more of its meaning, listening to the instructors in the rituals of their younger friends year after year. In initiation rites learning includes symbolic acts and articles, riddles, songs and dances. Much of this belongs to a frame of esoteric knowledge concealed from outsiders. Signe Arnfred has described in an enthused manner the secretive parts of the Makuwa women's ritual celebrations in northern Mozambique (Arnfred 2011). My one time attendance of the Makonde women's secret celebration as well as attendance in such an occasion in Rufiji gave me the impression that the women's celebration was secluded from all male observers and was more secretive than the Zaramo ritual events I had observed in Bunju. Even there I had to know the secret codes before being allowed to enter the most secretive part at the *mkole* tree.

All of the symbolic content of colours, forms, and actions are significant in working out people's knowledge system and in constructing an image of a society which corresponds with people's needs and resources. Associating with other women through different stages in the life cycle, women form flexible mutual support groups which serve also as social groups for entertainment and a variety of social interactions. For the Zaramo, the focus of the ritual is on the individual young woman as she comes into maturity. Nowadays it is carried out in two days in place of the earlier weeklong celebrations, and it is accommodated also as a ritual in the city of Dar es Salaam (M-L. Swantz 1970,

385-415). How much of the rich symbolic rites and meanings are included would need new anthropological research.

The southeastern ethnic groups in Tanzania, the Makonde, Makua and Yao, have retained their ritual ways to introduce their youth to reproductive aspects of life, but much of the rich symbolism is lost to the initiates because of their early age (M-L. Swantz 1998). The rituals have been arranged at an earlier age than before so that the youth would not be kept out of school. Furthermore, the government had forbidden the communally organized rituals annually and ordered them to be performed every third year because the consumption of food and drink exhausted people's reserves each year. The rituals for spirit rites and healing are continued in the countryside and are not hidden.

Another aspect, which requires a constructive use of anthropological knowledge, is witchcraft and the spirit and *jinni* phenomena, which raise people's fears. Only when something extraordinary happens, such as the attempts to kill albinos and taking limbs as a means of acquiring power, the officialdom wakes up to do something about it. I consider this to be part of the split between the epistemic system for the officialdom to perform its duties, whereas the people's practical knowledge finds its space in places and times where it is needed. The changes in life have led into the widening of the spiritual part of life in institutionalized and informal plural ways.

Ethno-sciences

The clear distinction that the "pure" epistemic knowledge makes between the ethnocentric knowledge is to prefix it with *"ethno,"* deriving from Lat. *etnos,* meaning a people, folk. Prefixing science with folk indicates that folk science, *ethno-science,* is not to be mixed with real science, which is the common axiom of an epistemic system, although there is the middle ground. *Ethno-logy* and *ethnography, ethnomethodology* are not sciences *by people* but *of people,* whereas *ethno-geography, ethno-biology, ethno-meteorology, ethno-philosophy, ethno-medicine, ethno-agriculture, ethno forestry, ethno-genetics,* belong to the category of *folk science.* They are generally conceived to be pseudo-scientific or knowledge belonging to the *techne* system.

An area of particular interest is that of healing, ethno-medicine, which is closely related with people's existential experiences and *cosmo-vision,* their central areas of symbolic knowledge. *Uganga,* traditional healer's medical skills and medicines they use, have been the interest of anthropologists and scholars of different disciplines (L. Swantz 1990; Feierman 1986, 1990; Harjula 1980).

As an idiosyncratic event I mention a course I was asked to run by a Tanzanian professor of medicine on Tanzanian traditional medicine for 12 Tanzanian medical personnel. The participants were brought to Lahti, Finland, from Britain, where they were attending a course. This came about while I was driving with the doctor in Bagamoyo district after the Jipemoyo project. We passed a house in a Kwere village where a diviner (*mganga*) was performing a divining ritual (*rungu*)with two shakers (*manyanga* or *mbizi*). I asked the doctor if he would like to see it. We were welcomed to come in and sitting there in the outer ring I was able to explain to him what was happening. The Kwere language and customs are close to the Zaramo and I was familiar with the Zaramo divining practices from my research in Bunju. The doctor was so impressed that after our conversations about the healing he suggested we run a course in Finland while the students were in Europe and I was living in Finland. We invited three Finnish doctors who had contacts with the Tanzanian health system together with two folk healers and a medical doctor from Kaustinen to come and take part in the two week course as part of the University of Helsinki extension programme. It included my lectures, discussions, role-plays, and a demonstration by the Finnish folk-healers of back healing and cupping besides various field visits.

Tanzanian elites varying degrees of knowledge of the healers and their services depending on their background, but it is not organized knowledge. Discussions and attendance in the healing performances helped to systematize their knowledge and think of the usefulness and dangers in relation to modern medicine. Many practising medical doctors know that the traditional *waganga* have treated the patients, especially children, until it was too late to save them when they were brought to hospital. This kind of experience makes the doctors reluctant to talk about cooperation with traditional healers. It is important to know what kind of healing the particular *mganga* practises (M-L. Swantz 1984). For instance, the Chagga families have their medicines tested over generations, which they use for specific illnesses, but when people are offered previously unknown solutions to new problems they can be attracted to experiment.

There are many more studies on the negative aspects of *uganga* relating to harmful use of medicines and *uganga* skills in witchcraft and sorcery than of their healing practices. It indicates anthropologists' interest in something more exotic than the healing processes. *Uganga* is also closely linked with reproductive knowledge. Here, as in all areas of life, the scientific analysis fragments life and influences people by splitting people's experience to different cognitive fields, but also dividing the human body into its parts. The medical personnel trained in school medicine tend to communicate with patients in a language which does not offer a unified experience of healing.

The collaborative approach of Reason and Rowan (1988) in doctor-patient relationships took elements from folk healing approaches. The efforts to bring the folk healers and organised health personnel together in Newala, Mtwara Region, turned out to be helpful, especially when the cholera epidemic occurred in the same area. The Health Officers in the Training Institute in Newala became involved in the discussions we had between them, the healers and the Health Officers and the groups were brought together. FINNIDA, at the time the development arm of the Ministry of Foreign Affairs in Finland, cooperated in bringing the two sides together in week long seminars, making visits to surrounding villages and pairing the participants from different types of medicine.

The aim here is to stay close to practical situations yet to interact with theoretical literature when it aids the main thread of the argument. The basic differences between the ethno and corresponding epistemic science are characterised by the attributes given in Marglin's table (1990, 234). What makes *episteme, algorithmic* knowledge true science is its claim to universality, replicability of its findings in other contexts, logical deduction or induction, and claims that knowledge gained is verifiable or verified. *Techne* knowledge, in contrast, becomes universal through successful practice (Marglin 2008).

Indigenous versus Western Technical Mode of Knowledge

Indigenous Technical Knowledge and Indigenous Knowledge in general are referred to as ITK and IK. In the course of innumerable developmental failures when too big jumps have been attempted in agriculture or in technical fields, the need to take a serious look into people's agriculture and technologies in general has become obvious.

Interestingly, the World Bank has taken serious interest in indigenous knowledge and has published a large volume of *Indigenous Knowledge, Local Pathways to Global Development* (2004). World Bank representatives spent five years collecting indigenous knowledge from Africa for development purposes. It covers 60 pages of chapters and 200 large pages of information about IK from many African countries. Two chapters are from Tanzania dealing with agriculture and medicine. Many writers quote Hirschman, one of the early analysts of development projects (Hirschman 1967). As an economist evaluating highly technical projects, he does not stress the local technical knowledge, but finds that canvassing the ground would save researchers from much extra work in the long run. Knowing the local conditions and taking into consideration the geography, social factors and history of the place demands time but is prudent as a research strategy.

Reference needs to be made to the Transfer of Technology research project TECO, for which I was responsible, carried out with a team of Finnish, Zambian and Tanzanian researchers. I refer to my book *Transfer of Technology as an Intercultural Process* (1989), which was the end result. A series of studies were made and published by other project members during and after the project. Margaretha von Troil wrote her licentiate thesis and the field leader, Taimi Sitari, summarized the research in several volumes (Sitari 1986, von Troil 1986). The research was done of the extensive water project covering two southeastern regions Mtwara and Lindi, the Valmet tractor factory, and industrial wood based projects in Tanzania in addition to the battery factory in Zambia, which had been initially started by the Finnish company Airam. Participatory research was used to the extent it was found to be possible. Margaretha von Troil took as her theoretical starting point Dilthey's methodology and the "hermeneutic circle." It was important to point out in the technical context, where the engineers were not used to exchanging ideas with the workers and not even with engineers from another culture. Partly prior to the technology project women's involvement in the water project had been made in the same regions. It helped to see the forgotten central role of women, especially as providers and carriers of water in the families. More attention has been drawn to that aspect later.

Von Troil brought out that the human activity should be treated as *meaningful* and as capable of *communicating meaning*. Technology, when taken as a means of knowledge, had its material element in the social sphere, its intellectual element in the cognitive sphere, and its organizational element in the intersection of the two others. The essential point in development work in general tended to be forgotten (von Troil 1986). As I put it: "(T)he preconditions for *receiving and giving knowledge* have not been given as a necessary element of development projects." It was forgotten in the water project by the Finns but as I had an opportunity to observe, also by the Canadians when developing the water system in the suburban areas of the capital (Swantz 1989, Italics added).

In the discussion of the suitability of the Western mould of development I brought up the question of rationality in preindustrial and partly preliterate society. Referring to Evans-Pritchard who claimed the Azande of Sudan acted rationally in interpreting oracles I brought out a differently interpreted concept of rationality. In the earlier discussion on rationality I indicated that in place of the concept "rational," philosopher von Wright had suggested the use of "reasonable" in traditional non-philosophocal context.

In *Understanding of Cultures* (1984), anthropologist Robert Ulin took the position from a specific cultural point of view that universality of rationality cannot mean solely Western ideas of rationality. Universal rationality could not be equated with human convention. Ulin established universality of rationality in and through the concepts of instrumental and communicative rationality. He showed how instrumental rationality had become the prevailing paradigm in social sciences. Ulin synthesized hermeneutics and critical anthropology and his communicative rationality was a modified adoption from Habermas, but he was critical of Habermas's later evolutionary presentation of instrumental and communicative rationality. Peter Winch's *The Idea of a Social Science and its Relation to Philosophy* (1967) was often referred to (Bloor 1991; Ulin 1984, xvi-xviii, 36-37, 173; Habermas 1970; M-L. Swantz 1989, 126-127; 1986, 26-27). Ulin saw that even Winch was not able to go further in his otherwise innovative way of using Wittgenstein's concept of language in the communicative theory based on ordinary language. According to Ulin, by privileging the native's categories, Winch allows the dialectical moment of communicative theory to escape. For Ulin, anthropologists must use their social categories as a standpoint from which the cultural object can be engaged. This means that communication with the people who participate in the research is mutual. In attempting to know something, an anthropologist starts from a certain standpoint in engaging the other side. A synthesis of distinct forms of life can be found in a context dependent perspective, "much as conversation between two communicators is a synthesis through their mutual understanding" (Ulin 1984, 36).

Within the sphere of communicative rationality there are substantial points of common ground for those who engage themselves from different levels in an act of communication. In becoming part of people's real life situations two modes of thought and two historical and social realities meet (M-L. Swantz 1986, 28).

How people cultivate, how they plant, how they classify their plants, what determines where, what and how they sow and which varieties are mixed in one field, are some of the aspects of practical knowledge which both indigenous and foreign development experts must know if any agricultural project is to succeed. The universal weakness in trying to retrieve information from the farmers occurs above all in the neglect to approach women who in most cases in Africa are familiar with the soils and plants. There are cases in which the husband does not even know where the wife cultivates, yet when an expert comes he is the "besserwiser," (know-it-all). There is a crucial difference whether the development agent retains his epistemic framework or whether he accepts true interaction between the people's (ethno/techne) knowledge and science-based knowledge.

The Westerner switches the discussion to a general level with the sense of superiority as a representative of a system of knowledge which they have appropriated. Development as the project on the world scale has been based on techno-economic rationality with over-emphasized instrumentality. The world continues being in the process of recasting the Western mould, which is being taken over by the Eastern countries. We are reminded of the destruction that advanced technology has caused and many are looking for a third way, which the new reformers see is in horizon with the people's power through the new electronic devices.

Tariq Banuri made a thorough study of the environmental effects of the new development model. In 1987, when he was a researcher in WIDER, Helsinki, he wrote about "the decline of the West" and of the "impersonality postulate" of the West as the basic characteristics of the Western "cultural map." The present time gives increasing voice to the critics of the Western sense of superiority of its economic and technological models, which the Eastern and Southern countries rise up to challenge. "The Third Way" presented by Schumacher in his *Small is Beautiful* was attractive because the inert necessity to stay small meant a refusal to grasp power. Chilean Max Neef believed in small action in many places. In such environments creativity can flourish (Neef 1982, 117, 159). If Finland can be taken to represent the Western mould, the idea of small being beautiful has no longer been part of the reality, as there is for economic reasons an overstretched emphasis on everything growing bigger, from companies, schools, municipalities, to shopping centres.

In doing PRA with villagers in Bagamoyo District in Tanzania, their knowledge of vegetation, the species of trees and the use of them were astounding. The knowledge extended to symbolic and healing aspects, connections with the spirit world and to indicators for coming of rains and vicissitudes of seasons (Kinyunyu and Swantz 1996). It is even more surprising that lower grade school children already had extensive knowledge of plant and animal world.

In a short while, children who had gathered around us two researchers in Msoga, Bagamoyo district, could give us the names and uses of all the trees and plants around us, as well as of the living habits of birds which we could spot. When the biologist picked plants for pressing them after getting to the lodging in another village Msata, where we were accommodated, it was already getting dark. Another group of children gathered to see what we were doing and could in the light of an oil lamp identify again names of the now drying plants. Within the RIPS project in Mtwara and Lindi Regions, people's knowledge was studied and appropriated through PRA approaches in cooperation with a specializing biologist, who was part of the RIPS team.

Standard six students in a village primary school in Magumchila, Tandahimba, were asked to go into the surrounding area and collect non-cultivated plant species for half an hour. The majority of the students were girls and there were also four boys. They were divided into two groups, which would compete to bring as many species as possible. Some farmers joined to identify the plants after the students returned (one woman and four older men). Group A brought 51 plants and Group B 57 plants. The plants/branches were then laid out in a line, 12 at a time. Each plant was held up in turn by a child and named by consensus, often in two local languages, Kimakonde and Kimwera. The use of the plants and their merits were then discussed in terms of their utility for firewood, medicine, fodder, food, oil, timber, rope, witchcraft and construction. People had an astounding knowledge of the vegetation, according to the *PRA Report on Magumchila Village - Newala District*. There is a great loss of knowledge when the schools are not making use of the local knowledge. By giving such exercises to students, the teachers could adopt a constructive approach of mutual learning to teaching, as often the teachers come from different parts of the country. As long as the examinations do not require two-way communication in a learning process, teachers' knowledge continues to satisfy the requirements.

Farmers experimenting on hundreds of cassava varieties name and group them differently from the scientific categories with Latin names, but their use of them and knowledge of what is appropriate for what purpose can best be found out by following their taxonomy. In Nandagala, Lindi region, a farmer was experimenting with a great variety of cassavas, which he classified according to colour or taste. He knew how he could get new varieties but he did not know the reason why the outcome was another variety than what was planted. This was a good case to demonstrate how scientific knowledge of the extension officer was of help, but only after he had understood what the man's problem was, what he knew and how he gained new knowledge. A video was used to illustrate how the pollination took place from the female to male plant and how the new variety was dependent on the plant from which the insect came (PAR information from RIPS)

Indigenous soil fertility as well as land issues were studied through PR processes. Farmers were found to practice soil fertility management in a great variety of ways. I quote from a report listing them. The 27-page report is extensive and gives detailed aspects of farmers' knowledge. The items listed are an indication of the type of information farmers worked with (1995):

- Ridge-making. Grasses and leaves are put in mounded lines with soil.
- Fallow system. Each of the 3-4 years cultivated has a different name.
- Cleared grasses/bushes are spread on the ground to decompose.
- Goat or cow manure is spread on cultivated soil.
- Spot burning. Cleared grasses and shrubs are piled in heaps and burnt.
- Deep-hoeing to mix top and sub soil. "Bringing up the fertility sunk."
- Thinning of cashew trees to reduce the canopy to give air to trees.
- Artificial fertilisers used by younger wealthier men.
- Mulching: Leaving weeds from fallow of one year incorporated into soil.
- Retaining soil-enriching trees.

About 25 trees, four local grasses and two climbers were identified which were said to improve soil fertility. Six grasses, shrubs and a tree were identified which deteriorate soil. Different soils required different management practices. Land types had their own local names and they were used with insight to their suitability for different purposes. Extension officers with simple conventional messages do not have anything to teach to these farmers who depend on differences in the micro-environment.

When knowledge is applied, it does not make much difference how it is classified if the application is successful. On the other hand, it does matter which kinds of power relations accompany the knowledge which is applied and in whose interests the scientists operate. For this reason, it is necessary to use epistemic knowledge in clarifying the systemic differences.

The bottom line is how people's knowledge is used: It might be as an appendix to shed additional light on scientific knowledge or it gives the scientist a new angle from which to proceed with his/her own studies. Another way is to enter into an authentic dialogue with *techne* knowledge, to take it seriously and to let the laypersons share in different phases of the research process itself. This is collaborative research, which requires a break in the scientific paradigm.

The rest of the categories listed above belong to the presentational symbolic area of cognition and senses. This account of indigenous knowledge has not dealt with women's specific knowledge systems. It shows the weakness in acquiring the above information. I refer to Ulla Vuorela's dissertation published after the Jipemoyo project was finished which deals with the patriarchal mode of production among the matrilineal Kwere, who she studied using the participatory approach. She brings out the fact that women could exercise some sexual power and adapt to nature, while in general the overall mode was patriarchal. Women controlled the relations of mating and the allocation of junior labour in bride service (Vuorela 1987).

Oral tradition in relation to literate culture

What does oral tradition contribute to the construction of society? While it is obvious that without literacy one cannot manage in today's world, we have to be very clear that illiterate people conserve huge treasures of hidden knowledge, poetry, narratives, and the whole rich spectrum of folklore genres, as the Finns know well because Finland has one of the largest folklore collections in the world.Music, drama, song, and dance belong also to oral culture. In Jipemoyo project Philip Donner studied them. Indeed, having learned to know the symbolic expressions of the Zaramo, I find it difficult to speak about any of the expressive traditions without combining them with the symbolic rites and rituals, which give them their deepest meanings. I cannot imagine that we ever could come close to the real social reality of people in Africa if we did not understand the symbolic meanings of communication and social sharing. Even then, they will always remain in many ways hidden as they are often locally interpreted.

In my research of the Zaramo (1970) I have shown how the myths of the beginning of the use of plants for food gave the first woman, Nyalutanga, the task of discovering the plants, preparing them into food and then giving them to the husband to eat. The adoption of Islam on the coast affected the situation of women, but in the 1960s and 1970s they still could assert their active role through the ritual performances and roles related to the acting out them. Zenya Wild rewrote my book on the Zaramo ritual symbolism into a more readable (American) English in *Blood, Milk, Death, Body Symbols and the Power of Regeneration Among the Zaramo of Tanzania* (1995) and the book has now been translated into the Swahili language by the Swahili Institute scholars at the UDSM and was published in 2014.

The borderline between oral and literate culture is conceptually very crucial, because most of literate humankind considers it to be the dividing line between the "civilised" and the "ignorant." Few other aspects have received as much attention in development work as literacy. It has been used as one of the basic measures of human development and it has been considered to form the crossing line to rational, logical thinking. It is also a clear dividing line between *episteme* and *techne* systems of knowledge because it is doubtful whether anyone not knowing to read could be considered to think in terms of *episteme* (Goody 1987, Luria 1971, Marglin 1996, Swantz 1985).

The question whether there are intellectuals in non-literate societies, connects closely with the issue of rationalism. It again is relevant when we discuss the motivation for economic action based on rational choice. Stephen Feierman in his study of *Peasant Intellectuals* does not doubt that preliterate societies have their intellectuals. It depends on the interpretation of "rational" as well as what the requirements set are for the use of the word "intellect."

Feierman quotes Goody's opinion that non-literate authorship is very different from the literate variety and it is "less capable of creating rational knowledge." This is so because of the difficulty in achieving consistency among ideas and eliminating contradictions without literacy. Feierman quotes Goody:

... a continuing critical tradition can hardly exist when sceptical thoughts are not written down, not communicated across time and space, not made available for men to contemplate in privacy as well as to hear in performance. (Feierman 1990, 110)

The borderline in knowledge creation between written and oral is not at all as clear as it is in conceptualisation in science-based knowledge, which besides consistency and capacity for scepticism requires the capability to create rationalised knowledge (Goody 1987, 68-69; Feierman 1990, 109).

For Weber, rationality had a complex network of meanings and ideas "coordinated into a coherent and consistent system." Interestingly for Weber, if unpredictable religious ecstasy was replaced with methodically planned rituals in order to achieve the same ends, it could mean "systematization and rationalization of the methods for attaining religious sanctification" (Weber 1978, 538). But "coordination and consistent system" hardly is possible without written records. Feierman adds, "Rationality also means choice of the most appropriate means of achieving particular ends." Weber connects the rationalisation process with the emergence of experts in place of generalists. Feierman is in agreement with sociologist Edward Shils, an author of works on peasants and interpreter of Weber's work (Shils 1972). Feierman has no difficulty in calling the illiterate healers and leaders of society intellectuals in Shambala, North-Eastern Tanzania. He studied the way the medicine men created their knowledge and found that "Goody understates the degree to which alternative ideas found a systematic, cumulative basis in pre-colonial African societies." The healing traditions offered a good case. In them people had choices to make and compared cures. The big difference was in the entire social organisation of knowledge (Feierman1990, 110).

Writing and written texts have been worn around the neck and different parts of the body since the Old Testament times. Deuteronomy 6:8-9, for example, describes how the law should be (written) and tied around one's arms and worn on the forehead as well as on the doorposts. Within Islam, Koranic texts are written with red ink which is washed off and drunk, and they are enclosed within amulets commonly worn by Muslims and traditional believers alike. Goody suggests that writing was first valued for its role in superhuman communication and that the initial interest of Islam was frequently magical (or magico-religious) (Goody 1987, 137). In the East African context, the teachers of Islamic learning differentiate between knowledge of the other world and worldly knowledge or *elimu ya ahera* and *elimu ya dunia*. What Goody calls magico-religious would be *elimu ya dunia,* worldly knowledge, whereas *ahera* means Paradise or Heaven. The great significance given to the written word as consolidated in the Holy Book in Arabic is carried to its extreme in Islamic countries manifest in the anger any offence against it raises in the population. The use of the Book as an opportunity for burning churches became evident even in Tanzania when a schoolboy was said to have urinated on the Koran. This would not have happened without provocation in the south-eastern Muslim villages, where the book is in possession of very few learned people. The power of spoken word in the form of a curse is also much feared and is equated with bewitching. Any statement which sounds like a threat can be taken as a curse. The reading of a *halubadili* is a binding act certain to cause death or severe illness to the guilty ones (L. Swantz 1993). I have seen devout Muslims fingering their beads and praying non-formally, but it is obvious that the small role that literacy plays in at least coastal Islam has prevented the same educational advance in the Islamic areas as in other parts of the country. Literacy alone is insufficient if there are no reading materials available.

Literacy is common among Protestant Christians who take the Bible into worship services and read it as it is interpreted to them. This difference in relation to the written word is also transferred to the attitudes toward school education as there is also interest in secular education among Christians, I would add among the Lutherans. Interpreting the Bible activates the brain, thus even the religious reading is a rational process. Lamin Sanneh, professor of Missiology at the University of Yale, a convert from Islam, puts a great emphasis in the spreading of Christianity in Africa on the fact that the Bible has been translated into so many languages. For him, the Bible translations and personal reading of the texts have freed Christianity from the colonial limbo. Its vernacular transformation has freed Christianity from the Western cultural hegemony. The expansion of Christianity to him has resulted in "unprecedented diversity and vigorous expansion" (2009, 12). The big point of the Comaroffs in *Of Revelation and Revolution* (1991) is the British capitalist garb in which Christianity was introduced through literacy in the 1800s. They also show how Christianity changed its mode when in its indigenous form it was freed from the English garb, which was shown already in Jean Comaroff's book *Body of Power Spirit of Resistance* (1985).

Societies slow to adopt secular education are often rich in oral culture, music and dance. There is no possibility to expand on these forms of knowledge within this treatise, but they are made use of fragmentarily here and there in the text. I regret that in a book, which claims that development can take off only if the flourishing cultural forms are given credence, the presentation of this side is given little space.

Symbolic knowledge, communication, performing arts and music

In the creative field of symbolic knowledge and communication based on it, the westerners are left as spectators with their dominant emphasis on rational thought and epistemic knowledge. Communication in plain discursive words is perhaps the clearest reminder that the epistemic mode of thought as the only knowledge system is poverty-stricken. It is also evident in the interest in a variety of new fashions of singing.

In my earlier analysis I made a distinction between symbolic knowledge, which opens up to a meaning and symbols, which have immediate power and which often are referred to as magic. *Meaning* comprehended with a conscious thought process gives association to further meanings. It creates a developmental process whereby new thoughts open up. In ritual use of symbols these meanings are socially shared. As long as a symbol has such shared meanings and has a power to transform these meanings into new meanings they have a creative potential. If writing is not understood but only applied, believing in it as an instrument of immediate power, its possibility of creating meaning is limited if not entirely non-existent. If it links up closely with other levels of meaning it might serve a religious and not only a "magic" function, as might be the case when an amulet is received from a religious leader and is considered holy (M-L. Swantz 1970, 338, 354-6; 1995, 134-6).

Elsewhere I have struggled with the issue of whether development can take place through practical knowledge learned through symbolic and practical experience and what the role of rationality in it is. Conscious rational thought arises from practice and plays a role in the process of healing or in the understanding of modes of agriculture of which the healer and the farmer make use. All traditional knowledge has also taken elements from previous contacts with other cultures, even if they have not been literate cultures. The adoption process is at times concealed from the actors but other times it is a conscious process.

I have personally responded to the line of thought that suggests that the symbol precedes scientific thought. It was in reading Mircea Eliade's *Comparative Patterns of Religion* that I discovered how scientific thought is born and how any epistemic thinking comes about: It is preceded with symbols which give the whole picture, *gestalt,* at one and the same time (Eliade 1958). Paul Ricoeur confirmed this (1981). It is only after seeing the whole picture that I begin to pull it apart. The archetypal symbols present in all cultures, have kept the universe together, giving people their "cosmo-vision." They have inspired Carl Jung and many others with him. The elements with which we as humans deal with everyday, sun and stars, light, water, earth, vegetation and regeneration have created symbolic visions or *hierophanies.* Because of their central place in the economy and ecology of our world they made people query what their origin and where their power comes from. They became gradually objects of scientific discovery, but the borderline between scientific and symbolic cosmo-vision has never been clearly drawn in the minds of people. My understanding of symbol as a forerunner of scientific knowledge does not imply an evolutionary process in which symbolism precedes scientific, epistemic knowledge. I see them as parallel ways of knowing, one supporting the other. For me it does not imply what several scientists of religion have indicated, a kind of science of a "savage thought" or a meta-science (Bloch 1986, 179; Lévi-Strauss 1966).

The role of symbolism as a giver of meaning to the world has been one of the central issues in science of religion and anthropology, also in philosophy. Lévi-Strauss argued that what we call religious phenomena are a type of knowledge, a form of intellectual activity. They interpret the world to the holders of certain symbolic systems (Bloch 1986, Lévi-Strauss 1966). In this book I have used the term "cosmo-vision." I want to avoid a fragmented scientific view of the world or universe, but neither does the term signify only a religious or symbolic way of experiencing and interpreting one's place in the world. People have also individualistic ways of combining meanings derived from different systems of knowledge. It is not possible to speak about knowledge systems without seeing the centrality of symbolic knowledge in all cultures, in this case in cultures of Tanzania. But symbolic knowledge should not be limited to religious, ritual and mythical dimensions of cognition. My intention is to give an integrated view of our being in the world as human beings, not only as an intellectual activity but engaging people existentially.

I find Bloch's differentiation between people's everyday life and basis of action and ritual communication useful to quote here (Bloch 1986, 188):

(The Merina of Madagascar) "… hold both views in different contexts and they do not see them as contradictory because the image of the ritual is isolated in a heavy world between actions and statements. For the ritual to conflict with other types of knowledge it would have to be removed from the communication that characterises ritual. The two images of the world — the ritual and the everyday — cannot in ordinary, non-revolutionary circumstances, compete with each other."

The leading issue in this book is what role people's knowledge plays in development, and in people's economy specifically. This question cannot be answered without broadening the scope of people's knowledge to comprise the variety of knowledge forms, which grow from the rich field of symbols. The dilemma that an anthropologist faces in trying to analyse ritual arises from the fact that rituals are on the boundary between statements and actions, between knowledge which can be dealt with in analytical terms and action which is given functional interpretation. Bloch's interpretation of what ritual expresses serves us also in understanding that people's knowledge reaches beyond the world of development and economics. It ties them to the past generations concretely. Bloch has found the organising principle for the use of money in Merina culture to be the ancestral tombs. It directly relates to the way they act economically. I put forth the thought that we face the same difficulty in trying to understand how people interpret intellectually, and take action in relation to such alien concepts as "development" or "economy." We cannot assume that they relate to them in purely analytical terms. Bloch writes about the anthropologist's dilemma in analysing ritual.

`The anthropologist is inevitably faced by a dilemma, stemming from the fact that he is trying to express in analytical language something that is in another medium and is different in nature because of the way it is communicated.

The same is the case when we deal with the "rational" concepts of "development" and "economy," which can be analysed both as `"statements" and "action." I suggest that trying to analyse the present situation (of people for whom ritual is a living reality, in between statement and action) within the world of development programmes and economic schemes, means recognising the existence of symbolic ritual netherworld and finding tools for placing it in the same field of experience as human and economic development. It is this moving in between worlds, which makes our task difficult.

Bloch's ideas about linking ritual and non-ritual knowledge are pertinent here. Bloch develops a theory about the indirect interrelationship of two types of phenomena, the ideological and the politico-economic, which are of different kinds and occur in different types of communication:

. . . .the ritual is saying that the world one knows outside ritual, where sex and birth lead to life, where labour leads to production, where time is irreversible and potentially productive, will not ultimately be the basis of the transcendental existence . . . The ritual does not replace the knowledge of this world by the transcendental one; it merely suggests the transcendental world, just over the horizon, after death. (Bloch 1986, 188-89)

In my study of the Zaramo symbolism I found that the prevalence of death symbols correlated with the situation of the community. The death symbolism was close to female symbols, as margins of life and death converge in female symbolism. The long periods of seclusion meant going through death to new life and renewing life. The commonality of the spirit rites, especially in the rite of affliction (*madogoli*), was another indication of this: through vibrant music and intensive dance the person in a deep trance would be brought back into life. But also the experiences of the *waganga* meant going through the valley of death. This was very well recounted by *mganga* Ndamba who had indeed gone through the deep waters to the living place of the main *madogoli* spirits, *kinyamkera*, mother spirit and the bearer of death *mwenembago*, who would have wanted to keep Ndamba there under water while the mother spirit appealed on behalf of the human Ndamba. The name Ndamba indicates that he might have been from the Mahenge area where the Ndambas live. From somewhere there came the *mganga* who had sensed the need and walked through the bush and fields to come in time to drum Ndamba out of his predicament (M-L. Swantz 1984).

Interestingly a study made in the same general area among the Ngindo in 2004 by David Kitolero, a researcher in the Ministry of Education and Culture and earlier in Jipemoyo, names the same spirit *kinyamkera* as an experience of some of Ngindo he interviewed (Kitolero 2004). This could indicate that the Zaramo have adopted it from their neighbours, but more likely a few Ngindo have been affected by the *kinyamkera* spirits when they had been moving toward the coast to cut forests at certain period, because the *madogoli* rites have been recorded among the Zaramo in historical records and the symbolism used fits into the general symbolic system. The Zaramo spirit experiences with the traditional spirits do not fit into the explanations given about women's need to use possession as a way of gaining attention, first expressed by I. M. Lewis (1966) about the Somali cases of possession and then repeated by scholars studying the phenomenon such as Marja Tiilikainen on the Somali in Finland and many others. The Zaramo women's sudden fits which compare with the Somali experience is a later introduction patterned by the costal experiences.

Conclusion

I have made a cursory review of knowledge forms as an indication of the richness that the interaction of knowledge systems could offer. In comparison to the vast interest in development issues on all the levels, the cultural actors influencing development are sadly neglected and scant attention is paid to the potentialities there would be for participatory research in action. The anthropologist's interest stops on the level of theory, but when she uses the knowledge in practical action, she becomes aware of the need to create knowledge together and give the partner full credit in the common creation of knowledge. The vast knowledge that people have should be applied in practice. Thus it would be most useful to work out the possibilities in cooperation with the people who still hold the cultural treasures.

The experiences we had in Mtwara region with the traditional *waganga* were one example where the cooperation between two lines of thought and experience could be made use of in a crucial situation. Another line of thinking that this chapter has brought out is the inspiration, which the rationally thinking development workers and researchers would gain if they were able to derive inspiration from the rich symbolic world and utilize it in education. With education and increased adult education ways open up for mutual knowledge exchange and appreciation of the wide scope of the traditional but fast disappearing knowledge in its meaningful mode.

The negative implications of the traditional knowledge has been overemphasized in scholarship, as was shown already in Lloyd Swantz's study of the medicine men in Dar es Salaam. The "magic" ways of healing and treating problems reduces the meaningful utilization of traditional medicine. When the treatment no longer refers to the common spirits recognized by the social group, the treatment of accidents and problems in life with medicines and meaningless actions lead even to redressing the cases with evil and harmful medicines or deeds which turn the former more positive rituals to their opposite. When the self-made medicine men utilize invented ways of remedies it leads to misuse of tradition, as has been the case in relation to the albinos.

In closing i add that understanding the symbolic ways of seeing the world would also open the secrets of the biblical world, for christians, who also have the Word as the guide.

References

Ahmad, Ehtisham. *Social Security in Developing Countries*. Studies in Development Economics. Oxford, England, New York: Clarendon Press; Oxford University Press, 1991.

Ahmed, Durre, Märta Salokoski, and Marja-Liisa Swantz. "Issues of Methodology and Epistemology in Postcolonial Studies." *Occasional Paper*. Ed. Arnfred, Signe. Roskilde: International Development Studies, Roskilde University, 1995.

Anderson, David M., and Vigdis Broch-Due, eds. *The Poor Are Not Us: Pastoralism and Poverty in East Africa*. Athens, Ohio: Ohio University Press, 1999.

Apffel-Marglin, Frederique. *The Spirit of Regeneration: Andean Culture Confronting Western Notions of Development (Spirit Regeneration)* London: Zed Books, 1998.

Apffel-Marglin, Frédérique, and Stephen A. Marglin. *Dominating Knowledge: Development, Culture, and Resistance*. Studies in Development Economics. Oxford, New York: Clarendon Press; Oxford University, 1990.

Apffel-Marglin, Frédérique and Stephen A. Marglin. *Decolonizing Knowledge: From Development to Dialogue*. Studies in Development Economics. Oxford, New York: Clarendon Press; Oxford University Press; World Institute for Development Economics Research 1996.

Appelbaum, Richard P. *Theories of Social Change*. Markham Sociology Series. Chicago,: Markham Pub. Co., 1970.

Arnfred, Signe, ed. *Issues of Methodology and Epistemology in Postcolonial Studies*. Roskilde: International Development Studies, Roskilde University, 1995.

---. *Sexuality & Gender Politics in Mozambique: Rethinking Gender in Africa*. Oxford: James Currey, 2011.

Baber, Zaheer. "Sociology of Scientific Knowledge, Lost in the Reflexive Funhouse?" *Theory and Society* 21.1 (1992): 103-19.

Baert, Patrick. "Realist Philosophy of the Social Sciences and Economics: A Critique." *Cambridge Journal of Economics* 20.5 (1996): 513-22.

Bamurange, Virginia. "Relationships for Survival – Young Mothers and Street Youths." *Haraka, Haraka-- Look before You Leap: Youth at the Crossroad of Custom and Modernity*. Eds. Rwebangira, M. K. and Rita Liljeström. Stockholm: Nordiska Afrikainstitutet, 1998. 221-46.

Banuri, Tariq. "Development and the Politics of Knowledge: A Critical Role of the Social Role of Modernization Theories in the Development of the Third World." *Dominating Knowledge: Development, Culture, and Resistance*. Eds. Apffel-Marglin, Frédérique and Stephen A. Marglin. Oxford, New York:

Clarendon Press; Oxford University, 1990.

---. "Modernization and Its Discontents: A Cultural Perspective on the Theories of Development." *Dominating Knowledge: Development, Culture, and Resistance*. Eds. Apffel-Marglin, Frédérique and Stephen A. Marglin. Oxford, New York: Clarendon Press; Oxford University, 1990.

Basso, Keith H., Henry A. Selby, and School of American Research (Santa Fe N.M.). *Meaning in Anthropology*. School of American Research Advanced Seminar Series. 1st ed. Albuquerque: University of New Mexico Press, 1976.

Bastide, Roger. *Applied Anthropology*. New York,: Harper & Row, 1973.

Beidelman, T. O. *The Kaguru, a Matrilineal People of East Africa*. Case Studies in Cultural Anthropology. New York,: Holt, 1971.

Berque, Jacques. "Decolonisation, Interieur et Nature Seconde." *Etudes de Sociologie Tunisienne*, I (1968): 11-27.

Bleicher, Josef. *Contemporary Hermeneutics: Hermeneutics as Method, Philosophy, and Critique*. London; Boston: Routledge & Kegan Paul, 1980.

Bloch, Maurice. *From Blessing to Violence: History and Ideology in the Circumcision Ritual of the Merina of Madagascar*. Cambridge Studies in Social Anthropology. Cambridge Cambridgeshire; New York: Cambridge University Press, 1986.

---. "Zafimaniry Birth and Kinship Theory." *Social Anthropology* 1.1b (2007): 119-32.

Bloor, David. *Knowledge and Social Imagery*. 2nd ed. Chicago: University of Chicago Press, 1991.

Brain, James L. "The Kwere of Eastern Province." *Tanganyika Notes and Records* 58 & 59 (1962): 231-41.

Bryceson, Deborah. *Research Methodology and the Participatory Research Approach*. Dar es Salaam: Tanzanian Ministry of National Culture and Youth, 1980.

Bryceson, Deborah, and Marjorie Mbilinyi. "The Changing Role of Tanzanian Women in Production." *Jipemoyo*. Ed. Anacleti, A. O. Uppsala: Scandinavian Institute of African Studies for the Ministry of National Culture and Youth and the Academy of Finland, 1980.

Bryceson, Deborah, and Kemal Mustafa. "Participatory Research: Redefining the Relationship between Theory and Practice." *Participatory Research*. Eds. Kassam, Y. and K. Mustafa. New Delhi, India: Grafique, African Adult Education Association, 1982. 87-109

Cahill, Caitlin. "The Personal Is Political: Developing New Subjectivities through Participatory Action Research." *Gender, Place, and Culture* 14.3 (2007): 267- 92.

Caplan, Pat. "Something for Posterity or Hostage to Fortune? Archiving Anthropological Field Materia." *Antrhopology Today* 26.4 (2010): 13-17.

Carsten, Janet. *After Kinship*. New Departures in Anthropology. Cambridge, UK; New York: Cambridge University Press, 2004.

Chambers, Robert. "Pra, Pla and Pluralism: Practice and Theory." *The Sage Handbook of Action Research: Participative Inquiry and Practice*. Eds. Reason, Peter and Hilary Bradbury. 2nd ed. London; Thousand Oaks, Calif.: SAGE Publications, 2008. 297-318.

Clifford, James, and George E. Marcus. *Writing Culture: The Poetics and Politics of Ethnography: A School of American Research Advanced Seminar*. Berkeley: University of California Press, 1986.

Comaroff, Jean. *Body of Power, Spirit of Resistance: The Culture and History of a South African People*. Chicago: University of Chicago Press, 1985.

Comaroff, Jean, and John L. Comaroff. *Modernity and Its Malcontents: Ritual and Power in Postcolonial Africa*. Chicago: University of Chicago Press, 1993.

---. *Of Revelation and Revolution*. Chicago: University of Chicago Press, 1991.

Cory, Hans. *African Figurines*. London,: Faber and Faber, 1956.

Danielson, R. Elmer. *Forty Years with Christ in Tanzania 1928-1968, World Mission Interpretation*. New York: Lutheran Church in America, 1977.

Diamond, Stanley, and Christine Ward Gailey. *Dialectical Anthropology: Essays in Honor of Stanley Diamond*. 2 vols. Gainesville: University Press of Florida, 1992.

Douglas, Mary. *Implicit Meanings: Essays in Anthropology*. London; Boston: Routledge & Paul, 1975.

---. *Purity and Danger: An Analysis of Concepts of Pollution and Taboo*. London,: Routledge & K. Paul, 1966.

---. *Risk Acceptability According to the Social Sciences*. Social Research Perspectives: Occasional Reports on Current Topics. New York: Russell Sage Foundation, 1985.

Douglas, Mary, and Aaron B. Wildavsky. *Risk and Culture: An Essay on the Selection of Technical and Environmental Dangers*. Berkeley: University of California Press, 1982.

Drèze, Jean, and Amartya Sen. *An Uncertain Glory: India and Its Contradictions*. Princeton, New Jersey: Princeton University Press, 2013.

Durkheim, Émile. *The Division of Labor in Society*. Free Press Paperbacks. New York: Free Press of Glencoe, 1964.

Durkheim, Émile, and George Simpson. *ÉMile Durkheim on the Division of Labor in Society; Being a Translation of His De La Division Du Travail Social*. New York,: The Macmillan company, 1933.

Edevbaro, Daniel. "A Review of Social Policy Implementation in Nigeria with Emphasis on Education." Helsinki: UNU/WIDER, 1996. 31.

Ekins, Paul, and Manfred A. Max-Neef. *Real-Life Economics: Understanding Wealth Creation*. London; New York: Routledge, 1992.

Eliade, Mircea. *Patterns in Comparative Religion*. New York,: Sheed & Ward, 1958.

Elliot, Henry C. "Similarities and Differences between Science and Common Sense." *Ethnomethodology; Selected Readings*. Ed. Turner, Roy. Harmondsworth,: Penguin Education, 1974. 21-26.

Emmet, Dorothy Mary, and Alasdair C. MacIntyre. *Sociological Theory and Philosophical Analysis*. 1st American ed. New York,: Macmillan, 1970.

Escobar, Arturo. *Encountering Development: The Making and Unmaking of the Third World*. Princeton Studies in Culture/Power/History. Princeton, N.J.: Princeton University Press, 1995.

Espmark, Kjell. *Minnena Ljuger*. Stockholm: Norstedts, 2010.

Evans-Pritchard, E. E. *Nuer Religion*. Oxford,: Clarendon Press, 1956.

Evenson, Robert Y., and Germano Mwabu. "The Effects of Agricultural Extension on Farm Yields in Kenya." *Paper presented at the 10th Anniversary Conference on Investment, Growth and Risk in Africa, Centre for Study of African Economics, Oxford April 1997.*: 1997.

Fabian, Johannes. "Language, History and Anthropology." *Philosophy of the Social Sciences* 1 (1971): 9-47.

---. *Time and the Other: How Anthropology Makes Its Object*. New York: Columbia University Press, 1983.

Fahim, Hussein M., and Wenner-Gren Foundation for Anthropological Research. *Indigenous Anthropology in Non-Western Countries: Proceedings of a Burg Wartenstein Symposium*. Durham, N.C.: Carolina Academic Press, 1982.

Fals-Borda, Orlando. "Investigating Reality in Order to Transform It. The Colombian Experience." *Dialecticalo Anthropology* 4.1 (1979): 33-45.

Fals-Borda, Orlando, and Md. Anisur Rahman. *Action and Knowledge: Breaking the Monopoly with Participatory Action Research*. New York; London: Apex Press; Intermediate Technology Publications, 1991.

Feierman, Steven. *Peasant Intellectuals: Anthropology and History in Tanzania*. Madison, Wis.: University of Wisconsin Press, 1990.

---. "Popular Control over the Institutions of Health: A Historical Study." *The Professionalism of African Medicine*. Eds. Last, Murray and Gordon Chavunduka. Manchester: Manchester University Press, 1986. 205-20.

Ferguson, James. "The Anti-Politics Machine: "Development," Depoliticization, and Bureaucratic Power in Lesotho." Revision of the author's thesis (Ph D). Harvard University, 1990.

Field, Les W., and Richard Gabriel Fox. *Anthropology Put to Work*. Wenner-Gren International Symposium Series. Oxford; New York: Berg, 2007.

Follér, Maj-Lis, et al. *Conflict, Displacement, Transformation*. Nordic Africa Institute2013.

Forssén, Anja. *Childhood in Four Societies*. Transactions of the Finnish Anthropological Society,. Helsinki: Finnish Anthropological Society, 1985.

---. *Roots of Traditional Personality Development among the Zaramo in Coastal Tanzania*. Publication - Central Union for Child Welfare in Finland No 54. Helsinki: Lastensuojelun keskusliitto, 1979.

Fortes, Meyer, and Jack Goody. *Religion, Morality, and the Person: Essays on Tallensi Religion*. Essays in Social Anthropology. Cambridge Cambridgeshire; New York: Cambridge University Press, 1987.

Foucault, Michel. *The Order of Things: An Archaeology of the Human Sciences*. World of Man. London,: Tavistock Publications, 1970.

Freire, Paulo. *Pedagogy of the Oppressed*. New York: Herder and Herder, 1970.

Freire, Paulo. *Education for Critical Consciousness*. A Continuum Book. 1st American ed. New York,: Seabury Press, 1973.

Freling, Dana, ed. *Paths for Change, Experiences in Participation and Democratisation in Lindi and Mtwara Regions, Tanzania, Phase Ii*. Rural Integrated Project Support (RIPS) Programme, 1998.

Freud, Sigmund, and James Strachey. *Beyond the Pleasure Principle*. The International Psycho-Analytical Library No 4. Rev. ed. New York: Liveright Pub. Corp., 1961.

Garfinkel, Harold. "The Origins of the Term 'Ethnomethodology.'" *Ethnomethodology; Selected Readings*. Ed. Turner, Roy. Harmondsworth,: Penguin Education, 1974. 21-26.

Geiger, Susan. "Women in Nationalist Struggle: Tanu Activists in Dar Es Salaam." *International Journal of African Historical Studies* 20.1 (1987): 1-20.

Geschiere, Peter. *The Modernity of Witchcraft: Politics and the Occult in Postcolonial Africa = Sorcellerie et Politique En Afrique: La Viande Des Autres*. Charlottesville Va.: University Press of Virginia, 1997.

---. *The Perils of Belonging: Autochthony, Citizenship, and Exclusion in Africa and Europe*. Chicago: University of Chicago Press, 2009.

Godelier, Maurice. "Introduction: The Analysis of Transition Processes." *International Social Science Journal* 39.447-458 (1987).

Goldschmidt-Clermont, Luisella. *Unpaid Work in the Household: A Review of*

Economic Evaluation Methods. Women, Work, and Development,. Geneva: International Labour Office, 1982.

Goody, Jack. *The Interface between the Written and the Oral*. Studies in Literacy, Family, Culture, and the State. Cambridge Cambridgeshire; New York: Cambridge University Press, 1987.

---. *The Logic of Writing and the Organization of Society*. Studies in Literacy, Family, Culture, and the State. Cambridge Cambridgeshire; New York: Cambridge University Press, 1986.

Gould, Jeremy. *A Different Kind of Journey: Essays in Honor of Marja-Liisa Swantz*. Transactions of the Finnish Anthropological Society,. Helsinki: Finnish Anthropological Society, 1991.

---. "Localizing Modernity. Action, Interests and Association in Rural Zambia." University of Helsinki, 1997.

---. *Needs, Participation, and Local Development: Proceedings of the Eadi Basic Needs Workshop, Helsinki, December 13-15, 1979*. Publications / Finnish National Commission for Unesco,. Helsinki: Distribution University of Helsinki, Institute of Development Studies, 1981.

---. *The New Conditionality: The Politics of Poverty Reduction Strategies*. London; New York: Zed Books, 2005.

Green, Maia. "Making Development Agents: Participation as Boundary Object in International Development." *Journal of Development Studies* 46.7 (2010): 1240-63.

---. "Participatory Development and the Appropriation of Agency in Southern Tanzania." *Critique of Anthropology* 20.1 (2000): 67-69.

---. *Priests, Witches and Power: Popular Christianity after Mission in Southern Tanzania*. Cambridge Studies in Social and Cultural Anthropology. Cambridge; New York: Cambridge University Press, 2003.

Greenwood, Davydd. "Doing and Learning Action Research in the Neo-Liberal World of Contemporary Higher Education." *Action Research* 10.2 (2012): 115.

Greenwood, Davydd, and Morten Levin. "Pragmatic Action Research and the Struggle to Transform Universities into Learning Communities." *Handbook of Action Research: Participative Inquiry and Practice*. Eds. Reason, Peter and Hilary Bradbury. London; Thousand Oaks, Calif.: SAGE, 2001. 103-13.

Griaule, Marcel. *Conversation with Ogotemmêli*. London: Published for the International African Institute by the Oxford University Press, 1965.

Gudeman, Stephen, and Alberto Rivera. *Conversations in Colombia: The Domestic Economy in Life and Text*. Cambridge; New York: Cambridge University Press, 1990.

Gupta, Akhil, and James Ferguson. *Anthropological Locations: Boundaries and Grounds of a Field Science*. Berkeley: University of California Press, 1997.

Habermas, Jürgen. "Concept and Theory Formation in the Social Science." *Sociological Theory and Philosophical Analysis*. Eds. Emmet, Dorothy Mary and Alasdair C. MacIntyre. 1st American ed. New York,: Macmillan, 1970a. 48-66.

---. *Knowledge and Interest*. Sociological Theory and Philosophical Analysis. Eds. Emmet, Dorothy Mary and Alasdair C. MacIntyre. 1st American ed. New York,: Macmillan, 1970b.

Habermas, Jürgen. *Theory and Practice*. London: Heinemann, 1974.

---. "Towards Theory of Communicative Competence." *Inquiry* 13 (1970c): 360-75.

Hall, Budd. "Participatory Research: An Approach for Change." *Convergence* 8.2 (1975): 24-31.

Harjula, Raimo. *Mirau and His Practice: A Study of the Ethnomedicinal Repertoire of a Tanzanian Herbalist*. London: Tri-Med, 1980.

Havnevik, Kjell J. *Tanzania: The Limits to Development from Above*. Uppsala, Sweden; Dar es Salaam, Tanzania: Nordiska Afrikainstitutet; Mkuki na Nyota Publishers, 1993.

Havnevik, Kjell J., Emil Sandström, and International Fund for Agricultural Development. *The Institutional Context of Poverty Eradication in Rural Africa: Proceedings from a Seminar in Tribute to the 20th Anniversary of the International Fund for Agricultural Development (Ifad)*. Uppsala, Sweden: Nordic Africa Institute, 2000.

Heron, John. "Quality as Primacy of the Practical." *Qualitative Inquiry* 2.1 (1996): 41-56.

Hill, Polly. "Landlords and Brokers. A West African Trading System." *Cahiers et Etudes Africaines* 6.3 (1996): 349-66.

Hirschman, Albert O. *Development Projects Observed*. Washington,: Brookings Institution, 1967.

Hobsbawm, Eric J., and Terence O. Ranger. *The Invention of Tradition*. Past and Present Publications. Cambridge Cambridgeshire; New York: Cambridge University Press, 1983.

Hodgson, Dorothy. "Critical Interventions: Dilemmas of Accountability in Contemporary Ethnographic Research." *Identities* 6.2/3 (1999): 201-25.

Hodgson, Dorothy Louise. *Being Maasai, Becoming Indigenous: Postcolonial Politics in a Neoliberal World*. Bloomington: Indiana University Press, 2011.

Horton, Robin. "African Traditional Thought and Western Science." *Africa* 10.71 (1967): 155-87.

---. *Patterns of Thought in Africa and the West: Essays on Magic, Religion, and Science*. Cambridge England; New York, NY: Cambridge University Press, 1993.

Hurskainen, Arvi. "Cattle and Culture: The Structure of a Pastoral Parakuyo Society." University of Helsinki, 1984.

Hyden, Göran. *No Shortcuts to Progress: African Development Management in Perspective*. Berkeley: University of California Press, 1983.

Hydén, Göran. *Beyond Ujamaa in Tanzania: Underdevelopment and an Uncaptured Peasantry*. London: Heinemann, 1980.

Hymes, Dell H. *Reinventing Anthropology*. Pantheon Antitextbooks. 1st ed. New York,: Pantheon Books, 1972.

Ihde, Don. *Consequences of Phenomenology*. Albany, N.Y.: State University of New York Press, 1986.

Inkeles, Alex, and David H. Smith. "Becoming Modern." *The Gap between Rich and Poor: Contending Perspectives on the Political Economy of Development*. Ed. Seligson, Mitchell A. Boulder: Westview Press, 1984. xii, 418 p.

Jacobson-Widding, Anita, and David Westerlund. *Culture, Experience, and Pluralism: Essays on African Ideas of Illness and Healing*. Acta Universitatis Upsaliensis Uppsala Studies in Cultural Anthropology,. Uppsala, Stockholm, Sweden: Academiae Upsaliensis; Distributed by Almqvist & Wiksell International, 1989.

Jellicoe, Marguerite. *The Long Path: A Case Study of Social Change in Wahi, Singida District, Tanzania*. Nairobi, Kenya: East African Pub. House, 1978.

Jennings, Michael. "'A Very Real War': Popular Participation in Development in Tanzania During the 1950s & 1960s." *International Journal of African Historical Studies* 40.1 (2007): 71-94.

Jerman, Helena. *Between Five Lines: The Development of Ethnicity in Tanzania with Special Reference to the Western Bagamoyo District*. Jipemoyo, Saarijarvi; Uppsala, Sweden: Finnish Anthropological Society; Nordic Africa Institute, 1997.

---. *Cultural Process of Development,*: Institute of Development Studies, Helsinki, 1989.

Jipemoyo Project, Interim Report 2. *Utafiti Uliofanyika Na Mofisa Utamaduni (Mkoa Nad Vilaya) Katika Tarafa Za Miono, Msata Na Msoga, Wilayani Bagamoyo.*1976.

Jung, Carl G., and Marie-Luise von Franz. *Man and His Symbols*. Garden City, N.Y.,: Doubleday, 1964.

Kaartinen, Timo. *Songs of Travel, Stories of Place: Poetics of Absence in an Eastern Indonesian Society*. Folklore Fellows' Communications. Helsinki: Suomalainen Tiedeakatemia, 2010.

Kashaga, Frateline. "Back to the Roots: A New Social Policy Agenda for the Welfare of the Elderly in Rural Tanzania: The Case of Bukoba District." University of Helsinki, 2013.

Kassam, Yusuf, and Kemal Mustafa, eds. *Participatory Research*. New Dehli: Society for Participatory Research in Asia, 1982.

Katz, Cindi. "All the World Is Staged: Intellectuals and the Project of Ethnography." *Environment and Planning Development: Society and Space* 10.5 (1992): 495-510.

Kekkonen, Helena. "An Experiment in Outreach and the Pedagogy of Freire." *Convergence* X (1977).

Kinyunyi, L., and M-L. Swantz. "Research Methodologies for Identifying and Validating Grassroots Indicators." *Grassroots Indicators for Desertification: Experience and Perspectives from Eastern and Southern Africa*. Eds. Hambly, H. and Angura T. Onweng. Ottawa, ON, Canada: International Development Research Centre, 1996. 60-74.

Kitolero, David. "'Nchepela' Epidemiology of Spirit Possession and Its Contribution to Socio-Economic Activities: A Case of the Ngindo of Mahenge – Morogoro Region." *Institute of Social Work, University of Dar es Salaam*2004.

Koda, Bertha. *The Role of Local Government in Developing Women's Economy and Welfare in Iramba District Final Report on Research in 2003-2004 and 2006-2007*2008.

Kokkonen, Päivi. "Finnish Aid to the Tanzanian Health Sector, a Study of the Training of Rural Medical Aids and the Health of Women, Report 2, Effects of Finnish Cooperation on Tanzanian Women." Helsinki: Institute for Development Studies, University of Helsinki, 1985.

Krausz, Michael. *Relativism: Interpretation and Confrontation*. Notre Dame, Ind.: University of Notre Dame Press, 1989.

Kwasi, Wiredu. "On Defining African Philosophy." *11th Annual Conference of the Canadian Association of African Studies*. 1981.

Laitinen, Hanna. *Kenen Ehdoilla? Osallistaminen Kehitysyhteityössä*. Helsinki: KEPA, Kehitysyhteistyön Palvelukeskus, 2002.

Langer, Susanne Katherina Knauth. *Philosophy in a New Key; a Study in the Symbolism of Reason, Rite, and Art*. 3d ed. Cambridge,: Harvard University Press, 1957.

Lassiter, Luke E. *The Chicago Guide to Collaborative Ethnography*. Chicago Guides to Writing, Editing, and Publishing. Chicago: University of Chicago Press, 2005.

---. *Invitation to Anthropology*. Walnut Creek, CA: AltaMira Press, 2002.

Leal, Pablo Alejandro. "Participation: The Ascendancy of a Buzzword in the Neo-Liberal Era " *Development in Practice* 17.4-5 (2007): 539-48.

Lemeck, K., and Marja-Liisa Swantz. "Research Methodologies for Indentifying and Validating Grassroots Indicators." *Grassroots Indicators for Desertification: Experience and Perspectives from Eastern and Southern Africa*. Eds. Hambly, Helen and Tobias Onweng Angura. Ottawa: International Development Research Centre, 1996. 60-74.

Lévi-Strauss, Claude. *The Savage Mind*. The Nature of Human Society Series. Chicago: University of Chicago Press, 1966.

---. *Structural Anthropology*. New York: Basic Books, 1963.

---. *Totemism*. Beacon Paperback. Boston,: Beacon Press, 1963.

Lewis, I.M. "Spirit Possession and Deprivation Cults." *Man* 1.3 (1966): 305-29.

Liebenow, J. Gus. *Colonial Rule and Political Development in Tanzania: The Case of the Makonde*. Evanston,: Northwestern University Press, 1971.

Lienhardt, R. G. *Divinity and Experience; the Religion of the Dinka*. Oxford,: Clarendon Press, 1961.

Likanda, S.N.M., et al. *Indigenous Soil Fertility Improvement Study", Newala and Masasi Districts, First Technical Report. Mimeo. *. District Forestry offices, RIPS, Soils Section and Farming System research, MOA, Naliendele, Mtwara1995.

Low, Setha M., and Sally Engle Merry. "Engaged Anthropology: Diversity and Dilemmas: An Introuction to Supplement 2." *Current Anthropology* 51.S2 (2010).

Luria, A. "Towards the Problem of the Historical Nature of Psychological Progress." *International Journal of Psychology* 6 (1971).

Malinowski, Bronislaw. *A Diary in the Strict Sense of the Term*. 1st ed. New York,: Harcourt, 1967.

Mamuya, S. J. *Jando Na Unyago*. Nairobi: East African Pub. House, 1972.

Marglin, Stephen A. *The Dismal Science: How Thinking Like an Economist Undermines Community*. Cambridge, Mass.: Harvard University Press, 2008.

---. "Dominating Knowledge, Development, Culture, and Resistance." *Decolonizing Knowledge: From Development to Dialogue*. Eds. Apffel-Marglin, Frédérique and Stephen A. Marglin. Oxford; New York: Clarendon Press; Oxford University Press, World Institute for Development Economics Research. 1996. vi, 398 p.

Mattila-Wiro, P. "Women in Informal Markets: Women Traders and Marketing Networks in Mwanga and Moshi Districts." *Local Actors in Development: The Case of Mwanga District*. Ed. Omari, Cuthbert K. Dar es Salaam: Educational Publishers and Distributors, 1998.

Mazonde, Isaac Ncube, et al. *Indigenous Knowledge Systems and Intellectual Property in the Twenty-First Century: Perspectives from Southern Africa*. Codesria Book Series. Dakar, Gaborone; London, U.K.: Codesria; University of Botswana; World Association for Christian Communication, 2007.

Mbembe, Achille. "The Banality of Power and the Aesthetics of Vulgarity on the Postcolony." *Public Culture* 4.2 (1992b): 1-30.

---. "Provisional Notes on the Postcolony." *africa* 62.1 (1992a): 3-37.

Mbiti, John S. *African Religions & Philosophy*. London, Ibadan etc.: Heinemann, 1969.

McClelland, David C. *The Achieving Society*. Princeton: D. Van Nostrand Company, Inc., 1961.

McCloskey, Deirdre N. *Knowledge and Persuasion in Economics*. Cambridge England; New York, NY, USA: Cambridge University Press, 1994.

---. *Second Thoughts: Myths and Morals of U.S. Economic History*. New York: Oxford University Press, 1993.

McGrane, Bernard. *Beyond Anthropology: Society and the Other*. New York: Columbia University Press, 1989.

Mdachi, Patrick L. *Wanyaturu Wa Singida. Mila Na Desturi Zao*. Benedictine Publications, Ndanda, Peramiho, 1991.

Mead, Margaret, and American Museum of Natural History. *Culture and Commitment; a Study of the Generation Gap*. 1st ed. Garden City, N.Y.,: Published for the American Museum of Natural History, Natural History Press, 1970.

Medard, Jean' Francois. "Patrimonialism, Neo-Patrimonialism and the Study of the Post ¬Colonial State in Sub-Saharian Africa." *Seminar on Max Weber and Administration and the Politics in the Third World.* . Karthala, 1992.

Mertens, R. "Where the Action Was." *University of Chicago Magazine* April (2004): 30-5.

Mills, C. Wright. *The Sociological Imagination*. New York,: Oxford University Press, 1959.

Ministry of Health, Tanzania. "Ushirikishwaji Wa Jamii Katika Mafunzo Ya Afya." Dar es Salaam: Mwongozo wa utafiti. Kitabu cha mafunzo ya afya, 1989.

Mmuya, Max, and Göran Hyden. *Power and Policy Slippage in Tanzania - Discussing National Ownership of Development*. Stockholm: Sidastudies, 2008.

Moser, Heinz. *Aktions Forschung Als Kritische Theorie Der Socialwissenschaften*. München: Verlag, 1975.

---. *The Participatory Approach on the Village Level: Theoretical and Practical Implications*. Helsinki1980.

Moser, Heinz, Helmut Ornauer, and International Sociological Association. *Internationale Aspekte Der Aktionsforschung*. 1. Aufl. ed. München: Kösel, 1978.

Msuya, F.E. "Women Participation in Fishery and Economics of Nyumba Ya Mungu Fishing in Mwanga District." *Local Actors in Development: The Case of Mwanga District*. Ed. Omari, Cuthbert K. Dar es Salaam: Educational Publishers and Distributors, 1998.

Msuya, Flower. "Fishery and Economics of Nyumba Ya Mungu Fishng Communities in Kilimanjaro Region, Tanzania with Emphasis on Women Participation, Local Actor in Development ". University of Helsinki, 1993.

Mtei, Edwin. *From Goatherd to Governor: The Autobiography of Edwin Mtei*. Dar es Salaam: Mkuki Na Nyota Publishers, 2009.

Mustafa, Kemal. *Jipemoyo, Vol 1*. Workshop papers presented by the Bagamoy Research Project Team at a seminar, July 27-28th, 1976, organized by the Department of Research and Planning of the Ministry of National Culture and Youth in cooperation with the Department of Sociology of the University of Dar es Salaam.1977.

---. *Participatory Research Amongst Pastoralist Peasants in Tanzania: The Experience of the Jipemoyo Project in Bagamoyo District*. Geneva?: International Labour Organisation, 1981.

---. *Participatory Research and the 'Pastoralist Question' in Tanzania: A Critique of the Jipemoyo Project Experience in Bagamoyo District*. Helsinki1989.

Mwaikusa, Jwani T. "Maintaining Law and Order in Tanzania: The Role of Sungusungu Defence Groups." *Service Provision under Stress in East Africa: The State, Ngos & People's Organizations in Kenya, Tanzania & Uganda*. Eds. Semboja, Joseph and Ole Therkildsen. Copenhagen: Centre for Development Research, 1995. xiv, 242 p.

Myrdal, Gunnar. *Objectivity in Social Research*. Wimmer Lecture. New York: Pantheon Books, 1969.

Myrdal, Gunnar, and Twentieth Century Fund. *Asian Drama; an Inquiry into the Poverty of Nations*. 3 vols. New York,: Pantheon, 1968.

Nelson, Julie A. *Feminism, Objectivity and Economics*. Economics as Social Theory. London; New York: Routledge, 1996.

Nussbaum, Martha Craven snf Amartya Sen. *The Quality of Life*. Wider Studies in Development Economics. Oxford England; New York: Clarendon Press; Oxford University Press; World Institute for Development Economics Research. 1993.

Nussbaum, Martha, and Amartya Sen. "Internal Criticism and Indian Rationalist Traditions." *Relativism: Interpretation and Confrontation*. Ed. Krausz, Michael. Notre Dame, Ind.: University of Notre Dame Press, 1989. 299-325.

Nyerere, Julius K. *Freedom and Development. Uhuru Na Maendeleo. A Selection from Writings and Speeches 1968-1973.* A Galaxy Book, Gb 412. London, New York,: Oxford University Press, 1974.

---. *Freedom and Unity: Uhuru Na Umoja; a Selection from Writings and Speeches, 1952-65.* London, Nairobi etc.: Oxford U.P., 1967.

Omari, Cuthbert K. *Local Actors in Development: The Case of Mwanga District: Research Reports.* Dar es Salaam, Tanzania: Educational Publishers and Distributors, 1998.

Omari, Cuthbert K. . "Rural Market Women in Northern Tanzania." *What Went Right in Tanzania: People's Response to Directed Development.* Eds. Swantz, Marja-Liisa and Aili Mari Tripp. Dar es Salaam, Tanzania: Dar es Salaam University Press, 1996. vi, 184 p.

Pietilä, Hilkka. "Ecological Sustainability and Human Well-Being." *ISEE.* 2006.

---. "Ecological Sustainability and Human Well-Being." New Delhi: ISEE, 2006.

---. *Yli Rajojen.* Helsinki: Into, 2013.

Pietilä, Tuulikki. *Gossip, Markets, and Gender: How Dialogue Constructs Moral Value in Post-Socialist Kilimanjaro.* Women in Africa and the Diaspora. Madison, Wis.: University of Wisconsin Press, 2007.

Platteau, Jean-Philippe. *Traditional Systems of Social Security and Hunger Insurance: Past Achievements and Modern Challenges.* An Uncertain Glory: India and Its Contradictions. Eds. Drèze, Jean and Amartya Sen. Princeton, New Jersey: Princeton University Press, 2013.

Platteau, Jean-Philippe. "Traditional Systems of Social Security and Hunger Insurance: Past Achievements and Modern Challenges." *Social Security in Developing Countries.* Ed. Ahmad, Ehtisham. Oxford England; New York: Clarendon Press; Oxford University Press, 1991. xviii, 477 p.

Polanyi, Karl. *The Great Transformation.* New York, Toronto,: Farrar & Rinehart, 1944.

Pöntinen, Mari-Anna. *African Theology as Liberating Wisdom: Celebrating Life and Harmony in the Evangelical Lutheran Church in Botswana.* Studies in Systematic Theology. Leiden; Boston: Brill, 2013.

Rahnema, Majid. "Participatory Action Research: The "Last Temptation of Saint" Development." *Alternatives: Global, Local, Political* 15.2 (1990): 199-226.

Ranger, T. O. *Dance and Society in Eastern Africa, 1890-1970: The Beni Ngoma.* Berkeley: University of California Press, 1975.

Ranger, Terrence. "African Religious Research." *African Studies Center, University of California* 2.1 (1971): 46-49.

Reason, Peter. *Human Inquiry in Action: Developments in New Paradigm Research*. London; Newbury Park: Sage Publications, 1988.

Reason, Peter, and Hilary Bradbury. *Handbook of Action Research: Participative Inquiry and Practice*. London; Thousand Oaks, Calif.: SAGE, 2001.

---. *The Sage Handbook of Action Research: Participative Inquiry and Practice*. 2nd ed. London; Thousand Oaks, Calif.: SAGE Publications, 2008.

Ricœur, Paul, and John B. Thompson. *Hermeneutics and the Human Sciences: Essays on Language, Action, and Interpretation*. Cambridge Eng.; New York; Paris: Cambridge University Press; Editions de la Maison des sciences de l'homme, 1981.

Rigby, Peter. *African Images: Racism and the End of Anthropology*. Global Issues,. Oxford; Washington, D.C.: Berg, 1996.

---. *Cattle, Capitalism, and Class: Ilparakuyo Maasai Transformations*. Philadelphia: Temple University Press, 1992.

---. *Persistent Pastoralists: Nomadic Societies in Transition*. Third World Books. London; Totowa, N.J.: Zed; Biblio Distribution Center, 1985.

RIPS. *Paths for Change Ii, Reflections Along the Way. Maendeleo Ni Nini. Maelezo Kutoka Mikoa Ya Lindi Na Mtwara.* . Ndanda Mission Press2002.

Robbins, Joel. *Becoming Sinners: Christianity and Moral Torment in a Papua New Guinea Society*. Ethnographic Studies in Subjectivity. Berkeley, Calif.: University of California Press, 2004.

Robertson, A. F. *People and the State: An Anthropology of Planned Development*. Cambridge Studies in Social Anthropology. Cambridge Cambridgeshire; New York: Cambridge University Press, 1984.

Rodima-Taylor, Daivi. "Culture and Institutional Adaptation to Vulnerability: Self-Help Institutions in Decentralizing Tanzania." *Climate Vulnerability and Adaptation: Theory and Cases.* . ICARUS, 2010.

Rodney, Walter. *How Europe Underdeveloped Africa*. Washington,: Howard University Press, 1974.

Rossini, F.A., et al. "Interdisciplinary Integration within Technology Assessments." *Knowledge* 2 (1981): 503-28.

Rowan, John. "A Dialectical Paradigm for Research." *Human Inquiry: A Sourcebook of New Paradigm Research*. Eds. Reason, Peter and John Rowan. Chichester Eng.; New York: J. Wiley, 1981. 94.

Rowbotham, Sheila. *Dreamers of a New Day: Women Who Invented the Twentieth Century*. London; New York: Verso, 2010.

---. *Women in Movement: Feminism and Social Action*. Revolutionary Thought/Radical Movements. New York, N.Y.: Routledge, 1992.

Rwebangira, M. K., and Rita Liljeström. *Haraka, Haraka-- Look before You Leap: Youth at the Crossroad of Custom and Modernity.* Stockholm: Nordiska Afrikainstitutet, 1998.

Sahlins, Marshall David. *Historical Metaphors and Mythical Realities: Structure in the Early History of the Sandwich Islands Kingdom.* Asao Special Publications. Ann Arbor: University of Michigan Press, 1981.

---. *Islands of History.* Chicago: University of Chicago Press, 1985.

Samwel, Method. "Mabadiliko Katika Majigambo: Uchunguzi Wa Majigambo Ya Jadi Na Ya Bongo Fleva." Chuo Kikuu cha Dar es Salaam, 2012.

Sanneh, Lamin O. *Translating the Message: The Missionary Impact on Culture.* American Society of Missiology Series. 2nd ed. Maryknoll, N.Y.: Orbis Books, 2009.

Schneider, Leander. "Colonial Legacies and Postcolonial Authoritarianism in Tanzania Connects and Disconnects." *African Studies Review* 49.1 (2006): 93-123.

Schunsul, Jean J., and Stephen Schensul. "Collaborative Research: Methods of Inquiry for Social Change." *The Handbook of Qualitative Research in Education.* Eds. LeCompte, Margaret D., Wendy L. Milroy and Judith Preissle. Vol. 161-2000. New York: Academic Press, 1992.

Schütz, Alfred. "Common-Sense and Scientific Interpretation of Human Action." *Philosophy and Phenomenological Research* 14.1 (1953): 1-38.

---. "Concept and Theory Formation in the Social Science." *Sociological Theory and Philosophical Analysis.* Eds. Emmet, Dorothy Mary and Alasdair C. MacIntyre. 1st American ed. New York,: Macmillan, 1970. 48-66.

Scott, James C. *The Moral Economy of the Peasant: Rebellion and Subsistence in Southeast Asia.* New Haven: Yale University Press, 1976.

Seligson, Mitchell A. *The Gap between Rich and Poor: Contending Perspectives on the Political Economy of Development.* Boulder: Westview Press, 1984.

Semboja, Joseph, and Ole Therkildsen. *Service Provision under Stress in East Africa: The State, Ngos & People's Organizations in Kenya, Tanzania & Uganda.* Copenhagen: Centre for Development Research, 1995.

Seppälä, Pekka. "Utilizing Research in Finnish Bilateral Development Cooperation." *Nordic Africa Conference* 2013.

Seppälä, Pekka, and Bertha Koda. *The Making of a Periphery: Economic Development and Cultural Encounters in Southern Tanzania.* Seminar Proceedings. Uppsala; Dar es Salaam: Nordiska Afrikainstitutet; Mkuki na Nyota Publishers, 1998.

Shils, Edward. *The Intellectuals and the Powers, and Other Essays.* His Selected Papers, 1. Chicago,: University of Chicago Press, 1972.

Shuma, Mary, and Rita Liljeström. "The Erosion of the Matrilineal Order of the Wamwera." *Haraka, Haraka-- Look before You Leap: Youth at the Crossroad of Custom and Modernity.* Eds. Rwebangira, M. K. and Rita Liljeström. Stockholm: Nordiska Afrikainstitutet, 1998. 271 p.

Siikala, Jukka. *Culture and History in the Pacific.* Transactions / the Finnish Anthropological Society,. Helsinki: Finnish Anthropological Society, 1990.

Siirala, Aarne. *The Voice of Illness; a Study in Therapy and Prophecy.* Philadelphia,: Fortress Press, 1964.

Siirala, Martti. *From Transfer to Transference, Seven Essays on Human Predicament.* Helsinki: Terapeia Foundation, Helsinki University Press, 1983.

---. "On the Import of Our Basic Views in Medicine." *Journal of Social Medicine* II.A (1965).

---. "Our Changing Conceptions of Illness." *Journal of Religion and Health* 52105-118 (1986).

Singer, Merrill, and Hans A. Baer. *Introducing Medical Anthropology: A Discipline in Action.* Lanham, MD: AltaMira Press, 2007.

Singer, Merrill, and Pamela I. Erickson. *A Companion to Medical Anthropology.* Blackwell Companions in Anthropology. Chichester, West Sussex; Malden, MA: Wiley-Blackwell, 2011.

Sitari, Taimi. "Settlement Changes in the Bagamoyo Distric of Tanzania as a Consequence of Villagization." Turku: Turun Yliopisto, Maantieteen laitos, 1983.

Sokoni, Cosmas H. *Maendeleo Ya Makazi Vijijini Baada Ya Ujamaa, Magharibi Mwa Wilaya Ya Bagamoyo, Tanzania*: Turku University, Department of Geography 2010.

Stocking, George W. *Observers Observed: Essays on Ethnographic Fieldwork.* History of Anthropology. Madison, Wis.: University of Wisconsin Press, 1983.

Strand, Kerry. *Community-Based Research and Higher Education: Principles and Practices.* Jossey-Bass Higher and Adult Education Series. 1st ed. San Francisco, CA: Jossey-Bass, 2003.

Strathern, Marilyn. "Marilyn Strathern on Kinship (Interview with Marilyn Strathern)." *EASA Newsletter* 29 (1997): 6-9.

---. *Reproducing the Future: Essays on Anthropology, Kinship, and the New Reproductive Technologies.* New York: Routledge, 1992.

Swantz, Lloyd W. *The Medicine Man among the Zaramo of Dar es Salaam.* Uppsala, Sweden; Dar es Salaam: Scandinavian Institute of African Studies; Dar es Salaam University Press, 1990.

Swantz, M. L., E. Ndedya, and M.S Masaiganah. "Participatory Action Research in Southern Tanzania, with Special Reference to Women." *Handbook of Action Research: Participative Inquiry and Practice.* Eds. Reason, Peter and Hilary Bradbury. London; Thousand Oaks, Calif.: SAGE, 2001. 386-495.

Swantz, Marja-Liisa. *Beyond the Forestline: The Life and Letters of Bengt Sundkler.* Studia Missionalia Svecana,. Leominster: Gracewing, 2002.

---. "Community and Healing among the Zaramo in Tanzania." *Soc. Sci Med.* 138 (1979b): 169-73.

---. *Community and Village-Base Provision of Key Social Services, a Case Study of Tanzania.* Helsinki: UNU-WIDER, 1997.

---. "Community Based Research as Part of Academy." *Nordic Africa Conference.* 2013.

---. "Community Participation in Health Care" in Health and Science in Developing Countries." Eds. Lankinen, K.S., et al. London: MacMillan, 1994b. 433-41.

---. "The Ethnic, National and International Components of Culture in the Development of Tanzania." *Cultural Imperialism and Cultural Identity.* Ed. Sandbacka, C.. Vol. 2. Helsinki: Transactions of the Finnish Anthropological Society, 1977. 115-30.

---. "Evaluating Health Projects. How to Do It Better?" *Journal of Social Medicine* 29 (1992c): 277-85.

---. "Human Body as a Symbol of Resistance: A Case of the Zaramo of Tanzania." *Occasional Paper.* Institute of Development Studies, Helsinki1992a.

---. "Introduction to Local Actors in Development (Lad)." *Local Actors in Development: The Case of Mwanga District: Research Reports.* Ed. Omari, Cuthbert K. Dar es Salaam, Tanzania: Educational Publishers and Distributors, 1998. 1-19.

---. "Jipemoyo, Culture and Social Change in the Restructuring of Tanzanian Rural Areas." Helsinki: Bagamoyo Research Project, Institute of Development Studies, University of Helsinki, 1979c.

---. "Life and Research on Bengt Sundkler." *Swedish Missiological Themes* 97.4 (2009).

---. "Manipulation of Multiple Health Systems in the Coastal Region of Tanzania." *Culture, Experience, and Pluralism: Essays on African Ideas of Illness and Healing.* . Eds. Jacobson-Widding, Anita and David Westerlund. Acta Universitatis Upsaliensis Uppsala Studies in Cultural Anthropology. Uppsala; Stockholm, Sweden: Academiae Upsaliensis; Distributed by Almqvist & Wiksell International, 1989b.

---. "Methodological Notes on Cultural Research Amidst Planned Change. A

Case Study on Spirit Possession." *TEMENOS, Studies in Comparative Religion* 13 (1984).

---. "Notes on Research on Women and Their Strategies for Sustained Livelihood in the Southern Tanzania." *The Making of a Periphery: Economic Development and Cultural Encounters in Southern Tanzania.* Eds. Seppälä, Pekka and Bertha Koda. Uppsala; Dar es Salaam: Nordiska Afrikainstitutet; Mkuki na Nyota Publishers, 1998. 154-94.

---. "Participation and the Evaluation of the Effects of Aid for Women." *Evaluating Development Assistance: Approaches and Methods.* Eds. Berlage, L. and Olav Stokke. European Association of Development Research and Training Institutes, Eadi-Book Series. London; Portland, Or.: F. Cass, 1992b. 104-19.

---. *Participatory Action Research as a Practice.* Handbook of Action Research: Participative Inquiry and Practice. Eds. Reason, Peter and Hilary Bradbury. London; Thousand Oaks, Calif.: SAGE, 2001.

---. "Participatory Action Research as Practice." *The Sage Handbook of Action Research: Participative Inquiry and Practice.* Eds. Reason, Peter and Hilary Bradbury. 2nd ed. London; Thousand Oaks, Calif.: SAGE Publications, 2008. 31-48.

---. "A Personal Position Paper on Participatory Research: Personal Quest for Living Knowledge." *Qualitative Inquiry* 2.1 (1996): 120-36.

---. "The Place of People's Own Knowledge in Theorizing About the Economies of the Poor." *Issues of methodology and epistemology in postcolonial sciences* Ed. Arnfred, Signe. Roskilde: International Development Studies: Roskilde University, 1995. 15-30.

---. "Quality as Primacy of the Practical." *Qualitative Inquiry (Guest eds. Reason, Peter & Yvonne S. Lincoln)* 2.1 (1996b): 41-56.

---. *Rejoinder to Research Methodology and the Participatory Research Approach*1980.

---. "The Religious and Magical Rites Connected with the Life Cycle of the Woman in Some Bantu Ethnic Groups of Tanzania." Thesis. Turku University, 1969.

---. *Research as an Educational Tool for Development.* Dar es Salaam: Bureau of Resource Assessment and Land Use Planning BRALUP. Tanzania: University of Dar es Salaam, 1975b.

---. "Research as an Educational Tool for Development." *The Tanzanian Experience. Education for Liberation and Development.* Eds. Hinzen, H. and V. H. Hundsdörfer. Hamburg and London: UNESCO Institute for Education and Evans Brothers, 1979b. 229-38.

---. *Research in Action as a Programme for University Students' Participation in Village Development.* Dar es Salaam: Bureau of Resource Assessment and Land Use Planning, BRALUP, University of Dar es Salaam., 1973.

---. "Research in Action in Dar es Salaam." *Overseas Universities* 22.February (1975c): 19-22.

---. *Ritual and Symbol in Transitional Zaramo Society with Special Reference to Women.* Studia Missionalia Upsaliensia. Lund,: Gleerup, 1970.

---. *The Role of Participant Research in Development.* Research Report - Bureau of Resource Assessment and Land Use Planning, University of Dar es Salaam. Dar es Salaam: Bureau of Resource Assessment and Land Use Planning, University of Dar es Salaam, 1975a.

---. "The Role of Participant Research in Development." *Geografiska Annaler* 67.B (1976).

---. "Sallistuva Ja Osallistava Terveydenhuolto." *Kehitysmaiden Terveys Ja Sairaus.* Eds. Lankinen, Kari, et al. Helsinki: Kandidaatti kustannus Oy, 1989c.

---. "Transfer of Knowledge for Development." *The Cultural Dimension of Development: Report of the Afro-Nordic Seminar on the Cultural Dimension of Development: Organized by the Finnish Commission for Unesco, 22-26 April 1985.* Eds. Serkkola, Ari and Christine Mann. Helsinki: Finnish National Commission for UNESCO, 1986. 290 p.

---. *Transfer of Technology as an Intercultural Process.* Transactions of the Finnish Anthropological Society,. Helsinki: Finnish Anthropological Society, 1989a.

---. "Ushirikishwaji Wa Jamii Katika Mafunzo Ya Afya." Mwongozo wa Utafiti. Centre for Educational Development in Health, Arusha Tanzania. Institute for Development Studies, Helsinki University. 1984.

---. "Village Development: In Whose Conditions?." *What Went Right in Tanzania: People's Response to Directed Development.* Eds. Swantz, Marja-Liisa and Aili Mari Tripp. Dar es Salaam, Tanzania: Dar es Salaam University Press, 1996. 137-73.

---. "What Is Development?" *Perspectives to Global Social Development.* Ed. Perkiö, Mikko. Tampere: Tampere University Press, 2009.

---. "Women Entrepreneurs in Tanzania: A Path to Sustainable Livelihood." *Global Employment: An International Investigation into the Future of Work.* Eds. Simai, Mihály, Valentine M. Moghadam and Arvo Kuddo. London; Atlantic Highlands, N.J. Tokyo: Published for the United Nations University; United Nations University Press, 1995. v. <2 >.

---. *Women in Development: A Creative Role Denied?: The Case of Tanzania.* London; New York: C. Hurst; St. Martin's Press, 1985.

---. "Women/Body/Knowledge: From Production to Regeneration." *Feminist Perspectives on Sustainable Development.* Ed. Harcourt, Wendy. London; Atlantic Highlands, N.J.: Zed Books, in association with Society for International Development, Rome, 1994a. xiv, 255 p.

---. "Youth and Development in the Coast Region of Tanzania." *Research Report No. 6.* Dar es Salaam: BRALUP, University of Dar es Salaam. , 1974.

---. "Zaramo Jando Rites in the Mwambao Area,." *Research Reports*: Sociology Department, University of Helsinki, 1973.

Swantz, Marja-Liisa, Ulla-Stina Henricson, and Mary Zalla. *Socio-Economic Causes of Malnutrition in Moshi District.* Research Paper - Bureau of Resource Assessment and Land Use Planning, University of Dar es Salaam No 38. Dar es Salaam: Bureau of Resource Assessment and Land Use Planning, University of Dar es Salaam, 1975.

Swantz, Marja-Liisa, Salome Mjema, and Zenya Wild. *Blood, Milk, and Death: Body Symbols and the Power of Regeneration among the Zaramo of Tanzania.* Westport, Conn.: Bergin & Garvey, 1995.

Swantz, Marja-Liisa, and Aili Mari Tripp. "Development for 'Big Fish' or 'Small Fish'?: A Study of Contrasts in Tanzanian Fishing Sector." *Decolonizing Knowledge: From Development to Dialogue.* Eds. Apffel-Marglin, Frédérique and Stephen A. Marglin. Oxford; New York: Clarendon Press; Oxford University Press, 1996. vi, 398 p.

---. "The Limits of Self-Interest: Alternative Logics of Economic Decision Making among Small-Scale Women Entrepreneurs in Uganda and Tanzania." *Alternatives to the Greening of Economics.* 1993.

---. *What Went Right in Tanzania: People's Response to Directed Development.* Dar es Salaam, Tanzania: Dar es Salaam University Press, 1996.

Swantz, Marja-Liisa, and Arja Vainio-Mattila. "Participatory Inquiry as an Instrument of Grassroots Development." *Human Inquiry in Action: Developments in New Paradigm Research.* Ed. Reason, Peter. London; Newbury Park: Sage Publications, 1988. xii, 242 p.

Swantz, Marja-Liisa, with assistance by Jill Grönfors and Margaretha von Troil. "Health Workers' Village Workbook, Ministry of Health, Training Sector (Swahili and English)." 1981.

Tambiah, Stanley Jeyaraja. *Magic, Science, Religion, and the Scope of Rationality.* The Lewis Henry Morgan Lectures. Cambridge England; New York: Cambridge University Press, 1990.

Tapaninen, A-M. *Kansan Kodit Ja Kaupungin Kadut. Etnografinen Tutkimus Etelä-Italialaisesta Kaupungista.* Helsinki: Suomen Antropologinen Seura, 1996.

Tax, Sol. *Heritage of Conquest; the Ethnology of Middle America.* New York: Free Press, 1952.

Theobald, Robin. *Corruption, Development, and Underdevelopment.* Houndmills, Basingstoke, Hampshire: Macmillan, 1990.

Tripp, Aili Mari. *African Women's Movements: Transforming Political Landscapes.* Cambridge; New York: Cambridge University Press, 2009.

Turner, Edith. "Exploring the Work of Victor Turner, Liminality and Its Later Implications." *Suomen Antopologi — Journal of the Finnish Anthropological Society* 4 (2008): 26-44.

Turner, Victor W. *The Forest of Symbols; Aspects of Ndembu Ritual.* Ithaca, N.Y.,: Cornell University Press, 1967.

Ulin, Robert C. *Understanding Cultures: Perspectives in Anthropology and Social Theory.* 1st ed. Austin: University of Texas Press, 1984.

Voipio, Timo. *From Poverty Economics to Global Social Policy, a Sociology of Aid for Poverty Reduction.* University of Eastern Finland2011.

Vuorela, Ulla. "Establishing a Traditions Archive and Documentation Centre in the Ministry of National Culture and Youth, Tanzania. An Experiment in Archiving and Documenting." *Jipemoyo: Participation, Needs and Village-Level Development.* Ed. Paakkanen, Liisa. Vol. 18. Helsinki: Finnish National Commission for UNESCO, Department of Research and Planning, Ministry of National Culture and Youth of Tanzania, The Research Council for the Humanities, the Academy of Finland in cooperation with the Institute of Development Studies, University of Helsinki, 1980. 107-14.

---. *The Women's Question and the Modes of Human Reproduction: An Analysis of a Tanzanian Village.* Monographs of the Finnish Society for Development Studies,. Uppsala, Sweden: Scandinavian Institute of African Studies, 1987.

Weber, Max, Guenther Roth, and Claus Wittich. *Economy and Society: An Outline of Interpretive Sociology.* 2 vols. Berkeley: University of California Press, 1978.

Werbner, Richard P., and T. O. Ranger. *Postcolonial Identities in Africa.* Postcolonial Encounters. Atlantic Highlands,N.J.: Zed Books, 1996.

William, Thomas, ed. *Man's Role in Changing the Face of the Earth* Chicago: University of Chicago Press, 1956.

Willis, Paul, and Mats Trondman. "Manifesto for Ethnography." *Cultural Studies: Critical Methodologies* 2.3 (2002): 394-402.

Winch, Peter. *The Idea of a Social Science and Its Relation to Philosophy.* Studies in Philosophical Psychology. London, New York,: Routledge & Kegan Paul; Humanities Press, 1967.

Wood, Alan. *The Groundnut Affair.* London: The Bodley Head, 1950.

Ylhäissi, J. "Forest Privatization and the Role of Community in Forests and Natrure Protection in Tanzania." *Environmental Science and Policy* 6 (2003): 279-90.